D1084307

STATE STRATEGIES IN THE
GLOBAL POLITICAL ECONOMY

STATE STRATEGIES IN THE GLOBAL POLITICAL ECONOMY

Ronen Palan and Jason Abbott
with Phil Deans

PINTER
London and New York

PINTER
A Cassell Imprint
Wellington House, 125 Strand,
London WC2R 0BB
215 Park Avenue South, New York,
New York 10003, USA

First published in 1996

Contents

Acknowledgements

In completing this project we would like to express our gratitude to the following people whose support, encouragement and advice proved invaluable. We would like to extend a special acknowledgement to the Department of Politics at the University of Newcastle. This book was conceived, researched and written while all of us were based in the department and without both the financial and personal support we received it would have been a struggle to complete the book. We are extremely grateful for the perseverance and patience of our colleagues. A vote of thanks also goes to Barry Gills whose ideas were invaluable in conceiving the project, and to Brook Blair for the research contributions he made towards the book, especially for Chapter 9. In addition we would like to acknowledge our appreciation of all our other colleagues who commented on our work, especially Martin Harrop, Sean Breslin, Phil Cerny and Roger Tooze. Finally we would like to thank Pinter and Cassell, particularly Nicola Viinikker who showed faith in the project and supported us patiently throughout.

Introduction

Leafing through recent publications in business literature, industrial economics, sociology, history and politics, one cannot avoid encountering sooner rather than later the two current buzz-words: 'globalization' and 'competitiveness'. The evidence for the globalization of markets is at best mixed. In the minds of many, particularly those involved in the business of running the multinational enterprises, the world economy is verging on full integration. Terms like 'global village', 'borderless world', 'global marketplace' as much as the 'hollowing out of the state' and the 'erosion of sovereignty', have become commonplace and have captured the collective imagination. These buzz-words are controversial and lack any commonly agreed meaning. However, the controversies surrounding them cannot conceal that in one way or another, there is a growing cohort of people who believe that the world in the 1990s is dramatically different from the one we inhabited only twenty years earlier. As Drucker (1990) argues, we live in a world of 'new realities'.

Such alleged changes pose a stark challenge to international political economy. What is the role of the state, of political authority and of policies in a world that is increasingly integrated? How effective are they? Who are the significant actors? So far the answers to these questions have largely proved to be embarrassingly simple. Broadly speaking, they fall into three groups representing three putative research agendas.

The first group broadly interprets globalization to mean a qualitative transformation of the environment of accumulation from essentially nationally dominated 'economies' to an 'economy' and 'society' which span the entire world and are largely impervious to political borders. For this rather diverse group, the state appears exposed and outflanked, rendering, in Dendrinos' words, 'national boundaries and the political notion of sovereignty obsolete to a great extent' (1992, p.56). An assumption is drawn that under such conditions the experience of government intervention, which played a determinant role in stabilizing the post-war economy, has been frustrated. The resulting gulf between intent and content, and between governments' goals and aims and their ability to deliver has led, in the words of one critic, to an 'almost universal loss of faith in the capacity of any individual state to intervene decisively and effectively' (Phillips 1992, p.104).

It appears to us, however, that the 'withering' or the 'hollowing out of the state' thesis is rather ambiguous, consisting of a number of disparate and not necessarily mutually supportive arguments. To begin with, it emanates from the neo-liberal rejection of the Keynesian state. It is never entirely clear whether writers in this mould argue that the limited capacity of the state to affect outcomes is something particularly new, or whether the 1980s simply serve to reinforce older notions about the structural limitation of the state's capacity to intervene effectively in the economy and society. To underlie this ambiguity, the thesis is supported by post-Keynesian political scientists who maintain that the very policies advocated by neo-liberals and which were then undertaken in the 1980s as 'proof' of the folly of Keynesianism and the interventionist state are precisely the policies that are stripping the state of its logistical capabilities. There is a suggestion therefore that the thesis is as prescriptive as much as it is descriptive, that the more one accepts the decline of the state, the more one reinforces such decline.

This thesis is also supported for a number of reasons, not all of which are mutually compatible. Some political economists contend that modern technology has transformed the spatial dimension of 'natural' economic activity (Ohmae 1993). On the one hand, a number of key political issues such as financial regulation, trade regimes and environmental concerns can only be dealt with on a global rather than national basis. On the other hand, so the argument goes, faced with accelerating demands combined with greater openness and competition, regional economies and regional agencies are becoming better equipped to handle the challenge of globalization than national agencies. Hence Sabine and Piore's notion of 'flexible accumulation' has spawned a secondary literature which rejects the traditional spatial division between centre and periphery in favour of a global industrial map which consists of an archipelago of some thirty or so dynamic regions, connected together by the phenomena of the global cities (Sassen 1991). However, doubts are cast on this technological–economistic argument by the proponents of transnational class alliances who see globalization and the 'erosion of the state' as the ideological armoury of an emergent transnational coalition of classes dominated by financial interests (Overbeek and Van der Pijl 1993).

All this serves to underlie our conviction that the withering away of the state thesis contains a number of ambiguities. It is not entirely clear, for instance, whether the alleged decline represents an irreversible secular trend born out of the very structures that pull the world economy together in an ever closer interdependent web, or whether the alleged decline of the state and the increasing focus on change merely serve as an ideological or rhetorical device in the hands of certain interests that stand to gain from such changes. Nor is it remotely clear how 'social life' is to be conducted in such new conditions, where the existing organizational mode of social life has collapsed.

This possibility has not escaped notice. Talk of globalization, the erosion of the state or the 'new modernity' is by no means universally accepted. A second position, represented by an equally diverse group, tends to dismiss the literature on globalization as merely the latest craze, frequently exaggerating the degree of 'structural' change in the global economy.[1] 'There have been no major structural or processual changes in the world system in the last few decades,' writes Christopher Chase-Dunn: 'The new phenomena emphasized by many observers are largely predictable continuations of cycles and trends long in operation' (1994, p.95). Similarly, Robert Jackson and Alan James maintain that 'the fundamental characteristics of the international society formed by such sovereign political entities . . . give no indication of soon changing into something different or ceasing to exist' (1994, p.7).

In contrast to the first group, the second position is singularly unambiguous. Yet that may be its problem. In denying change it not only reaffirms old charges of a lack of historical sensitivity (Halliday 1994), it also serves as an open invitation to 'policy makers' to ignore developments around them. At the least, the second group of theories gives no indication how technological changes, the advent of a global financial market and the global corporation are to be addressed by governments, if indeed they are to addressed at all. There is some truth in the statement that globalization is a hype, but as we will argue in Chapter 1, the problem with the second position is that it particularly fails to understand globalization in its historical perspective. Indeed, it merely addresses the hype and erroneously takes globalization to denote a wholesale structural change that has no roots in history.

A third approach opposes the first two. The crux of the matter, says Strange, is not the 'withering away of the state' nor the diminished significance of the system of states, but that the 'nature of the competition between states in the international system has fundamentally changed' (Strange 1995, p.55); so much so that 'states are now engaged increasingly in a different competitive game: they are competing for world market shares as the surest means to greater wealth and greater economic security' (Strange 1987, p.564).

Rather than view globalization and the state as two conflicting dynamics, destined to pull in opposing directions, this third position stresses the adaptation of the state to the new conditions. Thus 'the very concept of the national interest is expanding to embrace the transnational dimension in new ways: the so-called competition state is itself obliged by the imperatives of global competition to expand transnationalization' (Cerny 1994a, p.225).

This third interpretation accepts that globalization is a distinctly new phase and a new reality, but at the same time it also accepts that states and governments still have a role to play (Stopford and Strange 1991, p.7). The idea that the entire institutional, cultural, political and psychological notions about society can simply be brushed aside by the 'forces of the market' is not credible. The third school argues that both society and the state are changing, but that such change should not be confused with decline. The state may be besieged but it can fight back and reorganize itself. In fact, social structures and historical experiences have proved to be far more resilient than was normally assumed. The nature of this reorganization, the alleged shift from the welfare state to what Cerny has called the 'competition state' (1990), is as much a response to changing global circumstances as it is an instrument of further change. Accordingly there is a notion of a dialectical relationship, i.e. a non-linear conception of change which evolves neither accidentally nor deliberately.

Although there is no generally agreed definition of the 'competition state', broadly it comprises two elements. The first is the pervasive belief in national competitiveness as the means for generating economic growth and rising standards of living. This idea is certainly not new. None the less, the suggestion is that there has been an intensification of the theme of national competitiveness during the past two decades. As a result, more and more governments are now predominantly concerned with competitiveness, particularly comparatively (Stopford and Strange 1991; Taplin 1992). As a consequence of this concern, policy areas traditionally defined as 'domestic', education, transport, health, taxation, etc. are now increasingly viewed and discussed in the context of the national competitiveness debate. National competitiveness has become, in other words, a central ideological defence for far-reaching socio-economic restructuring.

Second, the manner by which governments execute competitive policies in an integrated economic market has shifted from predominantly demand-side measures to supply-side measures. During the 1950s, while integration was encouraged through the Bretton Woods agreements and successive rounds of GATT negotiation, there was none the less an acceptance that at the same time the state had an important interventionary role to play in the economy. This role was associated with the demand-side intervention commonly associated with the Keynesian/Fordist state and included the nationalization of utilities and key strategic manufacturing sectors; the effective nationalization of the financial markets; the erection of formal and more often informal trade barriers, and the subsidizing of strategic or key industries. Since the mid-1970s, however, there has been a growing belief in supply-side intervention. Rather than directly controlling the economy, it is maintained that in an increasingly global market and complex economy, the state is better off providing the conditions for generating growth.

Competition state theory became popular in business studies and industrial economics. There, the debate on national industrial policies and the ways and means by which states can and should enhance their competitiveness has raged for years. This debate has been largely ignored in international relations and international political economy. The work of Cerny and of in particular Susan Strange is a welcome exception. Indeed, as we will argue in Chapters 1 and 2, in a number of books and articles Strange has put forward a framework for an alternative international relations theory in the age of the competition state. This book seeks to contribute to this literature in three ways.

First, we ask whether there is an emerging model of the competition state as many scholars seem to suggest – such as the neo-liberal or Alpine model (Albert 1993) or the 'Schumpeterian workfare state' (Jessop 1993) – or whether competitive pressures are generating a diversity of responses. In our opinion it seems incredible to suggest that such diverse countries as the United States, Sweden, China, Chad or the Cayman Islands should follow the same overall trends. We will demonstrate instead that there is little evidence of a worldwide shift from one state-form to another; nor is there a single universal model of a competition state emerging. We encounter instead a great number of competitive strategies that are pursued by states, often concomitantly, and rarely with great conviction.

We take it that much of the varied literature in IPE, development studies, industrial economics and state theory provides illustrations of the different ways in which states cope with changes in the world economy. The study we present argues that states are faced with a number of policy options from which to choose, of which we identify seven. Four of these options or competitive strategies are open primarily to the group of states represented in the OECD, while three others arc open primarily to the less developed countries. These options are as follows: (1) states may wish to join together in large regional blocks (see Chapter 3); (2) they may adopt the 'developmental state' model (Chapter 4); (3) they may embrace the 'social democratic' mode of selective integration into the world economy (Chapter 5), or (4) a select number of states may seek to dominate their regional economy or even the world economy to achieve hegemony (Chapter 6). On the other hand, poorer and weaker states are likely to opt for one of the following strategies: (5) they may try to exploit their cheap and abundant labour (Chapter 7) to attract foreign capital; (6) they may seek to exploit a parasitical niche in the world market such as tax havens (Chapter 8), or (7) they may be structurally impeded from joining the competitive game at all (Chapter 9).[2]

In identifying these strategies we raise a couple of ancillary questions, namely (1) how are such strategies being adopted? And (2) who chooses the options and how? In other words, how do we see 'the state', and what are state strategies? – an issue which is discussed in Chapter 2. In anticipation of Chapter 2 we only wish to state here that we agree with the position adopted by Michael Mann (1994); namely, that too often the state is taken as a unitary or functional social body, representing an exaggerated belief that social life is patterned and orderly and that the state is therefore (sic) a functional organization which operates in the service of identifiable interests. As Mann notes, one of the central issues in state theory is the degree of autonomy enjoyed by governing bodies. This has immediate implications for the study, to the extent that there is an important debate as to whether competitive strategies can be legitimately thought to originate in some distinct 'national interest' (Krasner 1978), or whether policies are shaped primarily by the constellation of interests and the struggle between them (Poulantzas 1973). Mann suggests that there cannot be a universal theory of the 'relative autonomy' of the state, but that diverse states achieve different degrees of autonomy.

To avoid this particular problem we propose to shift our attention away from the state as a unitary social formation and instead to examine the nature of competitive strategies individually, divorced, so to speak, from this or that state.

We define a competitive strategy as *a set of policies that are explicitly aimed at improving the climate for business (national and/or multinational) and hence at enhancing the 'competitive' advantage of such countries in the global economy*. Since policies that aim at enhancing the competitiveness of, for example, the manufacturing sector, are different from those aimed at enhancing the competitive advantage of the financial sector, such a definition allows us to examine a plethora of strategies which can be pursued concomitantly. By doing so, we would like to address the diverse roots from which strategies evolve.

A further question this book seeks to address is the overall impact of these strategies. We maintain that the current debate on globalization is problematic. Whether or not globalization is accepted as a 'fact', a growing number of multinational enterprises are already operating as if there is such a global market. In doing so they are not only changing and restructuring themselves, but they are also shaping an environment. Our study of competitive strategies demonstrates that similar processes are taking place at the level of the state. The state is not negated or about to disappear, but it is reacting by devising a number of strategies of competition. These strategies may or may not be effective in terms of improved competitiveness. Yet in devising strategic responses, the fact that so many states worldwide are shifting in this direction is an important development and represents nothing less than the institutionalization of globalization in the state system. In effect, an entire new infrastructure of globalization is emerging, which corresponds to a new political geography of accumulation.

Competition in historical perspective

As with the other two proto-empirical positions, the 'competition state' offers a deceptively simple argument whose roots are planted deep in the history of economic thought. Indeed, the competition state may be seen merely as a modern continuation of the idea that government has a role in promoting economic growth. For example, the reforms and policies of Jean-Baptiste Colbert are generally regarded as the first comprehensive attempts to promote indigenous industry. Colbert, of course, drew inspiration from the earlier theoretical work of the Carmelites and the mercantilists. While it is true that there has been a vast expansion in the literature on competition and structural adjustment, it is still often problematic in its assumptions. It tends to be prescriptive and uncritical, primarily concerned with identifying a secular or structural trend empirically. Thus for the most part the literature pays scant attention to both the underlying causes of such trends and the resistances and/or complications that arise. There is therefore a decidedly empirical slant to such research which by focusing on 'problem solving' often lacks an awareness of the significance as well as the sheer problems in treating the national unit as a competitive entity in a global market. There is, generally speaking, a lack of concern with the social implications and even less with the broader theoretical problems that are raised by the alleged rise of the competition state. In addition, the concern with 'problem solving' has generally led to over-simplifications for the purpose of coming up with hard-edged policy prescriptions.

At the same time, the concern with competitiveness is clearly more than the latest issue exciting some small circle of academics.[3] From a theoretical point, the concern with competitiveness has ushered in a new period of increasing interdisciplinary work which is to be welcomed. We can already see the beginnings of an overlap between research into public policy and international relations, organization theory, institutional economics and foreign policy.

While much has been written about the state and the economy, little has been written about the state *in* the world economy. Of the latter, there is a rather scattered and dispersed literature. However, if there is one common theme among such literature, it is the predominance of stark and rather unhelpful dichotomies in the representation of the options that are supposedly open to states.

This is not accidental. The political framework of the world was frozen since 1945 by the Cold War in a way that the economic realities were not. We have become accustomed to think about economic processes as if they were taking place within a homogeneous and relatively unchanging political environment. This was expressed often enough in the dichotomy of either being within or outside the market. Within the market, or the 'free world', was the world of the business literature. Outside was the realm of international relations and strategy which was never of great interest to the former.

This is not to deny that important dissenting voices were heard. Yet they too have tended to erect their own set of dichotomies or at best their own set of trichotomies. In one popular categorization, states were divided into two camps: planned rational capitalist economies such as Japan and perhaps France, facing the 'Anglo-Saxon' regulated economies (Johnson 1982). Alternatively, a dichotomy was drawn between *laissez-faire* economics and neo-mercantilism, while in yet another interpretation the world was divided into a centre and periphery, in which the 'centre' or the 'core' capitalist states were represented as a monolithic social formation, and the periphery another essentially internally undifferentiated form. To this Wallerstein added the ambiguous notion of the semi-periphery which, like Kornhauser's (1960) intermediate social organizations, act as 'shock-absorbers' to the inherent tension within the system.

Similarly, with the end of the Soviet menace and the ebbing of the challenge of the Third World (Taplin 1992), a new dichotomy appeared to be emerging between the Anglo-Saxon model of neo-liberalism and the 'Alpine' or Rhennish model of Social Democracy (Albert 1993). It

8 STATE STRATEGIES IN THE GLOBAL POLITICAL ECONOMY

is this 'battle of ideas', as Douglas Hurd the then British Minister for Foreign Affairs described it, that is at the heart of the European Union. Strategic trade theory may be situated ambiguously somewhere in between, calling for concerted government planning and intervention within a broadly neo-liberal agenda (Humbert 1994). This in turn may be related to other academics who see the decline in the functional capacities of the state giving rise to the 'residual' state (Cerny 1995) or the 'workfare Schumpeterian state' (Jessop 1993).

Such sets of dichotomies and trichotomies are not entirely false, but they are predicated upon an essentialist, static and narrow conception of the global political economy and hence of the possibility of political action within it. They were born out of a series of ideological battles which obscure the active and participatory political responses that emanate from nation-states. A sound body of work that is profoundly sceptical of the uniform conceptualization of the 'international system' and of state theory has subsequently emerged. However, this has tended to result in a dispersion of work into specialist areas which largely appear to avoid each other. A tacit division has emerged, for instance, between those interested in development and those whose main focus lies in the advanced industrialized countries, and although the fate of both are clearly linked, there is often little communication between them. On top of that, the East Asian specialists, in particular those concerned with Japan and the four tigers, have gone off in their own direction, developing what amounts to a (sub)discipline of their own. Similar processes appear to have taken place in the study of Latin America, and there is a clear danger that the study of the former Communist states of Central and Eastern Europe will take a similar course. There is, in addition, the more industrial policy-oriented research and the politically oriented, again with little or no understanding between them. Others likewise draw attention to the division between mainstream productionist and trade-oriented literature, and the finance literature.

The impression that one gets from surveying this scattered literature is of an increasing stress on national uniqueness and distinctiveness. Such uniqueness is the consequence of socio-economic settlements between social agencies and institutions operating within the national territory. The distinctiveness of such settlements are less the consequence of cultural legacies than of socio-political action. In particular, the outcome and institutionalization of action between capital and labour, states and firms, capital and capital, and distinctive factory regimes are extremely important in creating national uniqueness.

However, while each social formation is by definition unique, is it not the case that 'national uniqueness' merely ensures that different states respond in different ways to what amount to global 'environmental changes'? Some states are clearly learning to take advantage of changing circumstances more than others. Japan, for example, is regarded as having taken the lead in articulating clear and cohesive strategies of competition in the world economy. Others are now coming round by compulsion to a more 'holistic' perspective of their policies and institutions. However,

while the uniqueness of national social formations ensures that there
will not be a single unified response to globalization, there is little evidence
to support the idea that globalization is not having a profound and
transformative impact upon the entire spectrum of political systems
world-wide.

We are therefore faced with a classical theoretical problem: how to
balance the forces of diversity with the forces of homogeneity. How
should we recognize that both derive from similar origins: that diversity
is born out of certain conditions, and these conditions form a totality
because they are made up of diverse responses? We propose in this book
to do so by shifting attention away from the state as a unitary social
formation, and to examine instead the plethora of competitive strategies
that are pursued by states. Because we understand 'strategy' to be the
calculated and deliberate application of policy to achieve a unitary goal,
the study of competitive strategies continues to be concerned with the
question of state policy (even if not necessarily presented as 'foreign
policy'), and hence with the activities of states in the era of globalization.
However, it does so without assuming beforehand an overall coherency
and consistency in intent or content

Previous studies of international competitiveness have proved to be
unrealistic because they have rested upon 'models' that have largely
been constructed at the level of the state. We believe that such models
are unrealistic because social formations, class structures, institutional
structures and geographical and topographical conditions create a far
more complicated set of criteria. The strategies we present have evolved
as 'techniques' of adaptation and competition. Such techniques are
rarely articulated by technocrats from bodies such as the 'grand école'
but instead are driven and articulated by contending interests within
the state. Since state policies invariably represent either sectoral strategic
interests and/or political and historical compromises, to talk of states
pursuing coherent and consistent 'strategies' can be misleading. Consequently, what one invariably finds is that states are pursuing more than
one strategy and that these do not necessarily have to be complementary.
On the contrary, in a number of cases they can indeed be contradictory
and inconsistent.

Contradictory strategies can be seen, for example, with regard to
Britain, which continues to pursue three principal strategies and two
'residual' ones, all of which prove in the long run to be incompatible
with each other. In the financial sphere the so-called self-regulation by the
City of the UK financial market may be regarded as synonymous with
the parasitical strategy of 'off-shorization'. In industrial policy Britain
has increasingly adopted what we call a 'downwardly mobile' strategy
of flexible labour in order to attract investment (Chapter 7). The UK, in
seeking to expose the labour market to market forces, has abolished
wages councils, restricted workers' rights in legislation, and through the
discipline of high unemployment made trade unions compliant. These
have combined to make the UK an attractive low-wage 'springboard' into
the European market for foreign and especially Far Eastern investment.

However, we have labelled the third strategy the strategy of size which
the UK pursues within the context of the European Union. As the EU
becomes more unified, this strategy may undermine the first two,
particularly the flexible labour strategy which has already generated
acrimonious controversy among Britain's EU partners. Furthermore, the
UK still residually pursues a hegemonic strategy that harks back to the
UK's days as an imperial and world power (Chapter 6) and it is still,
despite sixteen years of Conservative rule, a welfare state (Chapter 5).
Such incompatibilities lie at the heart of the inadequate responses of the
Conservative administration to international competitiveness – it simply
cannot find a way out of this strategic malaise.

Similarly, not all states are either equally capable or willing to adopt
aggressive competitive strategies. One of our contentions in this book
is that the old Third World itself has now broken down into a number
of groupings, one of which contains states such as Chad, Burma or
Afghanistan which, as we will argue, are structurally excluded from the
competitive 'game' (Chapter 9). Such states represent the outer limits of
globalization. Yet even these unfortunate state-forms are not entirely
excluded. Many have focused instead on marginal markets. For example,
in the not inconsiderable global market for heroin (estimated at over US
$100 billion a year), Afghanistan has emerged as the recent 'market
leader'. Similarly, the Lebanese lira appreciated *vis-à-vis* the US dollar
during the fifteen-year civil war because Lebanon had become the
world's largest exporter of hashish. We argue therefore that by focusing
on competitive strategies rather than on the competition state, we are
better placed to understand the enormous diversity of responses to the
overarching dynamics of globalization.

This book is a study of the variations or the ingredients that underlie
and shape policy responses in this age of globalization. In discussing the
formulation of these state strategies we will be guided by the following
general principles.

- First, while an argument can be made for the 'erosion of sovereignty',
  the decline of the state and so forth, in practice governments are rarely
  prepared to accept the verdict of 'the market' hands down. Capitalism
  by its very nature creates winners and losers, but while companies may
  cease to exist, states rarely do so; they continually respond to their
  environment. A study of global capitalism without the state, even in
  the age of globalization, is therefore simply unrealistic.
- Second, the debates and controversies surrounding the desirability
  and effectiveness of national and regional industrial policies may shed
  interesting light. Yet the assumption, implicit in many academic
  studies, that governments are willing or able to pursue policies which
  academics consider rational, effective or logical is obviously false.
  We take the view that the majority of international political economy
  debates, including those asserting the ineffectiveness and erosion
  of government sovereignty and power, are in effect discourses that
  aim to shape political responses: they are about what governments

should do in the name of the public good, individual welfare or class position. They form the basis, the raw material, so to speak, for the examination of the modern state strategies.

• Third, and attendant to our second point, we should not assume that because governments pursue policies which either prove ineffective or appear irrational, their policies have no impact either domestically or internationally. As we will demonstrate, most of the strategies being undertaken prove on examination to be ineffective within narrowly defined parameters. None the less, when combined they have a profound impact upon the environment of accumulation, both nationally and globally. By pursuing these strategies of competition, states are not only changing the environment of accumulation within their territories, they are also helping, often unwittingly, *the process of re-shaping the global political economic map*. A new political environment is emerging which, unlike the previous one, is neither homogeneous nor unidimensional.

The new games that nations play have therefore developed in response to the changing world. Collectively they shape a complex political environment within which globalization is occurring.

Notes

1 Krasner notes: 'Change, globalization, transnationalization, the erosion of the state, the transformation of political life. New, new, change, change. Academic reflections about international political economy are beginning to sound more and more like American political campaigns' (Krasner 1994, p.13).
2 Two types of states are not discussed in this book. The first are those that rely principally on a single commodity export such as oil. These states, by and large, have never adopted competitive strategies because they are able to use (or squander) their revenues by shielding themselves from the impact of the world market. The second are those that are in transition from communism to capitalism. We believe that sooner or later both will have to adopt one or other of the strategies described in this book.
3 As a UN report observes: 'during the 1980s, a large number of countries changed their policies and regulations affecting transnational corporations . . . those changes were a component of policies aimed at improving the climate for business operation in general' (UNCTC 1991, p. 25).

1

Globalization, neo-institutionalism and the competition state

This book asks an empirical question: how do modern states respond, adjust and adapt to the conditions of an increasingly integrated global market? Although much has been written about the state in the world economy, the literature is by and large concerned with what governments *ought* to do in conditions of globalization; less attention has been paid to what governments *are doing*. This book examines the evolution of a number of competitive strategies as forms of adaptation and response to global environmental changes. To do this we need first to clarify the structural realm within which states and societies must not only operate but also survive. Second, we need to draw attention to the processes by which such complex social entities as states respond and adapt to the changing global environment.

The international environment is said to have undergone enormous changes in the past two decades, described invariably as globalization. Globalization is represented as a new phase in the process of internationalization and the spread of international production (Van Tulder and Ruigrok, forthcoming). It is therefore understood as 'a major environmental change' (McGee and Howards 1988, p.48). In this chapter we will argue that there are lingering theoretical and methodological problems with the standard depiction of globalization. Not only is the concept itself contested and open to a variety of interpretations, but more specifically the relationship between globalization, as an evolving environmental phenomena, and the state, understood here as the dominant mode of social organization, is not very well theorized.

Broadly speaking, we can say that the central if underlying theoretical concern of the globalization literature is the relationship between the 'particular' and the 'general', between the activity and fate of states, corporations and indeed, individuals, and the changing socio-economic environment which they inhabit. Possibly because of the policy orientation of much of this literature, with its focus on the practical implications for decision makers, the theoretical questions have been largely ignored. In the standard depiction, the assumption is often made that states and corporations (the reference being normally to multinational enterprises) have continuing interests which define their strategic positions in the world. It is assumed that in pursuing such strategic goals these 'actors' must modify their behaviour in response to the changing 'environment'. The changing environment is taken as an explanation for the changing behaviour pattern of the actors. Globalization therefore implies that states and firms have no other choice but to modify their tactical decision to accommodate such extraordinary environmental change.

This raises a number of questions, however. When the environment of accumulation is described in abstract terms, the place, function and autonomy of states and firms become unclear. It is difficult to see what is left of the environment once states and multinational enterprises are taken out of it. One may wish to argue that the environment comprises the sum total of the activities of these two bodies. The environment is therefore the 'general' which is an aggregation of 'particulars'. At the same time we must recognize that what we call globalization is an abstraction and therefore does not negate states and firms. Whatever global constraints there might be, there are still a number of options open to both states and firms, including the option of not reacting at all. This raises two further questions: first, how are such options decided? Second, when choices are made, how do they interact and shape the global environment? The theoretical problem is therefore that there is a gap which needs bridging between the actions and perceptions of policy makers that ultimately cannot be anticipated, and the structural forces that are said to operate now on a global scale.

Failure to bridge the gap leads invariably to two equally unsatisfactory, and yet recognizable, positions. There are those who continue to describe state action and policy as if globalization has not taken place. When (and if) globalization is introduced, it is often in a rather confused manner and as an afterthought, as if global dynamics are entirely divorced from the state. Alternatively, the relationship between globalization and the state is depicted in a way that can be described as the 'politics of reaction', a presentation in which states and firms are rendered merely executioners of pre-ordained structural forces – as if their activities can be summed up merely in their reaction to something which happens outside their will and control. In both cases, politics is trivialized and effectively mean-ingless. After all, what is the role of political practice which is inherently unstable, participatory and developmental if the environment in which changes are taking place remains unaffected by political practice?

It is the second position which is particularly worrying, because it has bedevilled much of the globalization literature. As a result, the global-ization thesis is often employed as a prescriptive notion, propagated by business gurus and company directors to push through such ideas as 'down-sizing' or 're-engineering' – all of which usually lead to sacking people from their jobs, and doing so in the name of a changing global environment which (and that is the beauty of the concept) is unfortunately out of their control. Globalization has also been adopted enthusiastically by the big Japanese multinational enterprises in order, so the cynics say, to distance themselves from the Japanese state's protectionist practices. Why should the USA or the European Union retaliate against perceived Japanese intransigence in trade negotiations by imposing quotas and tariffs on Sony, Toyota or Honda when these are, after all, no longer Japanese but global corporations (Chesnais 1994)? Similarly, globalization is also utilized by politicians to introduce and rationalize unpopular changes.

The globalization thesis is often employed to make a broader argument as well. The idea was discovered (or, more accurately, adopted from cultural studies), as Chesnais recalls, by the big American business schools in the 1980s in order to deliver a simple message: that any obstacles to the business activities of multinational corporations are likely to have deleterious effects on state and society (1994, p.14). The globalization idea, he suspects, is about adaptation to globalization, i.e. the adaption of states and firms to conditions of unfettered market forces (1994, p.16). It suggests an expanded realm of 'private' business activity, and business is assumed to have gained as a result of new freedoms in essentially unregulated markets. The ensuing liberalization and de-regulation undoubtedly facilitate the activities of the multinational enterprises.

The basic message of the globalization thesis, thus perceived, is one that essentially denies individual choice. The only realistic policy still open is to comply and adopt global market forces. Lord Rees-Mogg thus warns:

> the world has never seen anything quite like this before. Governments are unlikely to recover their control of finance. . . . Any future attempts to restore capital controls or regain taxing power are quite implausible . . . American and European welfare systems which depend on high tax may well become insolvent. In the new world 'tax the rich' has ceased to be an option; the rich are not going to sit around waiting to be taxed.
>
> (Rees-Mogg 1993, p.14)

This gloomy prediction is at the heart of the observation of globalization by some academics as 'global neoclassicism' (Schor 1992), a neo-liberal ideology masquerading in the guise of structural change.

But, even if globalization is an ideology, is it therefore an illusion? Can we simply conclude that 'ideology' and perception are unimportant? After all, the decision to 'go global' represents an expensive 'bet' placed by companies on the changing conditions of the world economy. A growing number of corporations are investing heavily in communication and computer technology and developing new managerial and hier-archical structures (Reich 1990) in order to establish presence in all major markets. The sheer sums that are involved are staggering and therefore cannot be regarded lightly. The discrete decisions of so many multinational enterprises, and the growing likelihood that more will follow, may attest to important structural changes in the environment of accumulation. Since these companies form the backbone of economic life in the modern world as providers of goods, services and jobs, re-orientating their business towards a 'global' market must have great implications for economic growth and social welfare. As Strange pointed out (1994a), there is no point in saying that the state-system has remained fundamentally the same; vital elements in the life of states are now decided differently.

The question we shall seek to address in Chapters 1 and 2 is how to think about globalization and the state in a way that incorporates politics, and how to understand global structural forces within a framework that does not deny the role of institutions and choice. In this chapter we concentrate on this controversial concept, globalization. By rereading Marx and Braudel we identify the importance they attribute to institutions and in particular to juridical political structures in the development of capitalism. Consequently this historical sociological interpretation permits us to address neo-institutional concerns such as adaptation, learning and choice. In Chapter 2 we link our particular conception of globalization with the state.

Globalization in historical perspective

Capitalism, as Marx observed, was transnational or 'global' from the beginning. 'The world market itself,' he says, 'forms the basis for this mode of production [capitalism]' (1970, p.333). In light of this, the question must be raised: what has changed in the past one hundred and twenty years to merit talk of globalization? What does 'globalization' mean in a system of production and accumulation which was 'global' or transnational from the outset? One of the difficulties with the standard depiction of globalization is that the history of capitalism as a 'transnational' form is ignored. We would argue that if the term globalization has any use, then it must denote something different from the mere physical extension of market relationships in scale and scope. An alternative conceptualization, whose roots lie in the work of Marx and Braudel, offers, by extension, a different interpretation of the concept.

There is some validity in the perception of globalization as the culmination of long-term developments whose roots can be traced back at least as far as the eleventh century. This was a period which saw the emergence and subsequent rise to dominance of the contract and market relationship (Sorokin 1941), and increasing market integration. This is demonstrated with the movement from isolated regional markets to the formation of the European national markets in the mid-nineteenth century, and subsequently to the internationalization of such markets (Marx 1973). According to Peter Dicken (1992), internationalization has occurred in different phases corresponding to the Marxist notion of the 'circuit' of capital. The first circuit to internationalize was finance, and indeed the late nineteenth century is considered to be the age of dominance by international private bankers. Trade followed finance, and by 1913, on the eve of the First World War, international trade was estimated at approximately 13 per cent of global Gross Global Production (GGP), a figure that was only surpassed in the 1980s. The third circuit of capital, production, has undergone three phases of internationalization (Ernst and O'Connor 1989). The latest began after the Second World War, accelerating from the 1970s.

This model of incremental integration is challenged, however. According to one popular interpretation the process of integration and transnationalization of the global market originated in the 'long sixteenth century', a period of general prosperity which began, according to authorities such as Hamilton (1934) in the United States and Simiand (1932) in France, in the final decade of the fifteenth century, and which ended around the 1630s – although it must be stated that the entire periodization had been subject to critical evaluation. According to Wallerstein (1974, 1979), this period saw the emergence of an organic pan-European economy which rapidly enveloped the entire world. He calls this 'the capitalist world economy'. Others, including Fernand Braudel and the historical sociologists Abu-Lüghod (1989) and Michael Mann (1984), maintain that the initial spark for the economic integration of a European market had been earlier.

Many scholars reject the idea of an organic, all-encompassing world economy spanning Europe and its colonies and the whole world starting this early. It has been the subject of searching theoretical and historical debate. It has been criticized for ignoring the varieties of intensity in the level of integration and in this sense is profoundly ahistorical (Skocpol 1972). Braudel refined such ideas, arguing that market integration did not follow a linear trajectory but occurred in juxtaposition to various market dynamics. By the sixteenth century the European world economy possessed three distinct markets denominated roughly around the three distinct species of copper, silver and gold. The basic market form, still very much village fair-based and local, was the market for basic foodstuffs, local tradesman and so on. This market was the only market in which the vast majority of the population participated. Above that, a middle-distance or European market for timber, fish, grain, cloth and so on had emerged. Separately, a long-distance market for luxury goods had similarly evolved. Braudel charts a complex non-linear movement in the evolution of a global market, and is closer to Marx than to Wallerstein in viewing the industrial revolution as the true origin of the modern world.

There is plenty of evidence to support the existence of a world economy. Braudel points out that 'Europe in the sixteenth, seventeenth and eighteenth centuries was already clearly obeying a general series of rhythms, an overall order' (Braudel 1979, Vol. III, pp.75–6). To this, Wallerstein (1974) adds a subtle but powerful demonstration of the existence of an international division of labour. Taylor (1993) subsequently suggests the convergence of such infrastructural forms as the state, the household and the family as additional evidence for the world system.

As opposed to the world system theory, the central message of this Marxist–Braudelian tradition is maintenance of an important distinction between the concepts of the market, capitalism and the state (Braudel 1979, Vol. II, p.557). What follows may appear like semantic hair-splitting, but it is not. It is only if we maintain these important distinctions that the concept of globalization obtains the historical specific meaning.

In Marx's view, market relationships precede the capitalist mode of production. For example, while a veritable world market was already in place in the fifteenth century due to the opening of the sea routes to America and Asia, capitalism became dominant only in the nineteenth century (Marx 1973, p.69; 1970 *Capital I*, p.915). A superficial reading may suggest that 'capitalism' is therefore a specific form of market relationship. In such a reading capitalism is taken to be a totality, describing a period in history in the way that 'feudalism' describes a different period. In a different reading, as proposed by the Japanese Marxist Kozo Uno (1980) (see also Albirtton 1986), Marx's concept of capitalism has to be read in conjunction with the Hegelian dialectics. In this reading, capitalism, market and the state represent separate levels of theoretical abstractions.

Uno observes that the specific methodological problem that Hegel and Marx sought to address was the relationship between structural trends and historical contingencies, accidents and so on. So while the concept of the capitalist mode of production reveals certain inherent contradictions and characteristics, Albirtton argues that Marx's capital is a 'purified' concept. It is essentially a study of a hypothetical scenario, 'with total reification the market completely governs socioeconomic life, the result that purely economic categories are also social categories' (Albirtton 1986, p.190). Marx's capital is therefore not the history of capitalism, but it 'acts as a guide to historical research. There is no general theory of capitalist history' (Albirtton 1986, p.228).

It is in this light that we should read Braudel's remark that 'it was within the context of the market economy that a certain capitalism and a certain version of the modern state first appeared' (1979, Vol. II, p.519). The emphasis here should rest firmly on 'certain'; it was a *certain* type of capitalism and a *certain* version of the modern state. This suggests, of course, that other forms of capitalism and the state could have emerged, but they have not.[1] This tradition therefore subscribes to a doctrine that can be described as the immanency of capitalism. While the capitalist mode of production is an 'ideal-type' concept, capitalism is historically embedded in given social and administrative practices. So when Braudel talks about a *certain* capitalism and a *certain* form of state, he leaves enormous scope for history and practice in defining what we call capitalism.

The significance of this formulation for our purposes is that it allows us to identify broadly three phases in the relationship between capitalism and the territoriality of political authority. In the earlier phase, capitalism was truly transnational, largely dis-engaged from the state-system. In the words of Bienkowski,

> The capitalist system of production did not originally arise, nor was it formed, as a national economic system. It emerged as a method of accumulating capital from profits acquired by individual capitalists. . . . What is currently referred to as the 'growth of the national economy', 'the process of industrialization', etc., was only a side-product. . . . Thus for the first

hundred years it was possible to speak of the capitalist mode of production, but there was no such thing as the capitalist economic system on a global or national level.

(1981, p.139)

There follows a long if varied period in which capitalism increasingly takes on a 'national' form. 'Nations' or national markets, says Braudel, were 'built up inside an economic system greater than themselves . . . the national market was carved out within this wider unit by more or less far-sighted and certainly resolute policies' (1979, Vol. I, pp.322–3). This was in response to the rising state which:

shaped itself around pre-existing political structures, inserting itself among them, forcing upon them whenever it could, its authority, its currency, taxation, justice and language of command. This was a process of both infiltration and superimposition, of conquest and accommodation.

(Braudel 1979, Vol. II, p.513)

Marx goes even further and associates the evolution of capitalism with certain state forms: Spain, Portugal, Holland, France and England (1970, p.915). Each of these states added an important element to the potent cocktail which culminated in the rise of capitalism to a dominance.[2] Thus Holland perfected the colonial system (extending market relationships worldwide), and the '"companies called Monopolia" (Luther) were powerful levers for the concentration of capital' (1970, p.919). Venice introduced the concept of the 'national debt' which was so central to the rise of capitalism, and so on.

While Marx appears to emphasize certain innovations, Braudel stresses the state as perfecting certain regulatory mechanisms. What we are looking for, says Braudel:

is . . . a large-scale economy, covering a wide area, 'territorialized' so to speak, and sufficiently coherent for governments to be able to shape and manoeuvre it to some extent. Mercantilism represents precisely the dawning of awareness of this possibility of manoeuvring the entire economy of a country.

(1979, Vol. III, p.294)

The state is viewed in this interpretation as a historical entity, a particular type of social organization which developed in a historical context and cannot be thought of as merely a 'superstructural' form responding to the functional requirements of some economic base.

This phase reached its zenith around the 1870s. From then on a third phase becomes apparent, a phase in which capitalist enterprises burst their national boundaries and became, to 'the great chagrin of reactionists' (Marx 1973, p.71), increasingly global. The stress generated by the transition culminated in the crash of 1929 which damaged the transnationally oriented sectors and interests and offered opportunities for their nationalization and for the emergence of a new 'nationally' based 'mode of regulation' in its place. It is ironic that the transnational activities of capital engendered a renewed stress on the nation-state: 'Never before has the space of capital been so closely identified with the national framework, characterized by the validity of the legal-tender credit-currency and the redistribution of revenues in the welfare state' (Lipietz 1993, pp.29–30). Thus in a period when finance, production and trade outgrew their national boundaries, global depression led to an apparent reassertion of national government and national industrial policies. Paradoxically, therefore, the foundations of a reinvigorated *trans-national capitalism* were placed within a 'national' regime of accumulation. This gave the period of Fordism its fundamental character of ambivalence between the national and the international, a dichotomy that was never to be resolved.

There is plenty of evidence of this ambivalence which afflicted the period of Fordism.[3] For example, as Cooper observes, the Bretton Woods agreement 'asserted the primacy of domestic economic policy aimed at the maintenance of full employment and at the same time established the responsibility of each nation to the community of nations in the realm of international financial policy' (1975, p.85). This is surely a problematic relationship, asserting on the one hand the primacy of domestic economic policies, while at the same time initiating a 'responsibility' towards the international community. But Bretton Woods was paradigmatic of the entire international arrangement associated with the period of Fordism. The same ambiguities between national and international sets of priorities bedevilled the United Nations and the GATT agreements. Indeed, as David Calleo's (1982) masterful study of the United States reveals, it was also found at the heart of US foreign policy.

The development since the 1970s of what we call globalization represents in this interpretation both the extension of the third phase of transnational capital and an attempted resolution of the Fordist contradictions. Not surprisingly, the beginning of this resolution is linked with the crisis of the Fordist state on the one hand, which happens to correspond with the collapse of Bretton Woods on the other.[4] On the domestic level this was represented by a shift from demand-side policies of national economic control to supply-side measures, thereby profoundly changing the nature of the state, while internationally it was represented by the movement from international cooperative regimes to the transcendence of the state altogether. Globalization, as Lipietz (1994) stressed, is an extremely unstable resolution which is unlikely to reproduce a new 'golden age'; none the less, it is rooted in a historical context of the crisis of the 'national' mode of regulation in the period of already well-entrenched transnational production and capital.

To summarize: we regard globalization not as a quantitative change denoting the global integration of markets but as a qualitative change which implies an intensification and extension of capitalist relationships. Concepts such as the market, capitalism or the state, however, are not 'invariables' but changing entities. Thus, seen from the perspective of the regulation school, globalization is an unstable situation because it lacks a concomitant global regulatory mechanism. There is, as Rosenau, Strange and a number of other scholars point out, a deficit in 'global governance'. In this book, however, we shall not explore any further the contradictions of the new phase, but concentrate on the changing character of the state. Indeed, as we sought to demonstrate, globalization cannot be theorized independently of institutional changes and societal structures.

Contemporary evidence for globalization

What then does globalization mean today? There are distinct definitions of globalization which vary between and across academic disciplines. In this book we are not seeking to develop a comprehensive definition of globalization (for such a definition see Amin *et al.* 1994), but more specifically to analyse the changing character of the global market and its implications for the state. For our purposes Michael Porter provides a fairly comprehensive definition that offers the six main characteristics:

1 *Growing similarity of countries* Referring to the growing similarity in available infrastructure, distribution channels, and marketing approaches. Accordingly, more and more products and brands are available everywhere, manifesting similar buyer needs in different countries.
2 *Fluid global capital markets* National capital markets are merging into a global capital market, characterized by large flows of funds between countries.
3 *Falling tariff barriers* Successive rounds of bilateral and multilateral agreements have lowered tariff levels.
4 *Technological restructuring* Industry after industry has been significantly affected by some technological revolutions that are reshaping competition – microelectronics, information systems and advanced new materials.
5 *Integrating role of technology* Not only is technology reshaping industries but it is bringing countries and firms closer together by lowering transport costs and facilitating the flow of data and communication.
6 *New global competitors* New players are emerging, particularly in East Asia, which have exploited the new global environment to leapfrog well-established rivals.

(Porter 1990, pp.2–3)

Of these six points, four are particularly pertinent, namely, the globalization of finance, the internationalization of production, the changing role of technology and the politics of de-regulation. These broadly fall into two areas of economic activity: finance and production; the latter includes a large number of service industries. In the financial sphere, globalization represents the emergence of an integrated global financial market (or markets) aided, not least, by a series of political decisions that have led, directly and indirectly, to what has been described as international financial de-regulation. In production the reference is often to the internationalization of production and the rise of so-called global corporations, a process aided and abetted by multilateral trading agreements.

Globalization of the financial markets

In the economic realm, perhaps the most far-reaching steps towards truly global integration have been taken in the financial markets. The 1980s saw what many view as a 'second financial revolution' (Adkogan 1995; Allen 1994; Cerny, 1995), in which largely national financial markets gave way to an international or genuinely transnational market. None the less, the globalization of the sector is far from complete. It is still the case, for instance, that 98 per cent of *private* Japanese savings remain in Japan; the figure stands at 96 per cent and 83 per cent for the USA and UK respectively (Lake and Graham 1990). Thus the globalization of finance has not affected individual saving opportunities to the extent that it impacted upon the firm and the state.

Financial markets are essentially instruments by which savings are channelled into investment. The traditional channels linking savers with investors were banks, the stock market, government debts and the futures market. All these types of markets were until recently predominantly 'national'. Only a small minority of investment bank operations spanned the entire world, but they were the minority described as 'haute finance'. This has changed in the past two decades due to improvements in technology and to international financial de-regulation. As a consequence, entire areas of financial activities have shifted from the national to the international. Consequently, when we talk about global financial markets the reference is normally to the increasing ease with which savings can shift from one locale to another and hence be attracted to a better return. The traditional conception of the national economy was that of a financial 'system' pumping liquidity around the system and serving as the life-blood of the market. National financial markets, however, have amalgamated into a global 'wholesale' financial market whose combined asset are valued nowadays at approximately US $5.5 to US $6 trillion, or 25 per cent of GGP (Adkogan 1995).

Essential to the integration of the world financial markets have been improvements in real time communication. This has transformed transactions that were once long periods of exposure into short-term positions. It has also allowed assets and liabilities to be matched more rapidly across the globe, as witnessed by the growth of the swap markets. Such increases in the speed of communication have meant that the potential for arbitrage between currencies has grown. The most immediate effect of this has been the growing convergence in the movement of interest rates worldwide. Allen (1994, p.12) maintains that an equilibrium position of globalized financial markets, known as interest rate parity (IRP), was attained in the 1980s. IRP requires that national and international interest rates for the same types of loans in the same currency have to be equal; otherwise, there is enormous scope for profit through arbitrage. The globalization of the financial markets, then, has created a globally integrated financial market in which corporations, cities, localities and states are both competing for, as well as investing, funds.

There have been several key mechanisms of globalization: the emergence of virtually unregulatable interest rate competition via the Euromarkets; the breakdown of Bretton Woods and the multiplication of international currency flows after 1971 (much exacerbated by the oil shocks of 1973 to 1974 and 1979 to 1980); inflation and the fiscal crisis of the state, again in the 1970s, followed by deflationary monetary policies; the Third World debt crisis; the knock-on effects of limited deregulatory measures through policy competition between states; the emergence of new financial institutional structures; and, allowing these linkages to develop through a new material infrastructure, the development of electronics and information technology to permit financial flexibilization and more complex decision-making processes in order to operate efficiently.

It must be pointed out, however, that the end result of these processes is not an evenly 'integrated, global 24-hour financial marketplace', as media images would have it. Gross financial exchange transactions, estimated at about US \$5 trillion dollars a day at the Forex markets by 1994 (Evans 1994), dwarf exchanges of goods and services which then totalled around US \$4 trillion a year. Similarly, gross capital exchanges between the United States, Europe and Japan (excluding intra-European exchanges) grew at an average annual rate of 54 per cent per year between 1980 and 1986, compared to a growth in trade of about 8 per cent per year over the same period. But, as research by international management consultants McKinsey points out, the development of transnational financial market structures has been uneven, leading to the emergence of distinct world markets for each type of instrument. Thus although the major trends are still towards global integration, some markets are highly globalized, some are still essentially national with some transnational interpenetration and others are a mixture of the two.

There are two basic reasons for the growth of the international financial market. The introduction of computers and digital information technology linking the major financial centres created the possibility of taking full advantage of excess liquidity. It also offered new scope for 'arbitrating'. A globally encompassing financial market existed for a considerable time, but information about activities in one market would take days to reach the other one, by which time new events may have taken place. For all intents and purposes financial markets were primarily regional. Before the introduction of the fax machine and electronic mail, it could easily take two to three hours to establish contact between one centre and another. But with the introduction of the new technologies and the contraction of time and space, in some respects it is immaterial whether one is trading with a person who sits in a different office on the same floor, or whether one is trading with a person sitting a continent away.

The other facilitating factor has been global financial market de-regulation which refers to a complex set of processes and has a number of causes (Khouri 1990).[5] The seeds of this financial revolution were planted in the early 1970s with the collapse of the Bretton Woods agreement. Mason argues that it was a particular response largely generated by the fiscal burden caused by the increasing role of the state. By the early 1970s many advanced states were unable or unwilling to increase taxation, and thus resorted, first in the USA and then the UK, to massive borrowing. Rapid growth in government debt in the 1970s forced government to relax the financial regulatory environment.[6] Sassen argues that while this is true in Japan, '[a] key factor pushing de-regulation in the US was high and volatile interest rates' (Sassen 1994, p.117). Allen, on the other hand, argues that financial deregulation is one of the tactics signalling the shift towards a competition state:

> [in the 1980s] governments began rushing toward financial market de-regulation and internationalization in order to capture a large share of the new profitability for their own money centres, and in order to attract new international funds into their own economies.
>
> (Allen 1994, p.7)

As we will see in Chapter 8, competitive strategies in the financial sector have stimulated the rise of off-shore finance and tax havens.

Financial deregulation and the globalization of finance illustrate a number of important principles that lie at the heart of the debate on the competition state (which we explore in greater detail in Chapter 2): of these, two are of particular interest here:

1. *The growing pertinence of financial orthodoxy.* In effect, several factors stemming from financial transnationalization have together altered not only the scope but also the substance of government intervention. In the first place, it is by now well known that growing transnational constraints have undermined Keynesian demand management policies through adverse effects on capital flows, the exchange rate, etc. Monetary policy has become the main instrument of macro-economic control. Yet, at the same time, these very 'exogenous' constraints have increasingly meant that monetary policy instruments have become blunted and that to work they are required to 'over-shoot', thereby reinforcing boom–slump cycles. The consequence is that governments, even where they seem to be able to live beyond their means (as in the United States), must increasingly measure their performance according to criteria acceptable to the financial markets: i.e. they must be either strong or sound in order to retain the confidence of the transnational financial community. Rather than a system of 'embedded liberalism' (Ruggie 1982), what we have today is a system of 'embedded financial orthodoxy' which sets an international 'bottom line' for government economic intervention more broadly (Cerny 1994a).

This has had a profound effect upon the nature of currency. Traditionally, currency has reflected the strength of the economy, but now Forex markets offer new types of manipulation, and a new relationship between currency and policy. Governments can 'manipulate' money markets by offering higher interest rates. As a result currency does not necessarily reflect economic reality but economic policy.
2. *Emerging markets.* The globalization of finance, on the other hand, places territories in competition with each other for capital. Again, negative interpretations of this stress financial orthodoxy. Positive interpretations, however, stress that if run properly, states and regions are in a position to take advantage of global wholesale markets and to generate an investment boom far more than their own savings could have achieved. In some areas the competition state sees unprecedented levels of growth.

Furthermore, financial speculators like to be the first on the scene and, to benefit from low stock capitalization, globalization of finance is likely to spread growth and, particularly those countries with cheap labour (Chapter 7) and possibly even those countries currently excluded from the competitive game (Chapter 9), can rapidly join in because they potentially offer the best return for speculators. The globalization of the financial markets, then, has created a globally integrated financial market in which corporations, cities, localities and states are competing for, as well as investing, funds.

The global corporation

In addition to the emergence of an integrated global financial market, the growth and proliferation of global corporations are cited as further evidence of globalization. While during the 1980s the number of multinational corporations that decided to establish a global presence increased, the dream of global corporations and global product standardization is none the less still a long way off. In making strategic decisions, not all enterprises have gone global to the same extent. A very convincing argument can be made that if there is any rule about the process of globalization it is that there is no rule: 'The pattern of international competition differs markedly from industry to industry' (Porter 1990, p.17). Porter insists that a distinction should be made between multidomestic and global companies. In multidomestic industries competition in each country is essentially independent of competition in other countries: 'A multidomestic industry is one that is present in many countries, but one in which competition occurs on a country-by-country basis' (ibid.). At the other end of the spectrum are what Porter terms global industries, in which a firm's competitive position in one country is significantly affected by its position in other countries or vice versa. Among these, Porter counts commercial aircraft, television sets, semiconductors, photocopiers, cars and watches.

Others (e.g. Hamel and Prahalad 1988) however, maintain that the distinction between multidomestic and global can be misleading. In their view the essence of global competition lies in what they call 'cross-subsidizing'. Basically, enterprises are able to take advantage of a successful operation in one market to subsidize an operation in another. This then allows such enterprises to gradually build up a global network of production and distribution.

The literature identifies at least five main causes for the globalization of the enterprise: to cut costs; to finance expensive R&D programmes; to be seen to be physically present in important markets; to take advantage of economies of scale and scope, and political imperatives.

1 *The need to match the lower labour costs of foreign competitors leads to the establishment of labour-intensive manufacturing operations overseas.* Lipietz (1987) argues that the current phase of globalization was sparked by the crisis of profitability in the late 1960s. The current phase of globalization is therefore, he argues, a response to a deeper problem experienced by capitalist accumulation. In attempting to resume profitable accumulation, companies took advantage of improving transportation, communication and managerial techniques to shift production to the Third World.

2 *International expansion to amortize investment in world-scale plant or to generate funding for world class R&D programmes.* Large manufacturing plants applying new technologies could produce at lower unit costs than could smaller plants. In order to benefit from the cost advantages of these new, high-volume technologies of production, entrepreneurs had to make large investments. Recuperation of huge R&D outlays and the financial risks associated with them benefit the largest corporation. This has led to an enormous concentration of capital with several industries dominated by fewer than ten global actors.

3 *Rationalization of national product lines to take advantage of scale economies in design, manufacturing, marketing and purchasing.* In a large number of cases the incentive for the acquisition or merger of enterprises was to gain more effective control of output, price and markets. For example, the conglomerate was in fashion in the 1970s. Conglomerates provide a classic example of enterprises which attempt to spread risk by branching out into new areas. The other principal way by which such rationalization has occurred has been through vertical integration – companies seeking to link up the supply of raw materials and the marketing of the finished products with the actual production itself.

4 *Presence.* Companies want to be physically present in markets which they believe are important for their business. They need to be able to respond to consumer demands and changing taste and to keep pace with the latest technological development. They also wish to establish their own brand name. Companies seek to establish global presence in order to reduce vulnerability to the economic cycles that are such powerful determinants for their operations. They also need to recognize the rise of new markets (Dunning 1985; Freeman 1995).

5 *In their investment decisions, companies respond to market as much as to non-market measures.* Consequently, while the investment decisions of multinational corporations are complicated and diverse, some factors can be manipulated by political authorities. Corporations react to market information as much as to subsidies and other forms of government incentives (Grubert and Mutti 1991). Indeed, there are persistent suggestions that multinational enterprises (MNEs) attempt to systematically undermine market forces (Galbraith 1967; Weaver 1990). The implications are, of course, that the political environment, both domestically and internationally, may radically affect the investment behaviour of economic actors.

Several recent studies, for example, have concluded that political imperatives play a significant if not the dominant role in the strategic decision making of MNEs concerning investment. A study by Thomsen and Nicolaides (1991) concluded that Japanese investment in Europe is driven primarily by the fear of an impending 'fortress Europe'. Similarly, the rise of protectionist sentiments in the United States, directed primarily at Japan and the newly industrialized economies (NIEs), stimulated the growth of 'implant' factories within the US. Consequently, some 25 per cent of Japanese cars and electronics are produced in such implants today.

The implications of this are that political decisions may affect investment decisions of multinational enterprises not only directly, i.e. through subsidies and other 'sweeteners', but also indirectly, when a proper understanding of the concerns of multinational enterprises are addressed or taken advantage of by states. Political authorities may distribute values in various forms which are potentially as important in determining business investment and trade policies.

One can see immediately that a number of state strategies have evolved in order to take advantage of these considerations. Some government agencies have advertised the low wages, skills, dexterity and obedience of their labour force and so on (for example, advertisements by Malaysia and Singapore and more recently Portugal in *The Economist*); others, alternatively, are trying to keep wages and the price of other factors of production 'artificially' low by introducing the concept of the 'free economic zone': free, that is, of regulation, taxation, unionization and social benefits. At the same time, others have joined together in large regional blocs to take advantage of scale economies in order to produce market size which are able to support enormous R&D outlays.

Neo-institutionalism

We describe certain changes in the world economy by using the notion of globalization. These changes are not accidental; they are rooted in technological development and the changing patterns of production and distribution. The argument put forward in the first section of this chapter was that such developments are in turn embedded in the socio-economic environment which allows such technologies and production methods to flourish and stimulates them. For the sake of description and analysis, we have abstracted a situation which we described as the 'environment' of accumulation. We did so in order to be able to identify the internal dynamics that shape and determine the environment. The merit of such an approach is that by abstracting, stripping it to the very core and principles, we can then point out certain trends. The reality, of course, is that there is no such disembedded environment.[7] We should recognize that a socio-economic environment has a particular reality, specifically an institutional reality. This brings us to neo-institutionalism.

Neo-institutionalism offers many advantages over traditional theorization. The central concern of institutionalism is the integration of economic activities with one another and with social activities. It is concerned with 'issues . . . involving the relations of the economic process to the political and cultural spheres of society at large' (Polanyi 1977, p.35). While neo-classical economics is primarily concerned with equilibrium and stability, institutionalism is that branch of economics which centres on resistance and change.[8] In that sense some branches of institutionalism evolved as a direct challenge and a rebuff to (neo)classical economics.[9] This offers institutional economics clear advantages over neoclassical economics in a period which is generally perceived to be experiencing intensified change.[10]

However, it is the institutionalist perception of the social realm which is the central issue here. Marc Tool (1994) offers a good starting point. According to Tool, the basic assumptions of institutional analysis are: first, that any given level of integration necessarily requires a defined institutional structure: 'economic orders or systems are comprised of institutions; as structural arrangements, they prescribe and proscribe behaviour in the pursuit of social and economic functions' (Tool 1994, p.409). Second, that 'any social and economic order must be created; it is not "naturally" emergent or specified a priori. It is a product of human agency: there is no other credible source' (ibid.).

Using this framework, we could say that institutionalists would suggest that 'globalization' is a 'created' social order and as such a product of human agency. This, of course, is in marked contrast to the 'politics of reaction' which represents globalization as an externally generated social order, a product of technological determinism and other changes. By arguing that it is a 'created' social order we do not suggest a voluntarist interpretation. On the contrary, institutionalists would suggest that globalization is a credible thesis only when we can identify the institutions which prescribe and proscribe behaviour associated with globalization.

The chosen form of analysis for the changing relationships between the varied activities within society has been the concept of 'social structures'. Because the discipline of economics has had a longer history, born from natural law, such concepts could be incorporated into the orthodox body of thought (Mayhew 1987, p.975). Veblen, and later Polanyi, were different because they approached economics from an anthropological perspective and in doing so they were able to view human society as being in a state of constant evolution. Indeed, institutionalism was born out of the discovery of evolution and 'cultures' that accompanied the ideas of Darwinism and early anthropology.[11] This implanted the notion that existing structures and institutions emerged in response to certain situations and themselves would continue to evolve to meet new challenges.[12] Thus by stressing the importance of interactions between economic activities and society, neo-institutionalism arrives at a third tenet, namely that it is essentially evolutionary in character. The implications are that concepts of the market and the state, or indeed globalization, are not fixed but evolutionary or contextually related to time and place.

How the evolution of economic and social processes occurs has been a source of some debate. Polanyi argues in *The Great Transformation* that conscious political action is required to transform market activities into a market economy.[13] In contrast, Foucault and others stress the aggregationist nature of political change, placing the emphasis on various 'sites' of battles and societal responses which (although widely emulated in other sites) only in aggregate produce certain outcomes that are then perceived as 'social structures'.

Aggregationist assumptions are important in any assessment of globalization. Traditional sociological understanding (by which we mean the sociology which developed in the nineteenth century) of the processes of order and change assumed essentially that the social process is the outcome of the interaction of conflicting groups. Institutions were perceived as mediators between these social groups as well as 'institutionalizing' power relations into the very fabric of the social structure (Poulantzas 1973).[14] We may say therefore that the traditional model of social changes was that:

$$\text{Agency} + \text{Power} = \text{Outcome}$$

It was assumed that an understanding of a specific outcome, an event, a social structure or institution, requires an identification of an agency – class, group, state or individual – and the gauging of the power relationships between them. Such 'analysis' was (and still is) presumed to provide an explanation of a given outcome. Sadly, since power is intangible and profoundly immeasurable, one was left with the outcome, combined with one's preferred concept of the agency (both of which are inevitably controversial and debatable), which then served to identify the power configuration. Power is therefore deduced from this relationship between outcome and agency.

$$\text{Outcome} - \text{Agency} = \text{Power}$$

In our view, this is an 'ideological' interpretation, to the extent that both agency and outcomes are inscribed in one's theoretical perspective. Needless to say, the world has invariably proved far more complicated and unwieldy and has not lent itself to such linear causality.

An institutional approach, particularly in its aggregationist variant, could potentially provide for a healthy distance between outcome and cause. Global outcomes (which we may describe as 'Fordism', 'globalism' or 'neo-liberalism') may benefit certain social groups and certain identifiable interests (in other words, a relationship can be established between A, P and O). That does not mean, however, that such social groups have produced such intended outcomes (i.e. A + P = O), nor that they are in control of these outcomes. The rise of neo-liberalism and the globalization of finance undoubtedly benefited the financial sector (Overbeek and Van der Pijl 1993), but that does not necessarily mean that financial interests have consciously combined forces to bring about the rise of neo-liberalism. They were on the whole certainly in support of the tenets of financial orthodoxy, but equally there were other forces which helped to cement the new predominant ideology. Nor does neo-liberalism as an ideology provide increasing security for financial interests; thus they are certainly not in control of the situation, as the recent collapse of Barings has vividly demonstrated! It is therefore this relationship between agency, power and outcome that is further explored and refined in institutionalist texts. In this perspective, the notion of agency, choice and learning does not negate structure; it merely negates the A + P = O model.

With this in mind we can introduce our notion of social structure. Social structure is a compound and difficult concept, not least because it is drawn from a number of historical and philosophical sources. Due to the impact of anthropology and structural functionalism this century, the notion of structure is drawn primarily from biological analogy. Structure is viewed as the skeleton of social activity, an unchanging set of 'essences' in social life (Radcliffe-Brown 1952). The problem is, as has been noted all too often, that such a conception of structure denies agency of choice and ignores historical contingency.

The notions of agency (the subject) and contingency (error, accident) must therefore be brought into structuralist enterprise, or alternatively, some notion of structure and contingency must overlap with theories of agency. To put this in a different way, we wish to transcend the agency versus structure impasse. Such endeavours have taxed the minds of many sociologists and social philosophers with no clear-cut agreement in sight. It would be foolhardy on our part to suggest that we can resolve this problem. We propose therefore to describe our notion of structure with the aid of a metaphor which will hopefully provide some general idea of what we have in mind, although we do not pretend that the metaphor can resolve the questions of the relationships between structure, agency, trends and the tendency and line of causality. The metaphor we have in mind is that of a river in relation to the notion of energy. The downward stream of the river represents to us the notion of social structure; one may, of course, 'swim against the stream', 'buck the trend', rebel, dissent, but then one's movements are heavy, much energy is expended and success is never guaranteed. However, when one chooses to 'go with the flow', to conform, to 'follow the crowd', then everything becomes easier, everything flows naturally. Social structures operate in precisely the same way; flowing with the structure is easy – negating it is tremendously difficult.

Such a notion of structure is intuitively recognizable and works at a number of levels, both political and societal. When we characterize the international environment as undergoing a process of globalization, a process that is irreversible, we understand the term to denote a structural trend such as the one described above. Since we understand the concept to represent such a 'structural' form, it follows, in our line of argument, that globalization is likely to produce certain patterns of least resistance opposing patterns of most resistance: both, however, are not set in stone: they represent options, choices and therefore some intuitive notion of social energy. The environment, in other words, is not something external to the activities of states and firms. At the same time, we stress again that in our view the distribution of penalties and sanctions is not inscribed in the very logic of some 'system' (capitalism), but is the aggregated outcome of decisions and choices that were made. As we will see in Chapter 2, this notion of structure or structural trend serves as the basis for our interpretation of state policy in the age of globalization.

Notes

1 This idea has been explored by Kees Van Der Pijl. Van Der Pijl talks about the English state and its derivatives, the Anglo-Saxon colonial states, as an emerging 'Lockean Heartland' (forthcoming), a political compromise as much as a set of values, norms and a juridical system, all contributing to a specific type of capitalist state. The Lockean heartland, he maintains, has expanded in fits and starts to now comprise almost the entire capitalist world.

2 For discussion see Palan 1991.

3 For detailed discussion see Palan 1995a.

4 The link between international relations and the crisis of Fordism is not very well explored. In our view the regulation school tends to overemphasize developments which are internal to the mode itself, i.e. labour capital, production technologies, etc. to the detriment of the global political economic configuration. The rise of 'off-shore' finance, which again coincided with the 'crisis' and which robbed the Keynesian state of its regulatory instruments, tends to be ignored. Similarly, the important 'political' conflict between the USA and its European and Japanese partners, which led to the collapse of Bretton Woods, is overlooked.

5 'Deregulation is primarily the reduction or elimination of barriers which have inhibited the free interaction between various financial corporate and national entities' (Mason 1987, p.162).

6 'In countries where immature markets exist, the authorities were forced to alter regulation and encourage market development so that government debt instruments could be sold more easily' (Mason 1987, p.163). For the French case see Mason, for Japan see Ruhl and Hughes 1986.

7 This mode of abstracted analysis is described by Bourdieu as objectivism: 'Objectivism constitutes the social world as a spectacle offered to an

observer who takes up a "point of view" on the action and who, putting into the object the principles of his relation to the object, proceeds as if it were intended solely for knowledge and as if all the interactions within it were purely symbolic exchanges' (Bourdieu 1990, p.52). Bourdieu suggests that we need to complement this with a theory of practice.

8 'The central dilemma of growth is reconciling the demands of learning with the demands of monitoring. By economic learning I mean acquiring knowledge to make and do the things valued in markets. . . . The dilemma of economic development is that learning undermines the stability of relations normally required for monitoring' (Sabel 1994, p.137).

9 Hodgson says: 'we may define "neoclassical economics" as an approach based on the assumption of globally rational and optimizing behaviour by economic agents, in which the predisposition is to examine the attainment and characteristics of economics equilibria' (Hodgson 1994b, p.389). 'What is exogenous to neoclassical theory constitutes the very theoretical core of institutional economics'(Dopfer quoted in Tool 1994, p.407).

10 It must be recognized from the outset, however, that institutionalism or neo-institutionalism contains by now a variety of approaches, whereas the neo-institutionalism of Ronald Coase, Oliver Williamson and Douglas North offers refinement to neoclassical economics (Swedberg 1994). Others, in particular evolutionary economics which is associated with the European Association of Evolutionary Political Economy (EAEPE), evolved as a direct challenge and a rebuff to (neo)classical economics. But it is not necessarily the challenge to neoclassical economics and the notion of equilibrium, but the methodological and epistemological assumptions which are at the root of neoclassical thought and, more broadly, positivist thought, where neo-institutionalism is particularly interesting here.

11 See Veblen (1994); Polanyi *et al.* (1971); for a review see Mayhew (1987). To quote Terence Hopkins, 'To explain [the] variations in men's economic activities, then, one must turn to the wider system of social actions, the society, of which the economy as a social process is part' (in Polanyi *et al.* 1971, p.295).

12 Institutions can be defined as '[C]ollective action in control, liberation and expansion of individual action. Collective action ranges all the way from unorganized custom to the many organized going concerns, such as the family, the corporation, the trade association, the trade union, the reserve system, the state' (Commons 1931, p.649).

13 'The step which makes . . . regulated markets into a self-regulating market, is indeed crucial. The nineteenth century . . . naively imagined that such a development was the natural outcome. . . . It was not realised that the gearing of markets into a self-regulating system . . . was the effect of highly artificial stimulants administered to the body social' (Polanyi 1957a, p.57).

14 'When the state intervened against someone,' says Braudel, 'it was inevitably the masses who had to be contained and returned to the path of duty – that is to work' (1979, Vol. II, p.516).

2

The state in the global political economy

In Chapter 1, we emphasized the importance of the subjective projections of 'actors' in the construction of an emerging 'global' environment of accumulation. In doing so, however, we are not suggesting that globalization is somehow less real or merely imagined. Instead the argument we propose is that a mechanistic approach, in which the environment is deemed to be an external force that determines behavioural patterns, must be replaced by a more nuanced approach in which the perception of the environment is possibly the main cause for changing patterns of behaviour. In addition, such changes themselves intensify the perception that the external environment is in a process of change. Thus there is a notion of a dialectical relationship.

Controversies about the reality of globalization, and the kind of empirical validation they invite, are therefore insufficiently sensitive to the impact that the idea or even the 'myth' of globalization is making in modifying the behaviour of both states and firms. Such arguments ignore the fact that a growing number of corporations are responding to 'perceived' environmental changes by modifying their behaviour and institutionalizing structural changes. Such changes in the corporation are represented, so people like Reich would have us believe, by the move away from hierarchical structures of authority and control towards 'global web' structures (Reich 1990). Yet if multinational enterprises (MNEs) are responding and shaping the changing global environment, can states simply ignore such developments?

Competition state theory suggests that they cannot, and indeed, by and large, have not. Furthermore, the same process of institutional adjustment and adaption is taking place at state level as well. Yet in the same way that corporate decisions about change and response are not taken in abstract but in a specific institutional context, so the study of the state in the era of globalization must be equally sensitive to history, culture and social structure. Indeed, if the study of globalization is to be grounded in empirical research into institutional change, so the study of globalization cannot be divorced from the state because the state is regarded as the site of social relationships and institutional practices. With this in mind we can now begin to assess the advent of what Stopford and Strange (1991) call the 'new international competitive game'. We begin with a description of how the activities and responses of the state are understood and theorized in international political economy (IPE).

The state in international political economy

If state policy is changing and adapting to the new global environment, this begs the questions: how are policies shaped and determined by the changing environment? How are policies conceived? And indeed, what is our conception of the state? The activities of the state in the global economy have been at the core of international political economy. In the dominant approach, IPE is understood as a meeting place between political authorities and market forces, in short, states and markets. In Gilpin's famous words:

> The parallel existence and mutual interaction of 'state' and 'market' in the modern world create 'political economy'. . . . In the absence of the state, the price mechanism and market forces would determine the outcome of economic activities; this would be the pure world of the economist. In the absence of market, the state or its equivalent would allocate economic resources; this would be the pure world of the political scientist.
>
> (Gilpin 1987, p.8)

As we will see below, the 'system of states' is understood in this view to represent a stable and unchanging set of relationships (Krasner 1978; Waltz 1979; Rosencrance 1986; Gilpin 1987; Jackson and James 1994) which, as we have seen in Gilpin's view, comes into conflict with another set of stable and unchanging relationships described as 'the market'.

We have two basic problems with this orthodoxy. First, if by 'states and markets' one imagines the coming together of two 'ideal type' descriptions, namely a world dominated by market forces colluding with a world governed by political calculations, then sooner rather than later this facile image breaks down. Second, this dominant presentation is grounded in a statist interpretation which is not only misleading but rather unhelpful when it comes to an empirical study of globalization.

When Gilpin refers to 'the market' as distinct from 'the state', he has in mind a macro-economic form of regulation based on the price mechanism. Yet while this concept of the market is sound, Gilpin's theory contains an additional unstated assumption; namely that market 'actors' would ideally like to extend market forces whereas states would ideally like to infringe upon the market. Market and states are therefore viewed as two different if not incompatible sources of 'resource allocation'. It is this additional, essentially conservative assumption which permeates the 'states and markets' approach that we wish to dispute. Indeed, one can equally advance the opposite argument, namely that the 'market' is being extended and supported by the state system; so for instance, the OECD, the GATT and other multilateral arenas discuss practical suggestions that aim to extend and nurture 'market forces'.

Meanwhile, despite the undeniable diversity, if not eclectic policy responses of both corporations and states (Dunning 1985), one thing is clear: multinational enterprises (and as we argue later, states also) are either unable or unwilling to abide by the rules of the market, *especially under conditions of intensifying competition.* It has been long propagated that the multinational corporation has achieved a certain autonomy from the nation-state. Chandler, for example, maintained that 'manufacturing enterprises . . . have provided a fundamental dynamic or force for change in capitalist economies' (Chandler 1990, p.4). Chandler, however, prefers to talk of business and manufacturing *enterprises* rather than of the multinational or transnational corporations. He argues that these corporations have a function beyond their mere direct business and production concerns. They also operate, as Oliver Williamson suggested, as a 'governance structure'. In other words, these companies have adopted the internal as well as external 'trappings' of states. In his popular anthology of ITT, Anthony Sampson (1973) quotes approvingly from a report of the Tariff Commission:

> In the largest and most sophisticated multinational corporations, planning and subsequent monitoring of plan fulfilment have reached a scope and level of detail that, ironically, resemble more than superficially the national planning procedures of Communist countries. Both sides are preoccupied with the techniques of control and surveillance, which have been so expertly developed in the last decade.
>
> (Sampson 1973, pp.269–70)

This is not to say that the multinational enterprise has achieved or wishes to achieve autonomy from the state. On the contrary, multinational enterprises thrive on the state and the state system. The state in OECD countries, for instance, finances about half of their research and development costs (see Table 2.1); provides them with sweeteners and subsidies and essential infrastructural support, i.e. education, transportation and security. To the chagrin of the Thatcherite/Reaganite advocates of the free market, the facts tell a different story. Following a stint as an executive in the Ford corporation, Paul Weaver, an important ideologue of the New Right, expressed his utter disappointment with the men who controlled the corporations. In his words, they are:

> Contemptuous of existing ways of doing business and unmoved by the ideals of individual rights, limited government, free markets, and the rule of law. . . . Contrary to its image as a narrowly commercial institution, the corporation has always been up to its hips – and sometimes in over its head – in politics.
>
> (Weaver 1990, pp.17–18)

Like Chandler and Galbraith before them, these writers have come to the conclusion that the multinationals, rather than extending it, are in fact bureaucratizing the market.[1] To quote Weaver again, 'Wherever the corporation appears, it sets in motion a process of vertical and horizontal integration that leads traditional market relationships to break down and bureaucratic relationships to proliferate' (Weaver 1990, p.19).

Table 2.1 Research and Development expenditures in major OECD countries

Country	Million current PPP (US $)	% of GDP	Financed by government (%)	Of which earmarked for defence (%)
France	25,033	2.42	48.8	40.0
Germany	35,562	2.66	36.5	13.5
Italy	12,898	1.32	46.6	6.0
Japan	71,766	3.05	18.2	5.5
UK	18,735	2.08	34.2	44.0
USA	154,348	2.75	46.8	62.5

Source: OECD (1995) in 1994 figures (the figures relate to 1991).

Not only do MNEs seek to replace market forces with a stable bureaucratized environment, but states similarly distort market mechanisms, introducing what economists refer to as 'externalities' and 'frictions'. These represent the ways in which the market is manipulated, sometimes beyond recognition, by the wilful acts of political authorities. Put in simpler terms, states have tried and continue to try to rig or buck the market. Ironically, in a condition of growing market integration, states' actions gain a new significance. As Johns explains, 'The very process of internal integration of nations states creates the potential for government induced frictions and factor immobilities' (Johns 1983, p.4). It is therefore not surprising that the 'pure' theories of the market do not serve as good indicators of market behaviour in a global economy.

If multinational enterprises are operating within an environment that is fundamentally shaped by the state, they are nevertheless not passive actors blindly responding to macro- or micro-economic policy indicators. Not only have multinational enterprises confounded neoclassical economists, they have also produced subtle but important changes in the policy decisions of states. Clearly decisions made by these enterprises can have extensive implications for national policy. Consequently, countries both large and small may see their pattern of trade being determined by the strategies of multinational enterprises. As Sampson points out, such strategies may lead to the decision that 'perhaps . . . Switzerland will be supplied from Germany instead of France, or that all refrigerators will be made in Italy, and all radios in Germany' (Sampson 1973, p.111). Their independent, active responses have meant that the assumed link between money supply, exchange rate and the balance of trade has not yet been broken – but it is less clear-cut than in the past. To give two such examples of this. First, the rise of the yen relative to the dollar in the 1980s did not produce the expected equalization of the balance of trade between the United States and Japan. It led instead to several broad structural changes which further widened the trade gap. Among these were an increase in the number of Japanese 'implant' factories in the

United States, handsome profits which helped to propel Japanese MNEs to the leading edge of technology, and the transformation of the Japanese financial markets. Similarly, the emergence of massive 'off-shore' markets have decoupled the financial sector from production to the extent that exchange rates now respond as much to interest rates or even bank secrecy laws as they reflect economic performance. Macro-economic policy therefore needs to be attentive to such changes in the global environment and can no longer follow blindly the prescriptions of economic textbooks which conceive the economy as a *national* economy.

For these reasons, we believe that the state and market approach does not provide an adequate framework for thinking about the international political economy. The approach is liable to generate a succession of contradictions as we try to disentangle ourselves from its initial assumptions, namely that 'state' and 'markets' consist of two sets of 'actors' and dynamics that are profoundly different. To preface our discussion of the state there is a confusion here between the interests of the capitalist class and the interests of capitalist enterprises. The capitalist class clearly seeks to undermine the 'Keynesian' state which as a form of class compromise had become a huge distribution mechanism.[2] The capitalist class clearly seeks a 'smaller' and less 'interventionist' state – i.e. less tax and less regulation – and this interest, of course, is always presented as being in the wider 'public' or 'national' interest. At the same time, *capitalist enterprises* require the state to provide expensive infrastructural support and the political and social conditions of accumulation. The fact that the two are contradictory, namely less tax means ultimately less infrastructural support, is a central ongoing problem of capitalism, exacerbated in the age of the competition state (Palan 1993, 1995a).

The competition state

Competition state theory arguably offers the first serious and comprehensive attempt to go beyond the state and market approach in international political economy. Many of the basic assumptions upon which the competition state is based are discussed in the works of Cerny and Strange. In particular, they point to a number of important developments: the shift in strategic interests from military and territorial enlargement to market share; the decreasing significance of bilateral diplomacy and the concomitant increasing importance of multilateral arenas such as the OECD, GATT, the G7, etc. where the 'rules of the game' are devised; and the blurring of the distinction between 'domestic' and 'foreign'. In addition, attention is drawn to the way in which traditionally domestic policy concerns, such as education, transportation, energy policy, law and order, as well as fiscal and monetary policies, are increasingly understood and defined in the context of comparative international competitiveness.

This changing international economic climate is clearly demonstrated by a wealth of articles in recent OECD publications (Vickey 1993;

Gonenc 1994) which stress the drift away from the classical instruments of industrial policy towards policies that create the 'framework conditions' for business and industry to thrive. As a senior OECD bureaucrat remarks,

> This reflection takes in not only macroeconomic factors, such as excessively high interest rates, taxation or labour costs [but] a host of other, more qualitative factors. . . . Among them are the management style of firms, the relationship between shareholders and management ('corporate governance'), short-versus-long-term returns on investment, the degrees of skill of the workforce and investment in training, the state of physical infrastructure for transport and communications and . . . the quality and effectiveness of public administration.
>
> (Gassman 1994, p.17)

At the same time we must bear in mind that competition state theory is grounded in a number of assumptions, not all of which are universally accepted. Certainly, not all these assumptions govern policies and are acted upon with equal fervour. The competition state theory is therefore essentially an 'ideal-type' description of the activities of the state based upon four essential assumptions:

- That governments are concerned primarily with economic growth and that they are willing and likely to undertake measures to improve the standard of living and growth in their territories. 'The principal economic goal of a nation,' says Porter, 'is to produce a high and rising standard of living for its citizens' (1990, p.6). This assumption is controversial to say the least. The Iranian Islamic revolution or the Yugoslavian warring parties were prepared to accept a catastrophic decline in the standard of living in the name of other values. In addition, economists are not particularly interested in the political implications of this assumption, or to put it in Lasswell's (1977) words: 'who gets what, when, how'. Economists are quite happy therefore to define economic growth in national terms, leaving aside the question of distribution and values.
- That the place, ownership and type of production facilities are a matter of profound concern for political authorities. Governments are rarely prepared to placidly accept the 'rules of the market' or the dictates of comparative advantage. *On the contrary*, political authorities have always attempted to manage what is produced, how it is produced and often even the very ownership of production facilities. They have erected tariff barriers and non-tariff barriers to trade; they have sought to subsidize their favoured (champion) industries; to limit and control the movement of capital, and even to control the movement of population.
- That technological advances in the past two or three decades have had a striking impact on the way in which multinational enterprises are run and this in turn has affected their investment decisions. While the rising cost of technology, combined with an accelerating turnover in

technological innovation, are forcing a growing number of enterprises
to seek a global presence (Stopford and Strange 1991; Dicken 1992),
improved communication and transportation enhance the mobility of
such enterprises. Such mobility is further augmented by a fairly free
or de-regulated trade regime and the integration of the world capital
market.
- That the *source* of economic growth lies in encouraging economic
  actors to invest. Conversely, traditional protectionist measures and
  subsidies are no longer regarded as being efficient and productive.
  Tariff barriers and other existing or potential impediments to trade
  have acted as enormous incentives for MNEs to internationalize their
  operations. Capital controls such as the infamous Tax Equalization
  Act of 1963 and regulations Q and D for capital control gave an
  enormous stimulus to the globalization of finance (Johns 1983; Strange
  1986). None the less, states possess various means at their disposal to
  'persuade' capital to flow into or remain in their territories. The aim
  of modern industrial policies is therefore to improve and enhance a
  state's natural endowments in order to win inward investment. Hence
  the new concept of 'competitive advantage' (Porter 1986, 1990) has
  largely replaced the Ricardian notion of 'comparative advantage'.
  Combine these four assumptions and we have the framework of a new
  global competitive game, one that can be interpreted both negatively
  and positively.

It can be interpreted negatively, because the logic of the situation
forces states increasingly into a zero-sum-game as they compete over
market share (Strange 1987, 1995). In a market-driven environment,
states are increasingly seeking to attract investment into their territory
and to improve their position in the international division of labour.
Growing integration and interdependence have greatly intensified such
competition, to the extent that the 'competition state' finds itself in the
grip of a 'beauty contest', trying to outbid other states by offering more
attractive incentives to capital. Those who fail to compete for capital
early enough are drained of productive investment and manufacturing
capacity and are therefore likely to experience a catastrophic decline in
economic activity. The prospects of such a gloomy scenario force a
growing number of governments to adopt an active role in promoting
growth. Thus, as Stopford and Strange observe, 'Governments, both
host and home, continue to play a crucial, and perhaps paradoxically,
an increasing role' (1991, p.7).

Conversely, this new game can be interpreted positively, as the
OECD, IMF and other multilateral agencies seem to do. Liberalization
and the provision of a stable and friendly environment for business are
regarded as offering states the best prospects for growth. Such agencies
of course do not like to dwell on the negative competitive impact of
globalization.

The competition state theory is therefore at the heart of a new
rationale and a redefinition of the relationship between states and

markets. As state and corporate policy complement each other, a new orthodoxy appears to have taken shape on a number of levels. At the collective level, there is a shared assumption that 'the free market best maximizes the real income a country can derive from its resources' (Dornbusch 1993, p.4). Such a view, expressed for instance by the OECD Ministerial Communiqué (1994) on globalization, argues that 'hindrance or reversal of globalisation, world-wide competition, technical progress or structural change, runs counter to the long-term interests of member countries'. Moreover, the structural difficulties experienced by states cannot be resolved by traditional means because 'governments do not have very much fiscal room for stimulating growth. Social expenditures and, with the notable exception of Japan, already high burdens of public debt are set to rise in the major . . . economies' (Stevens 1994, p.19).

Yet at the same time, this new orthodoxy offers a re-definition of the role and function of the state. The state should provide a stable environment for accumulation, not only by ensuring political stability but also by providing financial stability, infrastructure, an educated workforce and a favourable tax system. Redistribution, which was the mainstay of the Fordist state, has been relegated to a distant third. The Communiqué continues by calling upon member states to 'provide economic agents with a framework which gives the confidence and encouragement to move forward, macro-economic policy must pursue three interrelated objectives:

- reduce budget deficits over the medium term
- ensure lasting price stability
- support demand as necessary and appropriate'.

Whether interpreted negatively or positively, the competition state theory presents us with the rationale for the changing practice of state policy. At the same time, the general consensus, as represented by the collective response of multilateral organizations, should not blind us to the *diversity* of individual state responses to the challenges presented by the new global environment.

Beyond states and markets

How then are such responses decided? And who is responsible for creating such outcomes? These sorts of questions underpin the entire discussion of the competition state and of the evolution of competitive strategies. Indeed they also form one of the enduring problems of international relations theory, namely whether countries can be legitimately thought to pursue a distinct 'national interest' independent of social and political interests, as statist interpretations would have us believe (Krasner 1978), or whether policies are shaped primarily by the constellation of interests and the struggle between them (Poulantzas 1973).

The state and market approach has generally adopted a 'statist' conception of the state (Krasner 1978). This stresses the state as a cohesive unit of action – a unitary state. The origins of this conceptualization are to be found in idealist philosophy in which the state was deemed to possess a personality of its own (Palan and Blair 1993; Blair *et al.*). The juridical school which emerged in the middle of the nineteenth century signals a fundamental shift in the theory of international relations. Following the Romantic tradition this school asserted that it is the state – not the people, the prince or select institutions – which acts in the political sphere.[3] Such a concept of the state can be found in the work of Morgenthau (1967) and Schwarzenberger (1951). We understand such a statist interpretation to be 'an interpretation in which the state is understood as a macrocosm of the human individual and that the state as such is understood to behave in a way which maximizes its personal advantage' (Blair *et al.*, forthcoming).

In the 1970s, statist theory registered a shift from the 'metaphysical' theory of the personality of the state to the so-called neo-Weberian formulation of the unity of the state.[4] As the title of Auster and Silver's influential book reveals (*The State as a Firm* (1979)), in the neo-Weberian formulation the state is deemed to represent a social body or a social organization which, like a firm, pursues specific goals: 'The state provides the service, "protection" and punishment, and through these it manipulates the level of order' (1979, p.7). Much of the competition state literature draws, whether implicitly or explicitly, on one of these statist interpretations (often confusing the two).

Statist interpretations in international relations are generally concerned with strategic issues. So when Jackson and James reject the globalization thesis, they do so because, for them, 'The world is still, in territorial terms, made up of separate political entities, each of which, by virtue of its independent status, enjoys certain basic rights. . . . Each state still has its own interests to advance and defend' (Jackson and James 1994, p.7). Their suggestion is that the state is *still* predominantly concerned with strategic considerations such as the defence of the territory and so forth. Although realists have asserted the continuing importance of defence and strategy increasingly, though belatedly, there has been an acknowledgement that economic considerations and competitiveness are important. Such acknowledgements have emerged in the growing work of neo-realist writers.

Gilpin, in *War and Change in World Politics*, made probably the first influential attempt to understand the dynamics of economic competition in the international system. Gilpin defines the international as a form of social system. In his view, 'the purpose or social function of any social system, including the international system, may be defined in terms of the benefits the various members derive from its operation' (1987, pp.9–10). Since the 'international system' is defined as a 'system of states', this cost/benefit analysis is then conducted on a purely statist level: 'A state will seek to change the international system through territorial, political, and economic expansion until the marginal costs of further change are equal or greater than the marginal benefits' (1987, p.10). Citing North and Thomas, Gilpin asserts in a neo-Weberian fashion that 'the state is an organization that provides protection [and welfare] . . . in return for revenue' (p.15). But he concludes soon enough that 'the objectives and foreign policies of states are determined primarily by the interests of the dominant members of ruling coalitions' (p.19). Yet since this shift from state to 'élites' is equivalent to a shift from a statist to a societal interpretation of the 'state', Gilpin in effect conveniently adopts both statist and non-statist interpretations concomitantly.

Rosencrance offers a different route from a traditional statist interpretation to 'competition state' theory. In his view, 'As long as a state could get bigger and bigger, there was no incentive to regard trade with others as a strategic requirement' (1986, p.14). However, now that states are interdependent, he considers that trade had become a central goal of the national interest.

Superficially therefore, statist interpretations could easily accommodate the competition state by viewing economic competition merely as an extension of the national interest – the latter understood to be pursued by, and in the name of, a distinct social body – the state. Indeed, statist analyses have certainly added to our understanding of the competition state. Developmental state theorists like Johnson (1982), Amsden (1989) and Wade (1990) draw heavily on neo-Weberian statist theory. Nester (1993), for example, explains Japan's pursuit of neo-mercantilist policies in power politics terms. Such policies have elevated and continue to elevate Japan's position in East Asia and the world economy and in so doing reassert Japanese power. Similarly, there is a school of thought that interprets regionalism in Europe and the United States in statist terms (Silva and Sjogren 1990; Prestowitz et al. 1991). However, is it realistic to assume that countries can be legitimately thought to pursue a distinct 'national interest' independent of social and political interests? In this book we argue that ultimately, competitive strategies are shaped primarily by the constellation of interests within the state, and by the struggle or accommodation between them. Consequently, we adopt a relational theory of the state. Before we go on to address this theory we will illustrate why we feel that statist approaches are insufficient in explaining how and why divergent responses to the new competitive global environment have emerged.

Arguably among the most interesting and successful works on competition in the world economy has been the statist interpretation of 'social democracy' by Katzenstein (1986) and Dohlman (1989). These works have explored a dimension of the social model of small European states in a way that is largely ignored by welfare theorists. These scholars are at the forefront of explaining the importance of the international dimension for the study of these societies, and in many ways they are correct. Wilde (1994a, 1994b), for instance, demonstrates that Swedish political scientists of the Left had grossly underestimated the significance of changes in the international political economy. In doing so they hastened the final collapse of the 'Swedish road to socialism' through ill-thought-out policies and demands. As late as 1991, Pfaller *et al.*, who largely failed to take account of the changing global conditions, were sufficiently confident to celebrate the continuing virtues of the Swedish model just months before Carl Bildt's right-wing coalition were elected to begin dismantling it! However, while these statist interpretations of social democracy have some merits they remain ultimately limited by the confines of that very interpretation. This we will now demonstrate, and in so doing reveal why we do not adopt such an interpretation in this book.

Both statist and society-based theories agree that social democratic states represent a complex and yet discrete model of integration into the world economy. Katzenstein characterizes them specifically as a corporatist 'third way', offering a uniquely beneficial form of integration. Confronted with such beneficial outcomes, the question must arise: who is the agent of change? Who is responsible for creating such an attractive outcome? Statist interpretations clearly identify the agent of change as the state itself. It is the 'state' that forged a third way between capitalism and socialism; it is the state that understood the needs of the world economy and of its own population, and it is the state that maintains control over outcomes. And yet the statist interpretation goes invariably fuzzy at crucial moments, precisely when the agent of change is finally about to be identified.

Katzenstein maintains that the 'small states' in Europe *understood* that large-scale and widespread protectionism was not in their interest. They also understood that their weak positions gave them a collective interest in pursuing multilateralism (Katzenstein 1984, pp.38–47). Katzenstein's thesis is attractive and undoubtedly illuminating. Unfortunately, he does not demonstrate the manner by which countries like Sweden or Switzerland came to 'recognize' or 'understand' the realities of the international political economy. For Katzenstein the state is represented as an undifferentiated collective mind, united in its appreciation of global realities. Other scholars have pointed out, however, that the relative economic strength of the industrial and manufacturing sectors of such states is underpinned by a strong, if small, oligarchic ruling class whose commitment to internationalization can be traced back to the end of the last century. For example, in Sweden it is estimated that the Wallenburg family controls about 40 per cent of companies listed on the Swedish stock market (*The Economist* 1994).[5] Katzenstein's 'state' is therefore in reality a rather cohesive if small 'élite'. It was they who 'recognized' the realities of small states in the world economy.

Dohlman, another statist, implicitly recognizes that the Swedish commitment to trade liberalization corresponds to the interests of its industrialists. In her words:

Industrialization began in Sweden as a process of exporting increasing quantities of raw materials . . . [thus] industries which were previously protected gradually developed a dependence on foreign imports and began to recognize (sic!) that the country would profit from more liberal trade if it lowered its tariff barriers.

(Dohlman 1989, p.61)

Yet even this implicit suggestion that parochial interests may have a role to play is avoided in subsequent pages when she begins to refer to 'official thinking'. Katzenstein similarly argues with reference to 'small states' that

> Their pursuit of economic liberalism is not based on disinterested notions of aggregated welfare but is rooted firmly in the awareness that their political autonomy and economic welfare are best served by diffusing dependence in a wider market.
>
> (Katzenstein 1986, p.44)

Here again, any notion that 'aggregated welfare' might be a contested (indeed hotly contested) political programme is brushed aside in the name of these countries' collective 'awareness'. The long and intricate road that took Sweden from a backward, poverty-ridden agrarian society to a 'modern' welfare state is simply brushed aside (Gould 1993). Milner, who seeks to introduce rational choice theory into the discussion, maintains that the tremendous insight and 'collective awareness' that these countries exhibit are rooted in a superior education programme and a lack of a strong commercial television sector (1994, pp. 109–13). Such factors consequently allow the populations of these states to make more superior 'rational choices' (1994, p.152) than their Anglo-Saxon counterparts.

We deem these sorts of explanations to be unsatisfactory. Statist interpretations, while correct in describing the uniqueness of a welfarist competitive model, fail to identify its ingredients. Katzenstein's approach is a sophisticated form of structural determinism. In his analysis global political economic structures mischievously determine the nature of a domestic political economy. His analysis oscillates between a pure structural determinist argument that centres on the size of their economies, and subjective arguments that seem to attribute these societies with superior intelligence, as if they 'understand' better than, say, American society the pitfalls of liberalism.

Towards relational theory

Ultimately, the problem in such statist interpretations is that they confuse form with content. While competitive strategies are policies and hence by definition devised at the level of the state, that does not mean that the state as a distinct social body or even social 'mind' lies at the origin of these strategies. The common thread in statist approaches is then the inability or unwillingness to consider the 'relative autonomy' of domestic political processes, and in particular, the important role played by social forces. However, by ignoring the role of these processes and forces in the determination of competitive state strategies, we are left to assume that such strategies are externally induced. While we certainly accept that globalization is inducing a change in the state, we would like to suggest that the manner by which states respond and adapt works differently.

A proficient body of work, profoundly sceptical of the uniform conceptualization of the 'international system' and of the state, has subsequently emerged. In such work there is a renewed stress on 'national uniqueness' and distinctiveness. This is driven to a large extent by empirical observations. Why, for example, asks Porter, do 'firms based in particular nations achieve international success in distinct segments and industries?' (1990, p.18). His conclusion is that 'Competitive advantage is created and sustained through highly localised processes. Differences in national economic structures, values, cultures, institutions, and histories contribute profoundly to competitive success' (1990, p.18). Porter, however, takes these different histories as given. He does not dwell on the way in which such specific histories affect the institutional and social make-up of states. For Hart (1992), the key lies in the relationship between the state and society – which is another way of saying that each country experiences a unique political process and that this process determines its external position. Hart, however, aggregates or heaps together 'domestic ingredients' without placing them in any political context. Elger and Smith (1994) push such ideas further by adding some sense of political struggle. 'National uniqueness', they maintain,

> is created by socio-economic settlements between social agencies and institutions operating on a national terrain. In particular it focuses on institutionalized arrangements between capital and labour, state–firm relations, capital–capital relations, and distinctive factory regimes within particular societies. These conditions are less the consequence of cultural legacies than of socio-political action.
>
> (Elger and Smith 1994, p.37)

Consequently there is an emphasis here on class and group interests, cultures, norms, etc. None the less, while each social formation is by definition unique, is it not the case that 'national uniqueness' merely ensures that different states respond differently to what amount to global 'environmental changes'? There is a danger here, however, that too much emphasis may be placed on internal arrangements at the expense of international factors. By focusing solely on the internal arrangements, we are in danger of losing sight of the way in which the external environment shapes and moulds competitive strategies. We therefore need to find a way of emphasizing both the domestic and the international.

There have been a few credible attempts to consider the state at both these levels. For us, the principal level has been the often misunderstood notion of the state as 'a "mode of cohesion" i.e. a form of social relationship . . . [whose] strength or weakness has to do with the quality of the relationships that have been forged' (Jessop 1985, p.337). This 'relational theory of the state' requires some further explanation.

The genealogy of relational state theory

The state, at least in the European context, evolved very slowly as an extension of the power of the prince. Slowly but surely the myriad over-lapping power relationships on the Continent were reduced to a smaller number of political entities, each of which covered increasingly larger areas governing more people. Combined with the resumption of economic activity after the Black Death, these entities could also command greater resources. The complexity of running such operations under conditions of military competition between these states forced a change in the pattern of governance. The king's and prince's personal envoys, often close family and friends, were assigned more formal roles in what was becoming an increasingly rationalized and bureaucratized mechanism of governance. The extension of the power of the prince, in particular the larger resources required by the growing 'government', created conflict with the estates and hence the class pattern of these entities was defined primarily in the struggle between these groups (Hintze 1975). At the same time, spontaneous or societal disciplinary mechanisms were being taken increasingly on board by the formal apparatus of the state.

The absolutist state already exhibited some of the basic features of the modern state in a number of ways. It was an apparatus of routinized control and discipline. Yet it was also a form of entrenched hierarchy, i.e. it was a form of institutionalization of social power. Like the modern state, its political processes were concerned with three main issues:

1 The control and suppression of the lower classes;
2 Adjudication between the conflicting interests of the ruling groups;
3 The achievement of targeted goals, internally and externally.

Subsequently, different schools of state theory have tended to focus on one or other of these themes, often to the exclusion of the other two. Traditional Marxist state theory concentrated on the first, the famous élite versus pluralism debate on the second, and various strands of public policy, including statist interpretations, on the third. However, since all three aims are and must be pursued concomitantly, the picture tends to be rather confused and contradictory, especially if seen exclusively from the perspective of only one issue.

The theoretical move initiated by Nicos Poulantzas (1973, 1978) to view the state as a social relationship rather than a concrete social body, was an attempt to capture all three themes in one synthetic state theory. The central aspect of this theory can only be briefly discussed here, but its principal concern takes us back to the time when the absolutist state was gaining prominence.

The question which lies at the heart of modern state theory was perhaps first identified by Rousseau.[6] Living in a period which saw absolutism reach its zenith, Rousseau already recognized that the new political asso-ciation was 'ethically defective', and hence likely to experience difficulties in maintaining the continuing loyalty of its members. Modern bourgeois society, he judged, suffered from an essential contradiction between the private individual on the one hand, and the citizen of the state on the other. The individual, he believed, was never free in a bourgeois society because he was not a 'whole', being always caught up between his Christian sensibilities and his patriotism. Rousseau sought to resolve this dichotomy by invoking the notion of the social contract and the *volonté générale*.

From the late eighteenth century, state theory evolved in diverging paths as contrasting philosophical traditions sought to grapple with this fundamental ethical question. In Lowith's interpretation (1964), Anglo-Saxon liberalism sought to resolve this problem by expunging religion from the equation, increasingly representing the state as an association, a means to an end, and hence an instrument of freedom. In Continental Europe, in particular in Germany, Anglo-Saxon liberalism was deemed to be fundamentally flawed. While the Anglo-Saxon world was spared the enormous upheavals of political disorder that reigned on the Continent,[7] 'The revolutionary onslaught on Germany brought home to the people the fact that they were inextricably bound up with the fate of the State' (Aris 1965, p.292). Anglo-Saxon empiricism, which sought to emulate the inductive mode of reasoning of the sciences, did not resonate well with continental philosophy. One of the early Romantics, Schleiermacher, pointed out that a social contract can only be conceived if the people who conclude it already have a strong consciousness of their membership of a social community – in other words, the social contract must presuppose the state (Aris 1965, p.301). Continental state theory therefore engaged itself at the level of this presupposition: how does the social contract come about? How is it maintained? How do people become conscious of their community? Hegel thought that liberalism was simply naive: 'Willy-nilly, the individual member of bourgeois society is educated behind his back to the generality of his personal interests. Bourgeoisie society . . . is forced against its will to become the true state as an absolute community' (Lowith 1964, p.242). The liberal formulation works therefore by assuming as an a priori that the state exists by 'forgetting' the many tasks and relationships between individual and community which give rise to the whole. Undoubtedly rooted in Christian theology,[8] it is still worth recognizing that the 'holistic' or 'metaphysical' theory of the state is grounded in an 'empirical' problem: how has the state-form survived for so long? Why are individuals prepared to sacrifice their life on the altar of the state? From where does this consciousness of the community arise? What are the historical implications of the state-form?

Marx accepted Hegel's objections, but he saw in the state not a separate social body, but the 'encapsulation' of the entire civil society. In addition, Marx also saw it not as a spiritual, but as a material entity, a form of class organization. In his rereading of Marx and Gramsci, Poulantzas (indirectly) offered a different solution to Rousseau's problematic (as well as Hobbes or Locke). He maintained that these contradictory impulses, the gap between 'citizenship' and 'individuality', are not historical accidents, problems that can be surmounted, but profound (if ultimately misleading) reflections of changing material conditions. They form an element in that contradictory unity which Marx defined as capitalism. The Hegelian-Marxist tradition strives therefore to comprehend what appear to be disparate processes, the legal, economic, political and cultural in their unity, as systemic expressions of a unified process. But it understands the unity to be contradictory. In *Capital*, Marx traced Rousseau's problematic ultimately to the contradiction embedded in the commodity form, between use-value and exchange-value. However, these sets of contradictions are then reproduced to take a variety of forms at various levels (Holloway and Picciotto 1978). Althusser (1969) maintained that the unity of the various structures in capitalism – the ideological, the political and the economic – was profoundly contradictory. He described the capitalist mode of production with the often misunderstood concept of the 'relative autonomy' of the structures.

It was Poulantzas who adopted this concept to develop the notion of the 'relative autonomy' of the state. This controversial and little understood concept is in essence not dissimilar to Locke's or Adam Smith's (in particular in the latter's discussion of money), namely the idea that capitalism needs to be defended from itself. Locke, for instance, advocated that 'the civil government needed to regulate the situation and adjudicate between unequal claims on natural resources in the interest of society as a whole' (Deane 1989, p.28). The idea that capitalism requires an external regulatory mechanism has been debated for centuries and is well understood. In European political thought, legitimate public authority, or the rulers, were entrusted with power so they could promote their subjects' welfare. Jean Bodin, credited as the progenitor of the modern doctrine of sovereignty, maintained that a good prince 'takes account of the wishes of the people in the task that God entrusted to him' (Bodin 1986/1576, p.196, our translation).

Rulers therefore had a 'sacred' duty to promote growth, which in a capitalist economy takes the form of the growth of capitalism. In exercising their duty, one of the central functions of public authority was always to defend capitalism from itself. If you attempt to quantify this regulatory relationship, if you asked Locke or Adam Smith, in the same way as Skocpol asked Poulantzas, to what extent 'government' is required to be autonomous of 'civil society', they would probably have answered: completely and not at all. Completely, because government needs the autonomy to pursue the true interests of its 'people' (and by implication, of capitalism), and not at all because government needs to be embedded in the social formation. In short, Locke, Hume or Smith would have been unable to 'quantify' the relative autonomy of the state in the same way as Poulantzas did not; the question therefore is misplaced.

For Poulantzas, the liberal 'problematic' as captured in the work of the classical economists is both profound and illusive. It is profound in that it tells us something fundamental about the relationship between political authority, social power and the economy in the capitalist mode of production – a point which has been largely ignored by Marxist political economists up to his age. As we will see in Chapter 9, those countries that fail to adapt and compete in the modern world economy, those that are 'not in the game', are precisely those where the state lacks a 'relative autonomy', where ironically it is acting more like a firm, taxing its people in return for 'protection'. In these countries capitalist accumulation grinds to a halt, and, contrary to Jackson and Rosberg (1986) as indeed to Wallerstein, these countries in fact provide evidence to support Poulantzas' theory, i.e. they form a 'structural barrier' to capitalism.

For Poulantzas the relative autonomy of the state is seen as encapsulating the solution to the fundamental problem posed by the contradictions within capitalism. It is not simply enough for the capitalist state to reflect these contradictions because ultimately this could lead to the self-destruction of the capitalist system. The state, understood broadly as the entire constellation of social forces, needs to fulfil an adjudicatory role between contradictory interests, and it is this function that Poulantzas refers to as the relative autonomy of the state. However, in identifying the solution to the contradictory nature of capitalism, Poulantzas fails to examine how this solution emerged historically, and to our knowledge there has been very little work undertaken to answer this question (Wolfe 1977; Mann 1994). To take another of Hegel's insights, it is clear that military competition in Europe was possibly one of the main catalysts for change as well as for diffusing 'best practice' organization which ended up as 'relative autonomy'.

We are not, however, simply singing the praises of Poulantzas. Like many other state theorists, he ignored the case of Japan as well as – perhaps unexpectedly – the Scandinavian case. Consequently his typology is far too restricted. However, we chose to pursue our argument through Hegel, Marx and Poulantzas for two reasons. First, to argue for a 'holistic' conception of the state in which the state is viewed not as a concrete body but as a form of social relationship. Second, there is a strong body of thought that seeks to redefine the state as a social relationship and takes this 'abstract notion' of the state as a problem which needs to be resolved (Easton 1981). However, the 'abstraction' of the state is viewed in the Marxist tradition as an expression of capitalist contradictions, and is in fact one of the key aspects of modern political authority; it also reveals the very fundamentals of the workings of this authority.[9] Whereas if one wishes to negate the abstraction of the state, to treat it as a mere problem that should be avoided, one invariably ends up by reifying the state into a social body contrasted with an equally reified construct called 'society'. However, as we have tried to demonstrate, our conception of society and indeed the historical emergence of such social entities cannot be separated from the evolution of the state.

Four sources of diversity in state strategies

So what are the practical advantages that such a 'holistic' theory of the state offers us in this book? As we have argued, the state does not possess the individuality and singularity of purpose that are attributed to it by statist interpretation: the state, in fact, is not a personality but a social construct, and its policies are shaped by social forces. Relational state theory therefore takes 'the state' largely out of the narrative. Although we talk about the state, the state is not considered in this book as the 'unit of analysis'. We do not assume that the state is imbued with distinct needs and interests; indeed, we tend to assume very little about the state as such: the emphasis is placed instead on the confluence between domestic and global forces. Therefore the 'choice' of strategy is not taken by the state as a cohesive body. However, this does not mean that 'the state' is unimportant, but that its importance needs to be gauged differently.

The state therefore is not absent from this study. It is not simply a 'black box', an arena of conflict between group interests. If it was, there would be no point in talking about competitive strategies; 'states' would be seen merely as 'introverted' social entities 'responding' by accident to external changes. So the state must be brought in, but in a roundabout way. If the notion of the state as an adaptive mechanism which possesses in modern times a 'relative autonomy' has any practical value, it is to highlight the fact that states are power organizations: that they centralize and concentrate social power. Power has to be concentrated, but it also has to be executed and directed, otherwise it is merely dissipated. 'Policy' is in effect the term we use to describe the application of this concentrated social power towards prescribed goals. Value is placed on coherency and consistency in policy making so as to ensure a higher probability of achieving results. But as resources and power are not distributed evenly in the international environment, consequently the question of who pursues a strategy is as important as the strategy itself.

This observation has two broad implications:

1 However diverse and incompatible social interests might be, one of the tasks of the state is to create ostensible coherence in its policies.[10] We therefore find that a 'facade' of coherency in policies and consistency in its 'world view' (or ideology) is maintained. Such 'facades', or as Poulantzas called them 'hegemonic projects', when taken at face value, are often mistaken for practice. This suggests to us that 'models' of state behaviour (which are in effect the ideological facet of coherency), whether presented under the rubric of 'neo-liberalism', 'Keynesianism' or 'social democracy', are merely mobilization ideologies mistaken for practices. However, as with ideologies, they are not without significance; they affect and, indeed, over-determine the plethora of strategies that are pursued 'on the ground'.
2 At the same time, we must bear in mind that state policies are geared not only to maintain internal peace (to 'adjudicate' between conflicting

interests), but also to provide a collective response to *perceived* environmental changes. We highlight the notion of perception here, which in light of the work of sociology and neo-institutionalism (Powell and DiMaggio 1991) demonstrates the intricacies of processes which take place under the notion of 'adaptation' and 'learning'. At the same time, the notion of the 'relative autonomy' reminds us that any form of adaptation and change is over-determined by the internal constellation of forces.

When we examine the plethora of strategies, we find that there are a number of considerations that determine which is pursued:

1 In the vast majority of cases we find that the original competitive strategy lies in a historical compromise which is determined to some extent by geographical and other logistical conditions. Significantly, in all cases under review, it was from about the 1970s that the successful historical compromises began to be viewed as offering a competitive advantage and hence began to be emulated from that time.

For example, the origins of the strategy of size (Chapter 3) can be found in historical, geographical and class-specific factors within the USA. These combined to create significant economies of scale and to lay the foundations for the emergence of both the modern industrial corporation and the mass market. For example, Chandler argues that the modern multinational corporation was created by necessity to accommodate the geographical size and rapid growth of the US domestic market in the early nineteenth century. This vast geographical space and the distances between urban centres meant that many more railroads had to be constructed. This in turn required better managed, coordinated efforts on a continental scale and stimulated the development of other mammoth industrial enterprises such as Standard Oil (Chandler 1990, p.55), as well as necessitating the creation of modern financial institutions.

None the less, it was only in the late 1970s that the idea of artificially creating a large market in Europe to stimulate the sort of industrial and financial organizations that could compete against the Americans and Japanese, was seriously discussed (Franko 1990). Similarly, the Swiss tax haven strategy, which today has been emulated by more than forty states worldwide, began because of Switzerland's inherent conservatism (Fehrenbach 1966). While Europe began to introduce personal taxation in the early 1930s, Switzerland failed to follow suit and thus became a haven for tax evaders. Similarly, the Nordic model was shaped by the specific outcome of a number of compromises made in the 1920s and 1930s between organized labour, agrarian interests and a conservative export-inclined oligarchic élite (Wilson 1979). The dual-natured economy that emerged from these compromises provided, by historical fortune, a trajectory of development which delivered buoyant economic growth, peaceful industrial relations and a shelter from the more harmful disintegrative effects of international market forces.

Porter points out that most of Sweden's multinationals may be traced in some way to Sweden's natural resource endowment (1990, p.342). The success of Swedish companies was that 'despite a loss of competitive advantage in natural factors, and in some cases because of it, Swedish firms moved into more sophisticated industries and industry segments' (p.343). Porter identifies what he calls 'selective factor disadvantages', such as high wages and benefits that forced companies to innovate, the long winters and cold climate that led to the development of sophisticated technology in energy conservation, the long distances between resources and cities that led to greater sophistication in transport and logistics-related industries, and the hard climate and rugged geography which forced upon the Swedes particularly tough conditions in Swedish mining, transport and manu-facturing companies (p.345). Thus the original 'models' for each strategy reflect specific historical conjunctures.

2 Once in place these successful strategies become widely emulated. In instances where 'the state' achieves a great deal of autonomy, the state itself plays a major emulatory role. The extreme case is perhaps represented by Japan. Morishima recounts for example that

> In a search of a model for their modern state the government sent many missions to Europe and America. . . . In each country they investigated the conditions of such things as the police, industry and finance. On the basis of the information relating to these subjects obtained from the missions the government made its decision as to which sphere should be patterned on which country. For example, the education system promulgated in 1872 was patterned on the French system of school districts. The Imperial Navy was a copy of the Royal navy. The telegraph and the railways followed the British example, universities the American. The Meiji Constitution and the Civil Code were of German origin, but the criminal Code was of French origin.
>
> (Morishima 1982, p.88)

In the end, the Japanese state was an eclectic amalgamation of foreign ingredients superimposed upon one another. The autonomy of the state largely corresponded to the strength of its 'élite' which pro-duced its own unique brand of state ideology, a nationalist-paternalist capitalist state which ensured that labour and socialist movements were viewed as seditious (Chapter 4). We often find, however, that emulation is not initiated by the government but by interested sectors. The origins of the Single European Act can be traced to the activities of Gylhammer from Volvo and Dekker from Phillips, significantly representing two of the major sectors suffering from Japanese and American competition. The Single European Act can be regarded as a defensive strategy ostensibly initiated by these two industrial sectors. Using their influence in both governmental and non-governmental arenas, such groups managed to persuade European government and the European Commission to pursue the strategy of size.

Similarly, in order to assist its fledging Euromarket operation and maintain the City of London leading position in the financial sector, the first act of the Thatcher government was to abolish foreign exchange controls. The US Treasury, however, was strongly opposed to similar provisions. With the active encouragement of the New York banking community, particularly Citibank and Chase, a swift *volte-face* took place culminating in the establishment of the New York offshore market, the New York International Banking Facilities (IBF) on 1 December 1980. In turn, the creation of the New York IBF spawned the creation of the Tokyo and Singaporian IBFs and so the effects of 'off-shorization' were spread much wider. Model strategies are therefore widely emulated, a process which all the evidence suggests has intensified greatly since the early 1970s. Emulation takes place in three stages: first, enterprises seek to emulate the 'best practices' of their rivals; second, in their emulation they enlist the state to support them and produce the environment within which they can compete, and third, the strategy becomes state policy.

3 'No nation can be competitive in . . . everything' (Porter 1990, p.18). At the same time, the national economy produces macro-economic conditions that generate selectivity. There is an important debate over whether the types of condition that stimulate a strong financial sector strengthen or inhibit a strong industrial and manufacturing sector (Nairn 1978; Albert 1993). A vibrant financial sector tends to be located in less well-regulated environments, to be fickle and short term in its outlook, and at the same time to generally support an overvalued currency. These are precisely the conditions that inhibit buoyant industrial growth.

Returning to Porter's initial enquiry, namely how is it that in a period of increasing market integration 'firms based in particular nations achieve international success in distinct segments and industries?' (1990, p.18), the answer appears to lie in the way economic growth operates in a 'national' economy. The export success of those industries with a competitive advantage tends to push up the costs of labour, inputs and capital, thus making other industries uncompetitive. In Germany, Sweden and Switzerland, for example, this process has led to a contraction of the clothing industry in favour of those firms in specialized segments which can support very high wages.

More broadly, we can say that not all goods can be produced everywhere and not all businesses are equally profitable. Thus a hierarchy in production has emerged on a global scale. This hierarchy is the obverse side of the 'international division of labour', and it goes some way towards explaining the diverging paths of competition. In effect, this hierarchy has two dimensions. Most of the analyses of the new competitive global economic environment assume a simple dichotomy between high value-added goods and low value-added goods. The advanced industrial countries are regarded as continuing to specialize in the production of the former while the developing world increasingly moves into the production of those low value goods that were once 'sunrise' industries. Furthermore, high value-added products compete on non-price variables such as quality and thus allow workers in such industries to command high wages. In addition, such goods are generally produced and consumed in societies with an excellent infrastructure, education and more importantly, a high standard of living.

However, to this a new dimension in the international division of labour was added. New lucrative markets in high value-added niches have increasingly been discovered in traditionally low value-added industries such as textiles. These have allowed some advanced industrial countries to remain in the global market for these products (Gereffi 1992). Italy, for example, has resisted low wage competition in footwear by increasingly exploiting the niche market in high-priced fashionable leather shoes (Gereffi 1992, p.104). Similarly, high labour costs in the Scandinavian countries encouraged diversification into high value-added market niches in intermediate technologies such as cars and household goods. As a result the fledging Swedish automobile industry was revived during the 1980s because companies were able to exploit design and safety features in return for higher prices.

4 Indeed, we recognize on numerous occasions in this book the re-markable resilience of political and societal structures. Accordingly emulation and innovation occur on a number of levels: at the level of individual firms; at the sectoral level, and indeed at the level of the state. Ultimately we find that social structures are fairly rigid and that states therefore pursue fairly predictable strategies. Indeed, because of the inherent uniqueness of each social formation, emulation is never completely achieved, and thus, by definition, each emulation produces something subtly new which contributes to the diversity of state responses to globalization. Finally, all competitive strategies are ultimately susceptible to 'crowding'. The more states and companies that try to compete for the same niche in the world market, the less valuable and effective the strategy becomes.

Notes

1 In the 1970s Anthony Sampson remarked on a certain naivety regarding the behaviour of MNEs: 'Many articles and books have emerged in the last few years . . . they explain that the giants are sensitive; but there is a striking absence of case histories of individual companies. "The multinational firm seeks to be a good citizen of each country where it has operations," says Professor Charles Kindleberger. "Contrary to the common impression," writes Professor Raymond Vernon, "large enterprises are remarkably reluct-ant to invoke the support of the US government in overcoming the obstacles created by other governments". Into this reassuring world of theory, ITT has stampeded with the subtlety of an angry elephant, leaving a trail of memos behind it to leave no doubt about its motives and intentions' (1973, p.276). ITT has not proved the exception to the rule.

2 OECD countries spend on average over 40 per cent of their budget on 'transfer' funds (OECD 1995).

3 'The state . . . must be conceived as a unity, this unity being, as Jellinek says "a form of synthesis necessarily imposed upon us by our consciousness" points toward a unity behind the empirical agencies of government. This is the state itself, a collective person, to which alone ultimate authority belongs and whose being consists solely in the fact that it is the repository of political and legal authority' (Sabine and Shepard 1922, p.xxxi).

4 The critique of international relations' conception of the state had been discussed on a number of occasions by one of us. See Palan 1988; Palan and Blair 1993; Gills and Palan 1994; Halliday 1994.

5 As *The Economist* observed, 'Peter Wallenberg has been pretty successful at persuading the left that what is good for his group is good for Sweden' (*The Economist* 1994, p.14).

6 The following thesis draws on Lowith (1964).

7 It is noteworthy that Hobbes, who lived through the English revolution of the seventeenth century, is so atypical.

8 According to Otto Gierke, the earliest mention of the social contract was at the Council of Paris and Worms at Paris AD 829 (Ullmann (1975) and Nisbeth (1974) date it much earlier), where it was stated that the ruler's mandate was 'to rule the Folk with rightouseness and equity, to preserve peace and unity' (Gierke 1900, p.142, n.125). Similarly, Guilelmus Occam contends 'a plenitudo potestatis incompatible with the best Form of Government, which should promote the liberty and exclude the slavery of the subjects' (cited in Gierke 1900, p.142).

9 As Marx argued, the 'abstraction' of the capitalist state is not a case of mistaken identity, a mystifying conceptual tool. 'The abstraction of the state as such belongs only to the modern era, because the abstraction of private life belongs only to the modern era' (Lowith 1964, p.245). For Marx therefore, the 'abstraction' of the state is not a problem to be avoided, shunted aside, resolved by clever definition as Easton seems to advocate (1981); the abstraction is central to our understanding of the political authority and capitalism.

10 That aspect is now at the core of modern organizational theory (Powell and DiMaggio 1991).

3

Large markets as strategies of competition in the modern political economy

> The nation state has become an unnatural, even dysfunctional, unit for organizing human activity and managing economic endeavour in a borderless world.
>
> (Ohmae 1993, p.78)

The passions and divisions generated during the debates over the North American Free Trade Agreement and the Maastricht Treaty bear witness to one of the central problems of the modern age, namely that independence, self-determination and welfare do not always go hand in hand. The very fact that first, the European Union, and latterly NAFTA were devised implies that, in some aspects at least, nation-states can no longer be considered to be the most efficient and functional entities for ensuring economic growth, jobs and rising living standards. Bloc formation, regionalism and integration are therefore the product of attempts to build new communities and institutions that transcend the nation-state.

It was clear for many years that the geographical size of the United States combined with its steadily growing population contributed to its emergence as a military and economic superpower. Similarly, the re-emergence of China on to the global economic scene in the last two decades is testimony to its two major natural factor endowments – its population and its geographical size. China will become the world's single largest economy and market sometime during the twenty-first century. Arguably, with that will come a shift in the international political economy of a magnitude not seen since the United States overtook Great Britain at the turn of the twentieth century.

Prior to the creation of the European Union it was merely given that some states were small and others large, possessing natural factor endowments that policy-makers could do little about. Indeed, in this light imperialism may be regarded as an attempt to overcome geographical and population constraints on national accumulation. Nevertheless, the second phase of European integration that began with the launching of the Single European Market represents the first time in modern history that a conscious strategy was adopted by states to create the conditions within which collectively their economic and political power could be enhanced. With the creation of the European Union, sheer market size became a strategy of competition. NAFTA, Mercosur, the Maghreb Union and to a lesser extent APEC as well as other regional organizations have emerged partly in response and partly in emulation and confirmation of the European example.

It is such collective attempts by states to create larger economic units that we have coined the strategy of size. In this chapter we will discuss the various arguments put forward to explain the pursuit of this strategy. In addition, we will assess both the effectiveness of the strategy as well as the broader structural implications that regionalism poses for the world economy.

Territory and competitiveness

The best illustration of the potential of large economic units is provided by the growth of the US economy in the nineteenth and early twentieth centuries. What most strikingly differentiated the United States from Britain and Germany in the late nineteenth century was the geographical size and rapid growth of its domestic market. Not only was the American population dispersed over a much larger land mass, but it was more rural than either Britain or Germany. By 1851, half of Britain's population lived in towns of 5000 or more, a figure not reached in the US until 1960. The vast geographical space and the distances between urban centres meant that many more railroads had to be constructed. This required better managed, coordinated efforts on a continental scale. During the 1850s, writes Chandler, 'American railroads became the pioneers in modern management. Because of the complexities of their operations they formed almost overnight the nation's first managerial enterprise' (1990, p.54). The railroads stimulated other mammoth industrial enterprises such as Standard Oil (Chandler, 1990, p.55) while necessitating the creation of modern financial institutions.[1] In order to cover the vast distances and a scattered population, American industry set up more production and distribution units in their domestic markets than either Britain or Germany. By the late nineteenth century a large, thriving domestic market, serviced by hierarchically organized, well-coordinated and controlled enterprises, consequently had emerged.

Due to westward expansion, brought on by the gold-rush and rapid industrialization, there was a shortage of labour in the US market which meant that frontier wages stood at about twice or three times the average European rate (Brogan 1985). This in turn stimulated the quest for mechanization, which further reduced the unit costs of production (Aglietta 1979). The combined effects of mechanization, relatively high wages, the size of the market and the managerial and technological skills of American companies created significant economies of scale and laid the foundations for the emergence of the modern mass market. During the early period of this century, this potent mixture entered into an internal virtuous circle of unprecedented growth.

The success of American corporations in technological innovation, lowering costs and augmenting their financial power and managerial skills demonstrated the benefits to industry of large-scale markets. Since the early 1920s, the American continental economy therefore served as a model of the economic dynamism that economies of scale could generate. Such ideas found a particularly attentive audience in Europe.

In contrast to the failed attempt at European *political integration* in the early post-Second World War period the more cautious European Economic Community (EEC) proved a spectacular success. From an index of 100 in 1953, industrial production in the EEC had risen to 188 by 1965 in comparison to 154 amongst the EFTA members and 149 in the United States. Similarly while world trade doubled between 1957 and 1968, trade within the EEC trebled. Despite initial caution over the question of sovereignty, this success prompted the United Kingdom to seek membership of the communities. This reflected a degree of alarm in the UK over its poor economic performance relative to its European allies. As we will see, neoclassical economics also provided justifications for the re-launching of European integration with the Single European Act.

Unfortunately, despite the fact that the theme of regionalism/bloc formation has been widely discussed and debated, the focus of this dialogue has largely concentrated on the hype, anxieties and hopes of this trend. There is little consensus therefore on what the trend towards regionalism actually represents. This is partly due to the diverse context and the polemical nature in which the debate has been conducted. In the popular press, the focus of discussion has concentrated on sovereignty and accountability (e.g. the so-called 'democratic deficit' within the EU), and the consequences that these new organizations have for age-old questions of nationalism, patriotism and materialism.

The academic literature has generally avoided such hyperboles. Since Viner's (1950) pioneering work on integration a bewildering assortment of literature has emerged which discusses the phenomenon. For simpli-fication this can be divided into three broad assessments of what the trend represents. First, that regionalism represents an extension of the present multilateral trading system; second, that regionalism is a political strategy pursued to improve and enhance the member states' competitive position and power in the world economy, and third, that it represents a structural response to the problems emerging with the globalization of the world economy.

1 *Deepening multilateralism* One of the arguments postulated for the failure of earlier attempts at regional integration in the early post-war period such as those made by the Latin American Integration Association, the Central American Common Market, the Andean Pact and the Latin American Free Trade Association, has been that the United States was firmly committed to the multilateral approach and did not endorse regionalism outside Europe (De Melo *et al.* 1993). The revival of interest in integration accompanied the increasing frustration of American negotiators over the failure to reach an early conclusion of the Uruguay Round. It is believed that the multilateral trade process cannot

now work with so many participants and an ever more complex agenda, in particular since the agenda has shifted to non-tariff issues and service industries. By grouping together into small but powerful blocs which bargain between each other, it is argued that GATT can be strengthened.[2]

In this view regional and bilateral trading arrangements between some states, particularly close neighbours, are one way in which the multilateral system can move forward. While regional trade provides many of the advantages of multilateralism it is generally simpler to negotiate and encompass issues that GATT has not resolved (particularly rules governing investment and trade in services). Such considerations do not necessarily signal the demise of the multilateral trade system. Indeed, the conclusion of the Uruguay Round bore witness to the United States using its commitment to NAFTA and APEC as a lever for ending European intransigence. Hufbauer and Schott (1993), for example, argue that a continued open world trading system is fundamental to the long-term success of NAFTA because '[it] will make North American firms more competitive in world markets and thus better able to take advantage of the increased trade opportunities created by the . . . Uruguay Round reforms' (p.116). However, this is not to say that protectionist leanings will not arise as the deterioration in US–Japan trade relations during the Clinton presidency illustrates.

2 *A strategic decision*   In addition, regionalism is viewed as a economic strategy pursued by states in order to improve and enhance their competitiveness in the global economy. 'One should see the NAFTA,' argue Hufbauer and Schott, 'as an integral part of a national competitiveness strategy, one . . . designed to . . . promote the ability of local industries to compete more effectively against foreign suppliers' (1993, p.116). In accepting this assessment of regionalism the emphasis is shifted on to the political motivations behind the decision to pursue such a strategy. Much of the literature that asserts such an assessment is derived from so-called strategic trade theory (see, for example, Reich 1983; Krugman 1986; Zysman 1983) which although encompassing a range of opinions interprets the trend in broadly statist/mercantilist language. It is less a strategy about economics than a strategy about 'powernomics' (Prestowitz *et al.* 1991).

3 *Structural argument*   Regionalism is also viewed as a response to the changing global environment which is undermining the traditional pre-eminence of the nation-state. The ever increasing internationalization of production, trade and finance coupled with the increasing global nature of economic and environmental problems appear to be questioning the functional ability of the state. The ERM crises of 1992 and 1993, for instance, starkly revealed the inability of European states to maintain their exchange rate targets in the face of the massive speculative flows in the international financial markets while issues such as transboundary air pollution and climate change necessitate concerted global action.

Regionalism, it is argued, provides the institutional conditions for the expansion of capital. Drache maintains that it is an instrument of domestic restructuration in a neoclassical framework: 'The external market is being used,' says Drache, 'to create a paradigm shift between domestic markets, regional economies, and states' (1993, p.74). If multinational enterprises have set the pace, expanding and integrating the world market, then the drift towards regionalism represents tentative and incremental political responses to the economic realities. Regional blocs are thus viewed as functional necessities for capitalist accumulation.

As will be argued below, underlying each of these broad assessments lies a specific rationale for interpreting regionalism in such a way: first there is the *neoclassical* economic rationale that underpins much of the literature discussing regionalism and multilateralism in a favourable manner, with its emphasis placed firmly on the efficiency of economies of scale; second, a *strategic rationale* that sees bloc formation as a consequence of competition between states for economic and political power, and third, a Marxist/structural approach that argues that the process of integration is driven by a particular *coalition of interests*, largely international business and financial concerns. It is to these rationales that we will now turn.

The neoclassical rationale

Broadly speaking, neoclassical economics is favourably predisposed towards larger markets on the grounds that they provide economies of scale for industry, which in turn improves the terms of trade of member states and creates a large internal consumer market that stimulates investment. Larger markets create an economic environment in which political boundaries are rendered relatively unimportant. Such economic space is created through the lowering of tariffs, the harmonization of laws and regulations and a commonly traded currency. According to this rationale larger markets are not strategically pursued; rather they are the natural consequence of allowing the 'invisible hand' to regulate economic activity. What then are the specific economic arguments for the creation of a larger market?

Economies of scale

The most common explanation for creating larger markets is that economies of scale can be achieved between the member states that would be impossible in isolation (Machlup 1977; De Melo *et al.* 1993). Modern industry is characterized by the growth of multi-unit firms which are able to reap dynamic economies of scale within a large market such as the European Union.[3] *Economies of scale* may be defined as those which result when the increased size of a single operating unit producing or distributing a single product reduces the unit cost of production or distribution (Chandler 1990, p.17), with benefits for both producers and consumers. Such a larger unit of production allows for a more efficient division of labour, greater specialization among the workforce and hence more efficient production that yields (or should yield) relatively cheaper products.

Economies of scale are a significant factor in the formation of all larger economic units. Such economies enable firms to meet greater market demand by moving down their long-run average cost curves. This then allows firms in member states, so the argument goes, to expand production until the marginal cost is less than or equal to the world price. As much of this production as possible should then be consumed within the trading area and the residual exported. Any good for which the minimum cost is above the world price will not be produced because free trade will ensure this (De Melo *et al.* 1993, pp.169–70). For example, economies of scale in the car industry within the EU have allowed France and Germany, in particular, to successfully penetrate other EU markets, while Italy has been successful in such products as refrigerators and washing machines (Harrop 1989). Although economies of scale vary from industry to industry, and some relatively small states such as Sweden and Switzerland have been able to produce some of the world's major multinationals, the EU has been aiming to provide a market size to match the economies of scale and the standardization and productivity levels of the United States. The argument for larger markets is therefore tied up with consumer gains.

Yet producer gains are also evident because economies of scale lead to an increase in intra-industry trade. Freer trade as a result of such larger economic units enables countries to concentrate production in fewer, larger plants. Although such trade has always existed, it has increased substantially in the EU. In 1980, intra-industry trade ranged from 50 per cent in Italy to 65 per cent in France and the Benelux countries. Such trade exists particularly in differentiated products in which multi-nationals are involved, for example, in the automobile industry.

An additional benefit accrued from economies of scale is a world class research and development programme.[4] There is indeed evidence to suggest the regionalization of large-scale research and development outlay. Following the US semiconductor manufacturing technology consortium (SEMATECH) initiative, a major new Pan-European research and development programme began in 1989. This was the Joint European Submicron Silicon Initiative (Jessi) with a budget of ECU 4 billion (Flamm 1990, p.282).

Also implicit in the neoclassical rationale on size is the assumption that a competitive internal market generates winners that are then able to compete in the world market, as De Melo *et al.* argue: 'technological diffusion is more likely to be rapid if increased competition from trade puts pressures on domestic firms to adopt . . . new technologies' (De Melo *et al.* 1993, p.184). Such heightened competition forces firms to innovate and adopt efficient technologies and managerial strategies that then place them in a better competitive position in the world economy (Chandler 1990).

Large markets therefore generate economies of scale that in turn facilitate the emergence of efficient, market-responsive, economic actors, benefiting both consumers and producers and generating in the process world class economic champions. According to this rationale, larger markets are thus seen to create an 'enabling' environment.

Terms of trade

The idea that integration can yield gains in member states' terms of trade was first formulated by Jacob Viner in 1950 and has since been accepted as an orthodoxy by scholars in international trade theory and indeed political economy. Viner argued that integration could both create or divert trade. In the former case integration among the members of a customs union can lead to the substitution of high cost domestic production from one member to lower cost imports from another. In other words, in a large trading area the costs of production can be reduced, and in substituting this production to another, member states' terms of trade may improve relative to non-members. For example, it has been calculated that member states of the EU have been able to improve their terms of trade by up to 1 per cent of GNP. However, critics of this theory argue that rather than trade creation, trade diversion may occur. Returning to Viner, trade diversion occurs when integration leads to the substitution of low cost imports from a non-member state to low cost imports originating in a 'preferred' member state. Trade diversion, however, is only likely to be small where member states have a high proportion of intra-union trade and a relatively low common external tariff (CET). The terms of trade theory suggest that large market size by its sheer weight generates further production within its boundaries, however, some of this production and manufacturing could otherwise potentially remain outside.

Inward investment

In recent years the growth and volume of FDI have exploded. The 1991 UN World Investment Report (UNCTC 1991) found that between 1984 and 1987 FDI outflows nearly tripled, and increased by 20 per cent between 1988 and 1989. Between 1983 and 1989 FDI outflows grew at nearly three times the world export growth and four times the world output. By 1989 total world stock of this investment stood at $1.5 trillion. With respect to inward investment, size strategy appears to be undoubtedly a winner. A large expanding market is conducive to a greater level of investment. As De Melo *et al.* observe, '[a]n enlarged market also increases the stimulus for investment to take advantage of the enlarged market and to meet the expanding competition' (1993, p.184).

Implicit in much of the literature is that by joining together in a bloc, states ensure either directly or indirectly that they receive foreign direct investment. This reasoning argues that internationalization and globalization necessitate a presence by major multinational corporations in the world's major markets (Dunning 1985; Porter 1986). Indeed, the evidence for such a conclusion is overwhelming. The largest share of FDI goes to the developed world and has actually been increasing in recent years, from 75 per cent between 1980 and 1984 to 81 per cent between 1980 and 1989. Within this concentration the United States, the European Union and Japan have traditionally dominated outward investment flows (84 per cent in 1980); however, in the 1980s they have also taken a growing share of inward investment (50 per cent in 1980 and 55 per cent in 1989). These figures suggest that the larger blocs are trading more with each other. A clear example of the use of size to attract inward investment is best illustrated with the catalytic effect the Single European Act had on FDI in the European Union. Although investment in the EU slackened in the 1970s, US and Japanese investment in the run-up to the completion of the internal market dramatically surged. In 1985 total inward investment to the EU from the US and Japan stood at $86 billion, and by 1988 this had increased to $134.3 billion. More dramatic was the increase in intra-EU investment. This increased from 25 per cent of total FDI in 1980 to 40 per cent in 1988, when it stood at approximately $140 billion.

A similar trend is evident in the rise of FDI to the People's Republic of China. As economic conditions have become more liberalized the attractiveness of China's immense internal market has begun to draw in increasing foreign capital. From just over half a billion dollars in FDI between 1980 and 1984, inward investment flows increased sixfold to $3.29 billion between 1988 and 1989. Although as a percentage of total FDI flows this figure is marginal, as a percentage of total FDI flows to the developing world it represents 11.2 per cent in 1988 to 1989, and 21.6 per cent of total FDI in East and SE Asia (4 per cent and 11 per cent respectively in 1980 to 1984).

However, even these figures under-represent the investment benefits of such a strategy because they do not take into account the sort of investments that would have otherwise shifted elsewhere. The fear of disinvestment, argues Bhagwati (1993), was the main stimulus to Mexican support for NAFTA.[5] Hufbauer (1990) calls this 'the magnet phenomenon', whereby states bordering a large trading area are compelled to seek ever closer ties with the area for fear that they will lose investment in relation to the members of the trading area. As the UNCTC Report reveals, this results in the formation of clusters of FDI between a single member of the triad and those states typically most proximate to it geographically. Such concerns may be regarded as a reason behind the decision of the EFTA member states and the states of Eastern Europe to seek closer ties with the EU.

Large, thriving markets, therefore, certainly ensure a slice in global investment. Curiously, in the debates over EU or NAFTA there has been remarkably little discussion about the ability to attract investment. The reasons are not difficult to ascertain. The problem is that whereas the bloc as a whole attracts investments, not all states within the bloc are likely to be equally attractive to foreign investors. Japanese firms, for instance, have shown a clear preference for the UK, the Netherlands and the financial centre of Luxembourg. These three countries have received the lion's share of Japanese FDI, growing from 46 per cent of the total EU inflow from Japan in 1980 to 85 per cent in 1988 (Thomsen and Nicolaides 1991). Foreign investment can therefore be a double-edged sword, as the members of a bloc enter into perverse competition in regulatory laxity and offer 'sweeteners' to foreign capital.

The strategic rationale

During the 1980s there emerged a radical new economic approach which challenged the neoclassical paradigm that had gained widespread acceptance under the collective impact of Thatcherism and Reaganism. *New trade theory*, as it became known, developed to counter the assumption that in a 'borderless world' (Ohmae 1990) national economic policy was becoming redundant, subject to the 'embedded financial orthodoxy' (Cerny 1993) of the market economy. This theory, which began life in the debate over industrial policy that took place in the United States as early as 1982, takes the view that government should join forces with industry to conduct a coordinated national competitive strategy. In particular, the new trade theorists (Reich 1983, 1990; Krugman 1986; Zysman 1988) have argued that in reality the global market does not match the perfect conditions of the neoclassical rationale and that political intervention can actually create comparative advantage, or as Porter succinctly describes it, competitive advantage.

The state's role should therefore be to facilitate the competitiveness of its firms principally, but not uniquely, by providing the environment in which that can take place. 'Size' as a strategy is seen as a means of both providing such a conducive environment and as a superior instrument for asserting the strategic trade interests of those states. Regionalism is interpreted as a development which is driven primarily by political ambitions:

> Although potential regional blocs are motivated in part by economic considerations, they are primarily motivated by *political ambitions* of regional powers and the effort of each bloc to improve its bargaining position.
>
> (Gilpin 1993, p.34, emphasis added)

According to this view, sovereignty is pooled rather than lost. Instead of transferring political authority to the new politico-economic entity, sovereignty is shared in the decision to pursue a certain set of policies to further the collective welfare of members.

Curiously enough, such 'mercantilist' ideas were very much in evidence in the construction of the precursors of the modern bloc formations, the Napoleonic continental system and the *Zollverein*. Arguably the first conscious attempt at creating a large socio-economic unit for competitive advantage can be dated back to Napoleon's continental system (1806–1814). The system came into effect as a result of the Berlin and Milan decrees (1806, 1807) and was adopted by both Prussia and Russia. The system was primarily an anti-British mercantilist device, attempting to divert trade by closing the Continent to the British, in order to starve them into submission. French industrial output, for instance, was switched from Atlantic trade through Nantes, Bordeaux and Marseilles to continental trade through the north-east regions of France. However, the system also aimed at shielding less productive sectors of the French economy from superior competition. Enhanced by the protection it received, and the expansion of the domestic market from twenty-five million to forty-four million people, the relatively inferior French cotton industry blossomed during the system's existence.

The Napoleonic continental system in many ways served as a model for the founders of the German customs union in the 1830s, the *Zollverein*. At the beginning of the nineteenth century Germany consisted of a mass of over 300 independent states, each of which in turn levied their own tolls and customs duties so that there were no less than 1,800 economic frontiers. Under Napoleonic rule the number of states was reduced so that by the Congress of Vienna the German Confederation consisted of thirty-nine states. In 1818 Prussia, the largest of the German states, took the lead in embarking on the liberation of its own internal market by the removal of internal tariffs. The following year tiny Schwarzburg-Sondershausen in Thuringa (population 45,000) signed a treaty bringing it into the Prussian tariff system, thus giving birth to the *Zollverein*. In response to Prussia's plans, two rival customs unions were formed: the South German Customs Union and the Central German Commercial Association. Neither alliance proved sufficiently formidable in opposition and so by 1836, except for the German coastal states, the *Zollverein* had grown into a common trading area of around 23.5 million. However, Prussia's motives were *not solely based on the rationale of free trade*. The *Zollverein* was also a *political device* aimed at strengthening the political position of Prussia in the Confederation at the expense of the Austrian Empire (Kann 1974, p.248).

The *Zollverein* also demonstrated that by joining together, smaller states were able to increase the bargaining or countervailing power of its members *vis-à-vis* other states. Like the EU's position in the GATT talks of today, the *Zollverein* was able to negotiate a series of trade treaties with other European powers (e.g. 1839 with the Netherlands, 1842 Great Britain, 1844 Belgium and Portugal, 1845 Sardinia, 1846 Denmark and 1862 France) that would not have been possible by its individual members (Machlup 1977).

Currently, under the broad heading of the new trade theory, there is in fact a diversity of opinion as to the precise nature of the political game that is being played. The shared view is that regional blocs should be interpreted primarily as a strategy designed to increase member states' power and influence in the international political economy. According to this view, whatever the official position may be, regional blocs strengthen their members' position *vis-à-vis* their rivals.[6]

One extreme if rather popular perception of bloc formation is that it represents the highest form of modern power politics. As the title of their book *Europe 1992 and The New World Power Game* suggests, Silva and Sjorgren regard the Single European Market as 'an unforeseen power move in a higher status chess match' (1990, p.112), a move which, they warn, will place both the United States and Japan on the defence.[7]

These commentators have little doubt that if the EU and NAFTA prove successful, other regional blocs will follow. It is arguable that the re-launching of European integration in the Single European Market (SEM) programme gave perhaps the greatest impetus towards North American integration in the 1980s. But whereas American commentators view the formation of the EU with certain alarm, some Europeans already feel that the game has passed them by. Under the provocative title 'Asia's doing it. America's doing it. Let's do it here too' (Attali 1993), the former president of the European Bank of Reconstruction and Trade, Jacques Attali, claims that Europe is actually falling behind in this new 'chess' game. Attali argues that with the Pacific region responsible for an ever growing proportion of world trade and industrial output, the only way Europe can remain in the game is by pursuing a stronger common European policy.

However, the reality is more complex. As mentioned earlier, one of the arguments put forward to explain why former attempts at regionalism outside Europe were not successful was because of the firm commitment by the United States to the multilateral trading system (De Melo *et al.* 1993). A crucial difference today is that, as the US has grown relatively weaker economically *vis-à-vis* Europe and Japan, there has been both a rising protectionist sentiment in the US Congress and an increasing tendency of the United States to pursue its trade goals on a bilateral or regional basis. The North American Free Trade Agreement, it is argued, represents the most important example of this tendency. However, this shift in the direction of US foreign economic policy can be traced back to the US-Israel Reciprocal Trade Agreement of 1984. This was further encouraged during the Uruguay Round when the US met with strong opposition, particularly from the West Europeans, over attempts to liberalize agriculture, textiles and to address aircraft subsidies. In pursuing a more strategic trade policy the US sought to strengthen its role further in these negotiations by warning the Europeans that the US could turn to both its hemispheric trade and through APEC (Asia-Pacific Economic Cooperation) to increasing trade with its Pacific neighbours should GATT fail. For example, following the ratification of NAFTA by the US Congress, officials in the Clinton administration were saying that NAFTA was only the first part of a 'triple play', with the second part being a strong statement from the APEC group backing completion of the Uruguay Round by the end of 1993. In this view then, size can be regarded as a means of increasing *bargaining power* within the context of the multilateral system.

Such bargaining power can be both structural and relational (Strange 1988, see also Chapter 6, this volume). 'Size' as a strategy can wield power of both descriptions. On the bilateral and regional level relational power clearly dominates in the context of the US trade policy. However, in the Uruguay Round negotiations both the US and EU can be seen to have used structural power to make the eventual agreement reflect their interests. The turning point in the relationship between Europe and the United States over trade came during the Kennedy Round of GATT. It was as a result of the Common Commercial Policy of Treaty of Rome (1958) that the community assumed sole responsibility for trade negotiations. Thus when the Kennedy Round convened, six members were represented by a single European delegation. With a concomitant increase in the structural power of Europe, European interests have come to challenge the pro-US agenda of GATT and have brought the two parties into increasing conflict. Pelkmans (1986) maintains that when the two are cooperative GATT is decisive, but when they strongly disagree nothing happens: they agree to disagree. Thus GATT is characterized by a *bickering bigemony* (Pelkmans 1986).

Bhagwati (1993) maintains that the competitive rationale has been accentuated by the hegemonic decline of the United States. As the US has become more aware of its relative decline in the world economy it has also become more conscious of its regional power base and the attractiveness of a huge North American and perhaps Pan American market. The American (half) century might be coming to an end but US hegemony still prevails on a regional level. In this light, George Bush's Enterprise for the Americas initiative, with its emphasis on creating a free trade area that runs from Alaska in the North to Tierra del Fuego in the South, is merely a reiteration of the policies put forward by President Monroe over 150 years earlier.[8]

The interest group rationale

As is often the case, the neoclassical rationale tends to assume that if regionalism extends free trade, then by implication it also stimulates economic growth and is of benefit to all. The strategic rationale echoes such sentiments, only that this time it is the state that is deemed to benefit from regional cooperation. The interest group rationale, however, probes deeper and asks who exactly is in favour of regionalism. Who is likely to gain in relative terms? And who is likely to lose? These questions are raised principally by commentators on the left. They do not discount the neoclassical and strategic rationales, but they deem them to represent an emerging consensus among élites on the future of the direction of capitalism. Bloc formation is therefore often regarded as evidence of 'deep structural transformations in the nature of world capitalist competition' (Grinspun and Cameron 1993, p.18). Such literature is also the most critical of such developments, in particular with respect to the social, labour and environmental aspects.

Beginning with Barnet and Muller's *Global Reach* (1974) and Vernon's *Sovereignty at Bay* (1971), a growing number of writers perceive an emerging independent power of multinational corporations *vis-à-vis* states. In more recent years others have developed this idea by stressing the importance played in decision making by corporate and political élites in non-governmental organizations such as the Trilateral Commission, the Council on Foreign Relations and the Bilderberg group (Eringer 1980; Sklar 1980; Van der Pijl 1989; Gill 1991). Such groups' interests are based on the dictates of profitability and hence falling profits can be regarded as an impetus to pursue a strategy of size in order to counter such trends. Ultimately, politics and political institutions are viewed in the broader context of the functional necessity for capitalist accumulation, and the more parochial concerns of key interest groups.

This literature is uniformly united in its predication that regionalism or bloc formation has been essentially a *business agenda*. This was quite clearly the case in the second phase of European integration that led to the Single Market programme. Similarly, although traditional interpretations of the first phase of European integration have stressed that the motives were primarily military strategic ones (i.e. to counter French alarm at the prospect of German reindustrialization and to bolster Western Europe against the Soviet threat), Robert Eringer (1980) argues that the impetus for European integration actually came from business/industrial interests. Although this is somewhat difficult to substantiate, there is some evidence to suggest that this is the case. A UN report compiled by the eminent economist Nicolas Kaldor in 1948 argued at the time that although the steel and chemical industries had been restored to their 1938 level by 1946, Europe was perilously dependent upon imported agricultural products and coal. These industries were seen as being the main bottlenecks hindering the industrial recovery of Western Europe (United Nations 1948). In this light the origins of the European Coal and Steel Community in 1951 can be seen partly as a response to this economic failure.

The second phase of European integration, however, was overtly discussed as a competitive strategy conceived by European business. Early Euro-euphoria at the economic success of the Common Market gave way to pessimism in the 1970s and 1980s: 'Eurosclerosis' had set in. In relation to her rivals, as the Albert and Ball report (1983) showed, the EEC was failing. Whereas between 1960 and 1973 growth averaged 4.6 per cent, between 1973 and 1980 it had fallen to 2.3 per cent. Even more alarmingly, industrial output in the EEC only rose by 8 per cent between 1973 and 1980, compared to 16 per cent in the US and 26 per cent in Japan. Coupled with an increase in consumption of 6 per cent, investment falling by one-fifth and public expenditure rising to an average of over 40 per cent of GDP, Europe was grinding to a halt while her competitors forged ahead.

Worse still was that Europe's competitiveness was not just declining in those industries in which she had been world-famous, i.e. German cameras and British motorcycles, but more importantly in products synonymous with the modern age: VCRs, hi-fis, televisions, computers, etc. (Dumont 1990). Between 1980 and 1985, for example, Europe's share in world production of electronic goods had fallen from 26 per cent to 21 per cent, a level able to cover only 88 per cent of demand within the European market. This sense of decline was most acute in two industries that had felt the challenge from the US and in particular the Japanese, namely the electronics and automobile industries.[9]

The cost of such barriers was illustrated by the Cecchini Report (1988) and provided an impetus for the Cockfield Plan to re-launch the EC by creating a single market envisaged by the Treaty of Rome in 1956.[10] Much of the support and initiative to make European industry more competitive came from the Roundtable of European Industrialists. Not surprisingly, most vocal within this forum were the presidents of Volvo and Philips, companies whose primary activity is in those industries that were under most competitive pressure. To meet the challenge, the then vice-president of the Commission, Lord Cockfield, drew up a White Paper in 1985 which proposed the removal of such barriers. His plan was to provide the blueprint of the Single European Act that was signed by all twelve members in 1987 and was to create a single market to come into effect at the end of 1992.

The single market, and the evolution of the European Union since 1985, aimed therefore to promote and support European business to enable them to meet the threat from the US and Japan, with the threat from the latter perceived as being greater. For these industrialists the Japanese 'appeared bent on market domination wherever they struck' (Franko 1990, p.22) and that 'competition with the Japanese felt more often like total war'. Whereas during the 1970s the solution to this had been increasing protectionism and the support of national champions, it was widely felt by the 1980s, and supported by the Cecchini Report, that these measures had aggravated the situation.

The debate over NAFTA showed similar traits. A dichotomy of opinion ran between business, which was overwhelmingly in favour, and labour, which was against. The former International Trade Commission chairperson Paula Stern argued in a report released by the Progressive Policy Institute that Americans should support the pact because increased trade with Mexico would create more US jobs (Bureau of National Affairs 1993). The International Congress on Trade (CCI) meeting on 17 October 1993 gave strong support to NAFTA (*El Financiero*, 18 October 1993; *La Jornada*, 18 October 1993). A poll of business leaders attending *Business Week*'s 1993 Symposium of Chief Executive Officers showed that 36 per cent 'loved' NAFTA, while 64 per cent said they 'like it in spite of the negatives'. US Treasury Secretary Lloyd Bentsen, who spoke during the Symposium, urged CEOs 'to get the message out to the people' that NAFTA was a good agreement.[11] However, an alliance of labour representatives, democratic candidates representing poorer areas in the United States, and environmentalists, disagreed. Representative David Obey (Democrat for Wisconsin) released a report claiming that studies of NAFTA were 'either flawed in design, limited in scope or unable to accurately predict the future or economic consequences of NAFTA'.[12] In the event, the vote in the House of Representatives accurately reflected this polarization of interests.

Beyond the hype: assessing the strategy of size

As we have seen, there is a diversity of opinion not only about the merits of bloc formation but also about the rationale behind it. To what extent, however, does each of these rationales explain, in its own terms, the fact that a growing number of states are keen on adopting this strategy? As we have seen, the neoclassical rationale equates regionalism with economic growth. Such ideas were prevalent, for example, in the numerous reports set up by the European Commission in the mid-1980s to account for the sluggish growth of the European Community in the decade 1973 to 1983. The Cecchini Report to the European Commission estimated, for instance, that the benefits of removing the above mentioned barriers would be dramatic. Europe's GDP would rise by 4.5 per cent due to a re-launch of economic activity; consumer prices would be deflated by 6.1 per cent, payments balances improved by 2.2 per cent of GDP and approximately two to five million jobs would be created. In addition, the Commission estimated in 1990 that the abolition of customs checks and formalities would save Ecu 13 to 24 billion while Ecu 17 billion would be saved by the opening up of public sector markets. Undoubtedly the projections in the Cecchini Report were drafted in part to mobilize political support for European unification. Other studies (e.g. Hufbauer 1990, p.8) suggested less spectacular gains (for example, a GDP increase in the range of 1.5 per cent to 2.5 per cent). However, despite the creation of the SEM during 1992, the economic benefits failed to materialize. On the contrary, 1992 to 1993 saw Europe enter a deep recession accompanied by record unemployment.

Similar developments are promised with the implementation of NAFTA, the Clinton administration claiming that the agreement will boost economic growth and create over 200,000 new jobs. However, there has been fierce controversy over the benefits of NAFTA to its member states. The harshest estimates about the deal have been espoused by the 1992 presidential candidate Ross Perot (Perot and Choate 1993) and the Economic Policy Institute (Faux and Spriggs, 1991; Faux and Lee, 1991). Both claim that because of fresh capital investment and on-the-job training, Mexican labour productivity will approach US levels at wage rates well below the US minimum. Consequently there will be a 'giant sucking sound' as firms relocate their plants to Mexico. The result will be a 'loss of millions of jobs' in which US 'standards of living are sacrificed' (Perot and Choate 1993, pp.52–5). Other estimates range from the astronomical figures asserted by Perot to between a loss of 490,000 jobs (Koechlin and Larudee 1992) and the creation of 171,000 jobs (Hufbauer and Schott 1993, p.14). Similar divergences are found when assessments are made of the impact upon wages and the balance of trade and investment. The simple facts of the matter appear to be that no one really knows yet what effect a closer European Union or the NAFTA will have for the economies of the member states.

Nevertheless, regardless of which set of figures are taken to be the closest approximation of the economic benefits of integration, they hardly seem to justify the pains of restructuring. Likewise, even if we accept that larger markets may indeed generate terms of trade gains in the range of, say, the 1 per cent improvement of member states' GNP, this figure seems hardly likely to be the crucial evidence in convincing policy makers to take political decisions of such magnitude. Therefore, although we find some of the neoclassical arguments convincing, in particular the arguments about inward investment, they cannot in our view serve as adequate explanations for the political decisions necessary to adopt such a strategy. It is our view, therefore, that the conventional wisdom regarding economies of scale, as cited above (the neoclassical rationale), has played a significant factor in *rationalizing*, and selling to the public, the rather painful process of political integration and the formation of larger economic units.

The principal weakness of the neoclassical approach to explaining the formation of regional blocs is that it is predicated upon a separation of politics from economics. As a result it can only assume that political decisions are carried out in an orderly and rational manner and that economic gains will naturally follow. The assumption that the state is limited merely to providing a regulatory framework is clearly too simplistic and narrow a description of the actual realities of economic statecraft. Furthermore, neoclassical approaches have no concept of group interest and of the political process.

A second critical viewpoint of this rationale rests on the fact that the free market economy upon which it is based is in reality an ideal type. The assumptions upon which it is based, namely perfect competition, constant returns to scale and the absence of externalities, are clearly at odds with the 'real' conditions of the global market (Borrus *et al.* 1986, p.112). Where such externalities are considered, economists commonly refer to real economic conditions as market imperfections, but as Krugman argues, 'in reality however it may be that such imperfections are the rule rather than the exception' (1986, p.12). Hence as we demonstrated in our evaluation of the strategic rationale, neoclassical economics fails to explain what is essentially a political decision driven by political motives. Clearly the economic arguments do provide valuable ammunition to vindicate such decisions but the decision is favoured for separate reasons.

In contrast with the neoclassical rationale, the strategic rationale has the advantage that it takes us back into the realm of political decisions. Strategies of size can be explained as a power move in which states unite against rivals. This is a popular argument, and understandably so, for it draws on the popular images of realist theory. The shift in emphasis of the United States towards a tougher policy on trade that began during the Bush administration would seem to provide empirical evidence for this thesis. Likewise 'the ever closer union' of the states of Europe, as we showed before, has generated genuine suspicion of an attempt to replace American hegemony, from the launch of the ECU to the attempts to create a European defence force. As we argued earlier, this was vividly demonstrated in the belligerent stance adopted by both Europe and the US during the Uruguay Round of GATT.

The competitive rationale is essentially a realist or state-based approach cloaked in the language of trade and strategic industrial policy. This may be a source of strength as much as a source of weakness. Clearly the advocates of this explanation for size regard economics as 'the continuation of policy by other means', a notion that is particularly attractive to the ex-strategist now out of a job in the post-cold war world. It is an approach which those less familiar with the intricacies of both economics and domestic politics find persuasive. But it runs the risk of over-simplifying political factors in the same way that the neoclassical rationale simplifies economic factors.

Like classic realism, this argument is simply inattentive to the internal debates which were at the core of such bloc building, by assuming a unity of purpose of the 'state', or now even less credibly the 'region'. While it is true that certain firms in certain industries will be supportive of a strategic approach to trade, others which are more successful and competitive in the global economy oppose such interference. When George Bush embarked on his strategic trade tour of the Far East in 1991, he was accompanied, interestingly enough, by the chairmen of Ford, GM and Chrysler, firms that were bearing the brunt of Japanese competition. Again, the same is true of the attitude towards Europe. Not all US corporations are opposed to further integration between the members of the EU. As Hufbauer (1990) sharply observes, opposition tends to be most vociferous from those sectors of US industry which have been unsuccessful in Europe or which compete from outside the 'region'. Conversely those affiliates that have been well established in Europe welcome deepening integration because of the opportunities it will provide.

The strategic rationale overlooks the fact that the multilateral system is sufficiently entrenched so that the economic fortunes of the blocs are interwoven. There may well be a desire to take advantage of both economies of scale and/or powernomics (Prestowitz et al. 1991) but the relations between the 'Triad' are certainly not mutually exclusive. The blunt use of economic power belongs more to the dictators of the 1930s than to the policies of the supranational polities or hybrid states that the EU or NAFTA may represent. As discussed earlier, foreign investment between the blocs has been growing in relation to total investment, suggesting that more and more trade is being conducted between the three areas. Furthermore, outside Europe intra-regional trade is low; therefore any attempt to assert power over a rival bloc will simply be an own goal with disastrous economic consequences.

The less brazen arguments about bargaining power are conversely more persuasive. But the argument that smaller states can increase their structural power by pooling sovereignty to create a larger organization cannot explain the degree to which any decision has to be sold to society. For example, the Norwegian government would find it difficult to 'sell' to its own people the notion that by joining the European Union Norway would be able to increase its structural power in the wider world of multilateral negotiation. This is not to say that such leverage is probably attractive. In today's world previous powers such as Britain and France are considered smaller nations, yet at GATT they have accentuated their voice by allowing Europe to negotiate for them. However, in pooling sovereignty to increase their net structural power, states run the risk of allowing themselves to be dominated by a regional hegemon (i.e. Germany in the EU, the US in NAFTA).

The interest group rationale is attentive to such internal debates, and hence to the mechanisms and bargaining processes within bloc formation. It also serves as a timely reminder that with each and every policy there are those that stand to gain and others that stand to lose – a point that both neoclassical and strategic trade theorists largely opt to ignore. However, while such considerations are found in the interest group rationale there is always a danger that the more we identify a given strategy with some underlying structural trend of capitalism, so conversely we diminish the significance of internal debates and controversies. In addition, there is also a lack of sensitivity to the concrete problems facing decision makers. Clearly all these do play a role. All in all, there is a distance between interests and policies, between policies and outcome, a distance that is all too easy to ignore. So we regard the interest group rationale as an important aspect in the study of bloc formation, but by its very nature it can serve only as an aspect.

We believe therefore that the three conventional approaches to this strategy are, if taken separately, inadequate to explain the trend of regionalism. Each focuses on only one dimension in the complex process of policy formulation. So whereas the neoclassical approach gives an economic rationale, it cannot explain the strategic aspect of policy making. What it does do is provide valuable ammunition to vindicate the decision to pursue size as a strategy. The 'strategic rationale', popular among international political economists, actually provides a means of understanding the nature of the decision. Of course, to assume that the decision takes place for an abstracted 'parochial national interest' misses the point completely. This brings us to a third rationale which emphasizes the various groups within a society supportive of the strategy. However, we cannot dispense with the other two rationales because the third rationale only provides us with the impetus for the response, not the mechanisms that will shape it.

Our viewpoint is able to synthesize such rationales because of the way we seek to define the construct of the state. Because the state reflects the constellation of social forces within a given territory it designates the relationship between dominant business interests on the one hand and policy makers on the other. It is through a network of bargaining that potentially incoherent and disparate interests can be formalized into actual legitimate policies. Consequently, if various social groups in different states feel threatened by the prevailing forces of the global market, a realization of a common interest may occur that will then give force to the idea of integration as a means to overcome this outside challenge. It is not so much that this shared interest undermines the authority of the individual states but that in order to remain competitive, a larger economic area may just hold the answer. Thus size becomes seen as a strategy of competition in the international political economy.

So far we have purposefully avoided a discussion of size as a strategy in East Asia. There has been a reason for this. The general argument put forward for explaining the lack of any formal integration in the third leg of the Triad is because, unlike in Europe and the Americas, there is no obvious regional leader. Clearly Japan appears to be the obvious choice. However, we suggest that there are two key reasons why Japan does not appear to be in a position to assume this role. First, there is the political and economic rivalry in the region between China and Japan. (Consequently, in APEC the United States' presence is widely accepted as a counterweight to these two giants.) Second, there is a deep suspicion felt in South Korea and Taiwan with regard to an overt Japanese influence which emanates from the colonial histories of these two states under Japanese occupation. Institutionalizing what is currently a primarily economic relationship would give Japan the overt political role that these states fear.

Looking deeper, however, it appears to us that the developmental state in Japan and the NIEs may ultimately be incompatible with regional integration. Because the developmental state involves a closely co-ordinated, indeed interwoven, relationship between the state and economy in pursuit of defined national goals, the surrender of national sovereignty to a supra-national authority could disentangle and delegitimize this. Hence we are unlikely to see the creation of a EU-like body in Asia. But neither are we likely to see integration following the NAFTA model because it could give formal predominance to Japan and this, as we have just shown, is fraught with problems. Consequently the most probable outcome is an evolution of APEC into an Asia–Pacific trading bloc that spreads power and influence between Japan, China and the United States.

None the less, perhaps *the* crucial reason why size as a strategy has been so tenuous in East Asia is that as a strategy it is defensive. It is a costly strategy in terms of 'pooled' sovereignty and control and therefore it is a strategy that is likely to appeal to countries that feel threatened by the changing climate. If East Asia is 'winning' economically why does it need to change its strategy? It is Europe and the United States that appear to be losing the battle for world market share. Clearly there are and have always been common interests between interest groups and policy makers in neighbouring states but there has not always been an impetus for integration. As we argued in the interest group rationale, the momentum behind the Single European Act was largely driven by

European industrialists who were feeling the strain of foreign competition. Faced with such pressures, disparate interest groups are more likely to unite for a common purpose, and the political will for integration is far higher in times of perceived 'crisis'. The fears generated by the success of others will in turn often generate the political will necessary to confront the complexities of integration. The strategy of size is, for the most part, a defensive response to changing realities in the global political economy but because the strategy aims to fight back, restructure and regain competitiveness, it also attempts to change and shape the global political economy.

Beyond strategy: global implications

Regionalism is not, however, merely a refined instrument of competition in the global competitive game. The beauty of regionalism is that it is a competitive strategy which also functions as an instrument of regional and global governance. Regionalism does a number of things *concomitantly*, and it is most probably its profound ambiguity or multi-functionality that is the main source of its strength. Indeed, there are three additional features of regionalism that we shall now briefly discuss. These features are not primarily concerned with the strategic economic considerations the strategy has but rather the deeper and more structural features that this 'trend' or strategy represents.

First, the strategy of size not only provides the macro-economic conditions in which certain businesses flourish, but it also creates specific institutions which manage and promote the expansion of the social, economic and political values of the trilateral areas globally (Sklar 1980, p.21). This involves, at least in the case of the EU, creating and expanding a network of like-minded bureaucrats, politicians and corporate leaders into both these institutions and national governments. Regional bloc formation has therefore proved to be a significant step in cementing transnational class interests.

Second, the strategy is also an instrument of domestic restructuration in a neoclassical framework. The institutional aspect of bloc formation in this sense serves to 'anchor-in' the market-based rationale of the embedded liberal project. The explanation is seductive; but exactly how and why it operates this way remains unclear and open to question. The formation of NAFTA perhaps most vividly demonstrated that an ulterior motive of the free trade area has been that it has served as an instrument of social change, institutionalizing neo-liberal economic ideology. Mexico and Canada's decisions to join in a 'bloc' with the US represent precisely such intentions.

In Canada, the election of Pierre Trudeau in 1980 on a nationalistic interventionist platform alarmed Canadian business leaders. Throughout the late 1970s and early 1980s Canadian business horizons were becoming more and more continental in scale and, inspired by the resurgence of neoclassicism south of the border, Canadian business began to pressure the government to adopt a more pro-market line. By 1982 they had succeeded in pushing Trudeau off his nationalist agenda, followed two years later by the election of the Conservatives to office. The first act of the Mulroney government in 1985 was a request for negotiations with the United States as to the creation of a free trade area. In 1989 the forerunner to NAFTA was born when the Canada–US Free Trade Area came into being. As Clarkson poignantly describes it,

> As the rationale for this continentalist accumulation strategy . . . had been inspired by neoclassical economics, the success of business meant that economics had triumphed. The neoclassical paradigm had moved from the blackboard to the boardroom and from business to politics.
>
> (Grinspun and Cameron 1993, p.67)

Noam Chomsky (1993), in a similar vein, argues that for Mexican capital, NAFTA is essentially about locking Mexico into a neo-liberal core.[13]

Similarly, by bringing in the three Mediterranean fascist and military dictatorships of Greece, Spain and Portugal, the EEC ensured that their transition to liberal democracy would be smooth and lasting. As a consequence, many today argue that the EU should aim to achieve the same goal with regard to the former communist states of Eastern Europe, while also seeking to arrest the development of Islamic fundamentalism in North Africa.

Finally, regionalism is turning into the primary tool of global governance. The rhetoric of neo-liberalism notwithstanding, Wilkinson observes, it is not exactly protectionism that matters, but that:

> The rhetoric of letting global markcts regulate economic decision making . . . has emanated largely from the United States and, to a somewhat lesser extent, from the EC and Japan. . . . What is all too often neglected, however, is that . . . it is not simply a matter of governments getting out of the way so as to let the market work. Rather . . . the governments of the Triad are only interested in encouraging unrestricted operation of the market, provided that the long-run interests of their corporations are being protected and extended.
>
> (Wilkinson 1993, p.32)

As the Trilateral Commission itself stated,

> domestic concerns – in Japan, Europe, and the US – make it difficult to resolve problems in ways which will not drive these regions apart. . . . But . . . because of their technological and economic interdependence, these areas have sufficient common interests . . . [to foster] closer cooperation among the three advanced regions.
>
> (Sklar 1980, p.83)

Hence the bargaining power of blocs in GATT, the IMF, the G7 and the proposed G3 can perhaps be viewed as a new oligarchic arrangement for running the world. Such blocs are much simpler to operate than multilateral institutions and supposedly more effective. Together, such blocs are possibly forming a new cartel which will continue to marginalize the Third World.

To summarize, the strategy of size is a complex, multifaceted and polyfunctional state strategy, whose advantages are not as clear-cut as its proponents wish us to believe. Due to the complexity and the enormous costs it exacts from member states, it is a strategy likely to be taken by countries and regions that feel under threat. None the less, it is a strategy that lies at the very core of the vast restructuration process of the state and political authority in the era of globalization.

Notes

1 'The unprecedented capital requirements for constructing the American railroad network led to the centralizing and institutionalizing of the nation's money market in New York City' (Chandler 1990, p.57).
2 As Krugman argues, 'the question of whether regional trading arrangements are good or bad is a moot point . . . [it] comes down to asking . . . what are the problems of the GATT that lead countries to turn to their neighbourhood instead?' (1993, p.73).
3 The concept of an economy of scale must be treated with care. Since economy of scale is technology dependent, the precise dimension of a size economy varies from period to period. In the early 1950s, for instance, the optimum size of steel plants was estimated at around two million tons a year, by the mid-1970s it stood at over seven million tons. Today steel production had been revolutionized by the so-called mini-mills (*The Economist*) to the point that, as McKenzie and Lee argue in *Quicksilver Capital*, technology is perhaps 'resulting in "economies of decreasing scale"' (1991, p.35).
4 As a former director of IBM, Jacques Maisonrouge, a forceful advocate of European Union, observed, 'in future, international competitiveness will depend largely on scientific and technological performance, then neither France, nor Germany, nor England nor any other European country can be truly competitive on its own in all fields against the United States and Japan. Even if returns on research were the same, there is still the question of scale' (1989, p.121).
5 'The fear that European investments would be diverted to Eastern Europe, once it is integrated with the European community, was cited by President Salinas of Mexico as a factor decisively pushing him toward the Mexico-US FTA' (Bhagwati 1993, p.30).
6 'European Commission officials say privately that, while the United States can push weak countries around, the Community can now stand up and slug it out with an aggressively protectionist United States' (Hufbauer 1990, p.346).
7 'Ironically, while the United States' gaze remains fixed on the skyline and ticker-tapes of Tokyo, Europe has been steadily growing into an economic power that will challenge and *ultimately stifle* the current samurai siege on world economics' (Silva and Sjorgren 1990, p.101, emphasis added).
8 Clear parallels can be drawn with the decline of British hegemony in the early part of this century and the subsequent drift into an imperial bloc, namely that as US international competitiveness has declined the idea of a large protected market has grown more attractive (Bhagwati 1993). Although few commentators fear that the US will abandon its commitment

to multilateral trade despite growing calls for support of this protectionist ideal, if the basis of this argument is accepted it does signify a significant change of direction in the global economy.

9 As Franko has observed, 'Few sectors have been under as heavy attack from the Japanese in world-wide competition, and few have been as Balkanized as these by non-tariff barriers to trade within the European Community's not-very-common-market' (1990, p.21).

10 The report's findings revealed the following:

- That the cost of existing barriers within the EC was about £130 billion, equivalent to 5 per cent of the Community Gross Domestic Product.
- These customs formalities were costing firms equivalent to 2 per cent of the value of the goods they traded.
- The administration of such customs facilities was costing public authorities somewhere in the region of £335–670 million.
- Purchases controlled by the public sector both at national and local level accounted in 1986 for more than the total value of intra-community trade: £350 billion vs. *c.*£330 billion. Due to the common practice among member states of national purchasing policies, designed to discriminate in favour of home suppliers, these public sectors paid some £14.5 billion more than necessary.
- Differences in national technical standards, health and safety laws and environmental protection all stood as barriers to freer trade. The Cecchini Report estimated that in the telecommunications industry such differences were costing £2.35 billion, in the motor industry £1.75 billion, in the construction industry £1.14 billion and in the foodstuffs industry between £335–650 million.
- Differing regulations in the financial and service sectors also hampered freer trade. The removal of such barriers was estimated to save the industry £15 billion.
- Finally, although the report concluded that investment in research and development within the EC compared unfavourably to her competitors because such research was conducted nationally, it often resulted in inefficient duplications. A successful R&D programme necessitated a coordinated European response.

11 'Bentsen calls on CEOs for trade pact support', *BNA International Trade Daily*, 25 October 1993.

12 'As Obey unveils report discrediting NAFTA studies', *Congress Daily*, 25 October 1993.

13 'These processes [those of neo-liberal economic integration] will continue independently of NAFTA. But, as explained by Eastman Kodak chairperson Kay Whitmore, the treaty may "lock in the opening of Mexico's economy so that it can't return to its protectionist ways." It should enable Mexico "to solidify its remarkable economic reforms," comments Michael Aho, director of Economic Studies at the Council on Foreign Relations' (Chomsky 1993). Similarly, Mary Lucy Jaramillo, sub-secretary of the Defense for Inter-American Affairs, maintains that 'NAFTA and the economic integration of Latin America are vehicles used by the Clinton administration to re-orientate the national security doctrine in the hemisphere and to create an intervention army to protect and stimulate democratic markets' (*El Financiero*, 19 October 1993).

4

The Capitalist Developmental State
in East Asia

This chapter will examine what has emerged as the key explanation of East Asian development: the thesis that institutional factors, in particular the state, have played a fundamental role in engineering economic growth, development and success in these countries. Institutions are understood to mean practices, customs and values as well as physical institutions. This approach has the advantage of avoiding the pitfalls common when addressing Japan (and other East Asian countries) with the tools of western political science. Chalmers Johnson states,

> It [the Japanese economy] operates one of the most successful commercial systems on earth, but does so without the aid of, and often directly contrary to what the Nobel Prize committee calls 'economic science'. It is a 'modernised' society, but one that offers a challenge to modernisation theory at almost every turn. It is today the most conceptually interesting and difficult case for students of political economy, not least because of the fog that surrounds it generated by pundits, journalists, competitors and the Japanese themselves with their persistent attraction to their self-regarding ideology of *Nihonjinron* (the science of the Japanese).
>
> (Johnson 1986a, p.57)

A number of excellent studies on the workings of the political economies of East Asia exist and this chapter will focus primarily on the theoretical underpinnings of this state strategy with reference to this work. To understand the capitalist developmental state (CDS) in East Asia it is essential to go beyond its current organization and post-war history to examine the circumstances surrounding the emergence of the developmental state in Japan in the nineteenth century and its consequent impact on other countries of the region. The CDS has been evolutionary and a simple summary of the political economy of one of these countries in the mid-1990s would therefore be of limited use as the historical context is vital to understanding the operation of this strategy.

This chapter constructs a five-fold definition of the CDS around the concepts of the fusing of 'public' and 'private'; the role of state ideology; the use of developmental legitimacy; plan rationality, and the existence of a relatively autonomous economic technocracy. The fusing or blurring of the concepts of public and private in East Asian developmental states is explained by examining the creation of market society in Japan in the nineteenth century, using insights from the political economist and economic anthropologist Karl Polanyi. It is argued that the way in which market society was created in Japan resulted in a different configuration of the relationship between politics and economics and between public and private than was the case in the West.

State ideology is understood to mean the way in which the state in East Asia has reinforced this fusing of public and private in order to increase its autonomy over society. By stressing the collective over the individual, identifying business interest with national interest and by strong repression of socialist and Marxist thinking, the state has been able to achieve both greater autonomy from society and control and to manipulate labour towards developmental goals. Developmental legitimacy is the key tool by which the state ideology is held in place. Plan rationality represents the way in which the politics–economics nexus is instituted in these states in order to achieve developmental goals; and economic technocracy is the key physical institution that directs the CDS. Clearly there is considerable overlap and strong interrelations between these categories.

This chapter addresses the CDS conception as applied throughout East Asia, but particular stress is placed on Japan. This is because (1) it was the first Asian developmental state; (2) it has served as a direct model for other Asian developmental states, especially Taiwan and South Korea; (3) Japanese colonial heritage has played an important role in these follower countries, and (4) Japan continues to have a fundamentally important role in the current international political economy of the region.

Following the exposition of this five-fold definition of the CDS, the benefits and costs of the CDS strategy are assessed with regard to both the domestic and international environment. The conclusion assesses the usefulness and applicability of the CDS as a strategy for other countries in the global political economy. It should be noted, however, that in no way was the state the sole element in rapid development in East Asia; other factors, in particular the post-1945 trading system which operated under American hegemony in East Asia, were important to the success of this state strategy. However, these issues have been well addressed elsewhere, so this chapter will focus on the internal dimensions of the CDS strategy and address the more strictly external factors only briefly.

The state and development in academic discourse

The theoretical tradition to which the developmental state conception belongs has a rich and valuable history which has sadly been overshadowed by neoclassical, Marxist and other schools of economic thought, especially since 1945. Theories of development were dominated by the contending approaches of the modernization theory and the neoclassical tradition on the one hand and 'Marxist' approaches such as dependency theory and world systems analysis on the other. From the late 1970s a number of academics were realizing that East Asian development conformed to neither the precepts of neoclassical economics, with its stress on free markets and minimal government, nor to the depressing predictions of dependency theory. These new studies began to focus on institutions and marked the reinvigoration of the study of the role of the state in national development.

While there are clear similarities between mercantilist thinking and East Asian practice, the term is not entirely accurate nor is it an adequate way to portray the operation of these political economies. The term 'developmental state' is a recent one, but it is often associated with the tradition of mercantilism and neo-mercantilism. A number of comment-ators have seen this as essentially the pattern followed by the Japanese in their development process, which has led to the critique of the Japanese state following neo-mercantilist policies (Nester 1990, 1991, 1993). Neo-mercantilism is regarded as inappropriate, however, as it remains poorly defined and highly ambiguous, sometimes being used to mean merely '[T]he modern advocacy of protectionism as a means to encouraging employment growth' (Rutherford 1992, p.321). More sophisticated definitions relate it to the ideas of Friedrich List (List 1904/1841), with its roots in seventeenth-century English thinking. Here, neo-mercantilism is understood as maintaining employment, a positive balance of payments and the promotion of growth based on the development of new technologies (Johnson 1974).

A second concern with 'neo-mercantilism' is that the existing defini-tions of neo-mercantilism inadequately account for the experience and practices of Japan or the East Asian NIEs: the aspects of development that fit the neo-mercantilist view are consequences, rather than aims, of the developmental state. Third, the term 'neo-mercantilism' has become pejorative and used by some commentators to mean a conscious desire for political as well as economic domination, and some interpretations using the term neo-mercantilism are couched in extreme terms which detract from serious attempts to understand this branch of political economy.[1]

Mercantilist writings have had a fundamental influence on Japanese thought, and Japanese thinking and practice have gone on to influence the other rapidly developing countries of East Asia, especially Taiwan and South Korea. From 1881 on, economic thinking in Japan became dominated by German ideas, especially those of Friedrich List and the German Historical School. This is of great importance because the work of List and the German Historical School provided a theoretical basis and justification for powerful state intervention in the developing economy. List's writings were concerned with protecting a growing national economy in the face of ones that had already developed, a situation with strong similarities to Japan. The admiration and emulation of Germany and Bismarck by the Meiji leaders at this time are well documented and this is particularly the case with regard to German economists such as Gustav von Schmoler, Ernst Engle and Lujo Bretano

(Morris-Suzuki 1989b, p.15). This approach became dominant following the 1881 incident when the promoters of liberal free trade were ousted from policy making by those sympathetic to German ideas (Sheridan 1993, pp.28–32). The importance of this for the Japanese political economy is that it meant the discourse on political economy and developmental strategy was dominated by a mercantilist, developmental ideology promoting active participation of the state in development.

This tradition has grown considerably, both on theoretical and empirical levels. There are a number of country-specific studies with wider theoretical implications: Johnson's 1982 classic on MITI has been joined by excellent studies of Japan by Sheridan (1993) and Williams (1994), by Amsden (1989) on South Korea and by Wade (1990) on Taiwan. In addition, there have been a number of edited collections which have contributed significantly to important thematic issues, in particular Deyo (1987) and Appelbaum and Henderson (1992). The growing literature on the CDS strategy has become increasingly sophisticated and the dimensions of the debate over the strong state have moved beyond simplistic state *or* market discussions. Most observers do now credit a role for the state, and the disagreements focus primarily on the degree and dimensions of that role and the importance of other social and cultural factors.[2] A problem with the CDS strategy in academic literature has been that the focus has been primarily on detailed case studies, without adequate recourse to theory.

This chapter will now attempt to assimilate the key literature on the CDS in East Asia to develop a five-fold definition of the ideal characteristics of the CDS. It is the author's intention to focus primarily on the internal dimensions that have made the CDS strategy so successful, as the external dimensions have been addressed adequately elsewhere (Haggard 1988, 1990). It is also acknowledged that there are important internal differences between the states in question but the categories are intended to be understood as Weberian ideal types.

Public–private distinction

The distinction between public and private is one of the key tenets of western political economy. Neoclassical, Keynesian and Marxist political economists accept this distinction as a basic premise, but the key argument of this section is that in East Asian developmental states the separation between public and private is far from apparent.

The blurred distinction between public and private is related to both the traditional understanding of 'economy' in East Asia and the way in which market economies were established there. It is the vital theoretical issue underpinning the developmental state. It should be noted that public–private are addressed here primarily in terms of political economy, i.e. with particular regard to ownership. The broader public–private issues such as the relationship between the individual and the state or the family and the state are mentioned in the following section on state ideology.

This section will argue that it derives from two key sources. The first of these is linguistic/cultural: the words have indistinct meaning in East Asian societies (Matsumoto 1978; Boling 1990), and the second is historical/institutional, i.e. the state in East Asia has played and promoted this distinction for its own ends (Johnson 1980, 1986b; Williams 1994, p.111). Before the integration of East Asia into the expanding western world system, East Asian political economy did not rely on the self-regulating market as its principal organizing element. A detailed examination of the Japanese economy before the Meiji Restoration is beyond the scope of this chapter, but some of the basic issues must be addressed. The key aspect for this analysis is to show that under the Tokugawa, Japan was a provisioning rather than a market-based society. Moulder states:

> As in China, the economic policy of the bakufu and han was of a provisioning kind. The major function was to produce revenue to supply the stratum of tax dependants and to ensure an adequate supply of necessities to the government and to the rural and urban populations.
>
> (Moulder 1977, p.78)

As a 'provisioning' society, Japan is similar in many respects to the pre-industrial Europe that Karl Polanyi addresses in *The Great Transformation* (Polanyi 1957a). In Tokugawa Japan, as in Europe until the impact of the writings of Smith and Ricardo and the creation of market society, there was no clear distinction between 'political' and 'economic'. In Polanyi's terms, the (substantive) economy can be seen to be firmly embedded in the social whole. Bellah states:

> The relation of economy to polity can only be understood in terms of the Confucian theory of state which had a very great influence in Japan. The keynote of the Confucian thinking on the matter is 'the unity of economy and polity.' Indeed, on the Tokugawa Period the word *keizai* translated in modern usage as economy meant, in the words of Dazai Shundai 'governing the empire and assisting the people'.
>
> (Bellah 1957, p.108)

The modern Japanese word for economy, *keizai*, had very different implications in Tokugawa times from its modern, formalist one concerned with allocation of scarce means and rational economic maximizing. The difference in the understanding of 'economic' can be gauged from the fact that when western economic texts were first translated after the Meiji Restoration a new vocabulary had to be invented and developed for the new western concepts (Morris-Suzuki 1989a, pp.50–1). Economy was not regarded as a detached sphere but a practical part of government. In Tokugawa Japan, therefore, politics and economics were not regarded as distinct areas.

In what Polanyi terms the 'economistic fallacy' economy has come to be understood only by its market (i.e. 'formal') definition, creating the 'artificial identification of the economy with its market form' (Polanyi 1957b, p.270, 1977). When the economy was disembedded in East Asia

– their 'Great Transformations' – this process was different from the western case, because of factors such as imperialism, foreign threat and the vital fact of late development. Japan's transformation into a society with a significant market element took place as the direct consequence of the Meiji Restoration (1868). The Meiji reforms and the integration of Japan into the modern world economy 'disembedded' the Japanese economy from its society. Because of the particular historical and social circumstances involved in Japan's transformation, however, the new Japanese political economy differed in some important areas from those of the western countries.

This led to the relationship between politics and economics being instituted differently in these countries, both socially and on the state market level. This blurring of public and private has profound implications for the dominant western economic theories – neoclassical and Marxist – and accounts for the profound difficulties that most western perspectives on political economy encounter when dealing with East Asia (Johnson 1988; Wade 1990). This understanding of the public–private distinction provides the basis for understanding, on both practical and theoretical levels, the operation of the developmental state.[3]

In China also the economy was interpreted quite differently from the market-oriented view that has dominated western thinking since Adam Smith. Commerce, trade and markets existed and were significant, but were not the central institutions of the Chinese political economy. What is significant is that categories of 'public' and 'private' central to most western discourse on economics were not as relevant to the Chinese economy (Moore 1984). As in Japan, the political and the economic were not distinguished. Schurmann states: 'consideration of economic problems apart from those of government administration was unthinkable. For them, economics meant primarily managerial economics, and the state, of course, was the great manager' (1956, p.xi).

Furthermore, in the twentieth century German economic thinking had an important impact on nationalist planners in the 1930s because of Chiang Kai-shek's admiration for Nazi Germany and use of German economic advisers (Fairbank 1986, pp.224–5). The Japanese experience is, however, more significant with regard to the CDS as a state strategy for two reasons: first, the impact of the Japanese model on East Asia as a result of Japanese imperialism (before 1945), and second, the copying of the Japanese model (after 1945).

The blurring of public and private is not simply a 'natural' result of the evolution of East Asian capitalism; it is also to a significant extent the result of conscious action by the state to increase its autonomy, to control labour and to achieve developmental goals. Johnson argues, 'In part it [Japanese development] is based on an intentional blurring of public and private. Achievements of privately owned and managed enterprises are regarded as national achievements, but any profit that results is treated as private property' (1992, p.74). This neatly encapsulates the importance of the blurring of public and private on the operation of the Japanese political economy (as can be seen in Japan's public policy companies

(Johnson 1978)), which is replicated in differing forms in South Korea and Taiwan. This chapter will now go on to address how the state has used this blurring of public and private to perpetuate a nationalistic ideology that has enabled it to dominate and control labour and other potentially 'dissident' movements that could have obstructed the developmental project.

State ideology and paternalist capitalism

In addition to the linguistic/cultural and the historical/institutional reasons behind the fusing of public and private, the indistinct meaning of these two ideas has also been interpreted as a conscious strategy on behalf of the state to promote development. This section develops the previous arguments surrounding the public–private distinction by examining the role of the state in controlling society, especially labour. A key result was that it enabled the state to achieve the autonomy necessary to implement the developmental project. State ideology rests on the twin foundations of the mobilization of nationalism and external threat and the use and manipulation of 'culture'.

An important factor in the state ideology and its blurring of public and private has been the role of the Confucian heritage of the developmental states of East Asia. There is considerable literature on 'Confucian Capitalism', much of which is flawed by its cultural essentialism and failure to understand the use of the discourse on culture as a mechanism for control. Chowdhury and Islam (1993) point out five elements in Confucian/culturalist explanations of East Asian development in the work of two of its key western proponents: Pye (1988) and O'Malley (1988): (1) an ethical/moral basis for government; (2) justification of hierarchical political systems; (3) a stress on respect and loyalty being translated into consensus and conformity; (4) collective industrial organization along community/family; and (5) a cooperative relationship between business and government. However, these works tend to view the cultural context as a given, and fail to examine the ways in which culture is constructed or used to achieve specific objectives. Furthermore there have always been significant differences in the interpretation and implementation of 'Confucianism' between the three countries considered in this chapter. I accept the argument of Henderson and Appelbaum (1992, p.17) with regard to East Asia that 'one cannot understand the significance of culture outside of its relations with other structural elements of specific societies'.

With regard to the CDS, a key element of the Confucian tradition mobilized by the state has been its stress on the collective over the individual. The Confucian ideal saw individual (i.e. private) desires as essentially selfish, as opposed to the collective (i.e. public) desires which implied virtuous action in accordance with universal principles. The moral superiority of the group (often identified by those in power as the state) over the individual has been a powerful tool for control in these societies. A key aspect of state ideology has been its use of nationalism and its creation of nationalist symbols in order to achieve specific developmental ends. The Japanese, South Korean and Taiwanese cases support Hintze's (1975) thesis that internal class relations are the product of both domestic and international factors, of which the second is of greater importance.[4] Matsumoto has explored the implications of this, arguing that

> the establishment of modern political institutions in Japan was dictated by external rather than internal necessity, and since the existence of the state as a self-justifying entity was considered self-evident it was exempted from explanatory analysis. As a result, any attempts to establish universal principles that would transcend the state and pass judgement on its existence and behavior met with great difficulty.
>
> (Matsumoto 1978, p.45)

In Japan following the Meiji Restoration the threat of foreign domination or take-over was clear, and this fear was used by the newly emerged Japanese élite to control the people. After 1945 the foreign threat was absorbed into the Cold War structure and became in particular a fear of the Soviet Union. The use of nationalism was important in the control of nascent labour movements in these countries. The blurring of public and private ensured that private interests should not be put before the 'national interests', and that labour and socialist movements were viewed as seditious. The circumstances surrounding the emergence of the modern state meant that public interest was identified solely with the state interest, while the private interest remained selfish.

Fukui (1992) demonstrates the importance of the external threat to Meiji Japan in creating a 'nationalist–paternalist capitalist state' and of how a strong nationalist ideology came to dominate post-1868 Japan. This was perpetuated by a rigid, doctrinaire and ultra-conservative educational system which stressed the nation above the individual and was vital in creating a compliant workforce. Fukui makes the important point:

> what happens in political and social arenas, especially educational institutions, rather than what happens in economic arenas per se, is critical to the economic performance of a late-developing capitalist nation, if not that of any capitalist nation.
>
> (Fukui 1992, p.219)

The educational system in Japan, both before and after 1945, has been vital in promoting nationalist doctrines that keep the Japanese people passive and provide an important social block to labour action. Before 1945 this was centred around the emperor cult and the hijacking of the Shinto religion and transformation of the Shinto religion by the state. Rozman (1990, p.185) has also explored how traditional 'directed society' leads to expectations continuing to 'centre on a paternalistic state capable of leading a harmonious society'. After 1945 the state ideology in

Japan became more subtle and complex, emerging as the discourse of *Nihonjinron* or the 'theorizing of Japaneseness'. The key insight of van Wolferen's (1989) controversial study of contemporary Japan is the presentation of the use of this discourse as an ideology for state control of the people and the operation of 'power in the guise of culture'.

The importance of labour and its control by the state in East Asia are well documented (Deyo 1987, 1989; Bello and Rosenfield 1990). The *Nihonjinron* discourse stresses the consensual 'nature' of the Japanese, thus putting social restrictions on the ability of Japanese workers to protest or agitate. The company is private, owned by its shareholders but regarded as a national asset. Therefore any campaigns against the company are regarded as socially subversive and/or 'unpatriotic'. This element of labour repression, coupled with the co-opting of unions in a corporatist fashion into the company, is a vital factor in accounting for the minor role of labour in Japan, especially after 1945, and the state ideology has also been a major factor in the subordination of women in Japan (Sheridan 1993, pp.232–7).

Although state ideology has not reached the level of sophistication achieved in Japan, it has also played a vital role in the other CDS of East Asia. For Taiwan and South Korea, external threats after 1945 were also quite clear, though in these cases it was from the rival half of the divided nation. The competition for international recognition and the still un-resolved civil wars of these countries became a leitmotiv legitimating military rule for much of the period since 1945. Taiwan and South Korea have been dominated by various forms of military rule since the end of the Second World War, with working democracy only truly beginning to emerge in these two countries in the 1990s. Both regimes have still not formally settled their civil wars.

Both the KMT in Taiwan and the various military-backed regimes in South Korea used nationalism and fear of take-over by their communist rivals as a key aspect of legitimating their rule. Labour movements and socialist thought were regarded as particularly seditious because of their association with the ideology of the rival regime and were therefore perceived as an even greater threat. Support of such groups was regarded by the state as being seditious or anti-nationalist, a great stigma in these societies.

As with Japan, both these regimes stressed elements of 'traditional culture' that could be used to control the populations in general and labour in particular. This strategy for controlling labour met with more success in Taiwan than South Korea because of the different conditions surrounding the two civil wars and the greater indigenous nature of Korean communism relative to communism in Taiwan. The roots of this ideology in Taiwan stem not only from Sun Yat-sen's 'Three Principles of the People', but also from Chiang Kai-shek's fascist-influenced 'New Life Movement' of the 1930s and 1940s. In South Korea, a stress on Confucian values became a key element in Park Chung-hee's attempts to secure his military dictatorship; Cho and Kim (1991, p.29) state, 'Park made explicit efforts to inculcate in the Korean populace the Confucian value of "chung hyo" (loyalty to the state, filial piety, and harmony).' Furthermore, the state ideology has been strongly patriarchal in nature, combining the partite of Confucian ideology with the militaristic partite of the developmental regimes. This has been an important element in the control of women, an issue of particular importance given the vital role of the female labour in these countries (Cheng and Hsiung 1992; Salaff 1992).

Control through state ideology alone was not enough to enable these states to maintain their developmental strategies. Legitimacy had to be derived from other sources, and the key source of legitimacy became economic development itself. This issue is addressed in the next section.

Developmental legitimacy

Developmental legitimacy is the third key element which defines the developmental state. Here development is the single most important legitimizing principle of that state; in this sense developmental legitimacy provides the *need* for successful development and therefore the developmental state. Legitimacy here is exercised on behalf of the state project, rather than society: the broader parameters of social order are accepted, but the aim is a radical restructuring of the economic order. Castells puts developmental legitimacy at the centre of his definition of the CDS:

> A state is developmental when it establishes as its principle of legitimacy its ability to promote and sustain development, understanding by development the combination of steady high rates of economic growth and structural change in the productive system, both domestically and in its relationship with the international economy . . . ultimately for the developmental state, economic development is not an end but a means.
>
> (Castells 1992, pp.56–7)

For the developmental states of East Asia, legitimacy was necessary in two areas. The governments of Japan (post-1868), Taiwan (post-1949) and South Korea (post-1953) all had weak links with their domestic societies. In order to maintain their position all these states strove to legitimate their rule through delivering economic success. Related to this was the vitally important consideration of international legitimacy. Japan had to prove to western imperial powers that it was a 'worthy' nation which should be regarded as an equal, and that after 1945 it was a nation which had forgone military exploits and had devoted itself to peaceful commerce. Taiwan and South Korea were both faced with rival, irredentist regimes, professing rival developmental ideologies and competing for international support. International recognition for these states was vital to bolster domestic support and also to compete in the 'game' of international recognition.

The Japanese élite following the Meiji Restoration was a revolutionary élite which had weak ties with the Japanese populace and was intent on carrying out a series of radical reforms. Economic development was promoted not just as an end in itself but as the key through which Japan could defend itself against western imperialism. Chalmers Johnson argues,

> Industrialisation in Japan was introduced from above, for political and not economic reasons, in order to counter the threat of Western imperialism, and with genuine foreign models as the only true measures of success and failure. Japan's modern achievements are imitative in their results but not in their methods.
>
> (Johnson 1992, p.72)

This meant that the goals of economic development and national defence became interrelated and vital elements in legitimating the rule of the new Meiji leadership. This is neatly encapsulated in the Meiji slogan *fukoku kyohei*, 'rich country, strong army', which operates as an underlying theme in Japanese history and political economy from the time of the Meiji Restoration to Japan's defeat in 1945 (Samuels 1994). Although a facade of democratic institutions were created as part of the project of building a 'strong country', this achieved only limited influence over policy making.

Following Japan's comprehensive defeat in 1945 there were important changes in Japan's political and economic system, but significantly, development remained the key legitimizing device of the new conservative leadership. The Allied (essentially American) Occupation of Japan (1945 to 1952) ensured that conservative rule continued in Japan, although pre-existing democratic elements were strengthened and a formal democratic system was established. In a number of respects, however, the Occupation is important not for what it changed, but for what it left untouched or improved about the pre-war system. In particular the hand of the Japanese bureaucracies was strengthened as they were hardly affected by the American reforms and became the key centre of expertise in the immediate post-war period (Johnson 1982).

The economic focus of the new conservative leadership should not be seen as a foregone conclusion, however, and the 1950s were marked by considerable labour unrest and often violent street politics that culminated in the political crisis attending the revision of the US–Japan Security Treaty in 1960 (Johnson 1992, pp.77–9). Following this the ruling Liberal Democratic Party (LDP) moved away from high-profile politics and focused primarily on the issue of promoting Japan's economic growth, a process most clearly seen with the inauguration of Prime Minister Ikeda's 'Income Doubling Plan' in the 1960s.

This concentration on the 'economic' rather than the 'political' became the basis for legitimating the two key aspects of Japan's post-war political structure, the 1955-system and the Yoshida Doctrine, which dominated Japanese political economy and international relations until the 1990s. The 1955-system refers to the dominance of the LDP over the Japanese electoral system following its formation from the merger of the two main conservative parties (the Liberal Party and the Democratic

Party) in 1955. It should be noted, however that, in Johnson's telling phrase, in Japan the bureaucrats ruled while the politicians reigned: LDP electoral success gave legal–rational legitimation to a system in which the Japanese bureaucracy has been the principal originator of economic policy and has played the fundamental role in planning and implementing Japan's CDS strategy (Johnson 1982). The Yoshida Doctrine has been the key feature of the Japanese state's external relations since 1952; its key dimension is reliance on the US as Japan's principal ally and security guarantor.[5]

Economic legitimation has also been present in the other developmental states of the region. The ROC regime in Taiwan has faced extreme legitimacy difficulties since 1949. The Nationalist (KMT) government was defeated in the Chinese civil war and forced to retreat to an island that had been a Japanese colony for fifty years, where they had only limited relations with the people. This was worsened by the inept and corrupt nature of the initial KMT ruler of Taiwan, General Chen Yi, which culminated in island-wide disturbances leading to the deaths up to 20,000 people. The KMT in Taiwan was then faced with threats to its legitimacy on two counts. Internally it had to win over a hostile popu-lation which felt betrayed by the process of retrocession and were developing an identity separate from that of the mainland Chinese (Wakabayashi 1992). Externally the KMT was faced with an irredentist rival professing an opposing ideology of economic development that had comprehensively defeated it in war. This rivalry was soon reflected in competition for international support, particularly in the diplomatic sphere.

The KMT attempted to solve its internal and external legitimacy difficulties by delivering economic growth that would incorporate the native Taiwanese and present a better developmental model to the world than that of communist China. By generating economic development the KMT provided opportunities for advancement for the native Taiwanese that had been largely denied them during the colonial period (Gold 1988). Although avenues for political expression for native Taiwanese were restricted, business expression was strongly encouraged. This, and the palpable success in improving the standard of living, helped to diffuse much of the domestic discontent. Developmental legitimacy could also be married effectively with the KMT's professed ideology of *San Min Zhu Yi* – Sun Yat-sen's 'Three Principles of the People' (Gregor *et al.* 1981).

Externally the KMT faced considerable problems. Unlike the other divided nations of the Cold War era (Germany, Korea, Yemen), the disparity in size between the two sides of the Chinese civil war placed considerable strains on the Republic of China (ROC) in its search for international legitimacy. The rigorous adherence to the Hallstein Doctrine by the PRC has further hampered the ROC's attempts to present itself as the legitimate government of the whole of China. The replacement of the ROC by the PRC in the United Nations in 1971 marked the beginning of a long decline in international recognition of the ROC in favour of the PRC which further called into question the legitimacy of the KMT's position as the sole, legal government of China, and of being the representative of the people of Taiwan. Delivering economic development was a key way of trying to maintain legitimacy, although from the 1990s legal–rational legitimation through elections has become increasingly important (Wakabayashi 1992).

The ruling regimes of the Republic of Korea (ROK) have been confronted with similar problems of legitimacy. Like the ROC, the ROK has been confronted by an irredentist rival championing a rival developmental ideology. Under the corrupt Syngman Rhee regime in the 1950s South Korea fell far behind the North in the competition over development. The need to redress this imbalance was a factor in the military take-over of Park Chung-hee in 1961. Under Park the state began to play the dominant role in guiding the South Korean economy, implementing strategic economic planning and targeting key industrial sectors (Cumings 1988; Amsden 1989). In addition to bolstering international legitimacy by offering a successful capitalist alternative to North Korean development, the high growth strategy also served to placate domestic dissatisfaction with the Park regime.

Developmental legitimacy is thus a core feature of the CDS. Economic development is not pursued in these countries as an end in itself, but as a means of securing a regime with weak links to its society. In order to achieve this end the state in the East Asian CDS has actively pursued policies of intervention in the economy, the subject of the next section.

Plan rationality

The fourth key element of the developmental state, which concerns the means by which developmental legitimacy is achieved, is the role of the state in the market and the way that this relationship is instituted. The state–market relationship in the developmental state can be understood as a 'plan rational economy'. Henderson and Appelbaum define plan rational economies as follows:

> plan rational political economies are those in which state regulation is supplemented by state direction of the economy as a whole. Here national economic goals are identified, and the state operates with various degrees of influence or pressure to urge companies to act in accordance with these goals.
>
> (Henderson and Appelbaum 1992, p.19)

In a plan rational political economy, the state performs more than just a regulatory function concerned with forms and procedures; it is also concerned with substantive matters such as setting social and economic goals.

A key consequence of the plan rational political economy is a fundamental interpenetration of political and economic concerns, and of state and market (Wade 1988). This overlap of political and economic is of vital significance to the meaning and operation of these political economies, and can be understood in terms of the blurred distinction between public and private. This interpenetration of state and market is more than just a case of the implementation of neo-mercantile policies or the capturing of the state by certain class interests; it is a fundamental aspect of the state–market relationship. Johnson argues that the state does not displace the market but becomes a player in it, and continues,

> Big business is not a separate interest group in Japan; it is the prime beneficiary and virtual *raison d'être* of the Japanese system, as the theory of the Japanese developmental state stipulates. For that reason it is meaningless to speak of the role of big business in Japanese politics; the two are indistinguishable.
>
> (Johnson 1992, p.81)

Taiwan since 1949 can also be interpreted as a plan rational economy: the state has played a fundamental role in regulating and directing the economy (Amsden 1979, 1985; Wade 1990; Henderson 1993b). One consequence of the ROC's use of economic development for legitimation has been the comprehensive involvement of the state in directing the economy rather than relying solely on neo-liberal economic beliefs, practices and institutions. Regarding the operation of the developmental state, White and Wade state,

> Taiwan and Korea restrain market rationality by the priorities of industrialisation. Industrialisation *per se* has been the main aim, not considerations of maximising profitability based on current competitive advantage. For this purpose the governments have intervened aggressively in (parts of) the market to bring about specific allocative effects – in addition to measures designed to safeguard the self-regulating parts of the market.
>
> (White and Wade 1984, p.6)

Henderson identifies eight elements which exist with East Asian plan rational economies: state equity; creation of industries; market protection; performance standards; controls on speculation; price controls; land, labour and collective consumption; and labour repression (Henderson 1993a, pp.94–104). It is the combination of these elements (with important differences in practice between the three countries involved) that creates the policies of plan rationality.

The success of plan rational economies is also in part explained by their adaptability and pragmatism. By balancing the discipline of the market (i.e. allowing unproductive companies to go bankrupt) with long-term strategy, a fine balance has been achieved that is greatly beneficial to economic development. The state targeted sectors for industry to invest in and worked with business to achieve clear goals. The flexibility accorded by this system has been fundamental to these countries' success. It also helps to explain their ability to cope with exogenous shocks such as the two oil crises of the 1970s and the problems associated with these countries' rapidly appreciating currencies.

Plan rationality then is the means through which developmental legitimacy is to be achieved. The state directs the economy and governs the market, but the institutions which direct and govern – in East Asia typically identified with the economic bureaucracies – are also fundamental to defining and understanding the developmental state.

Autonomous economic technocracy

The fifth and final factor which identifies a developmental state then is the existence of a technocratic élite, typically an economic bureaucracy, that is both skilled and committed to the task of economic reform in a position of 'bounded autonomy' (Zhao and Hall 1994) from specific interests. This aspect of the CDS has received the most attention in the literature on East Asian development, and it is the purpose of this section to give an overview of this work and relate it to the wider definition of the CDS given in this chapter. Wade argues, 'Governing the market requires a small number of powerful policy-making agencies to maintain the priorities expressed in the routine accumulation of particular negotiations and policies in line with a notion of the national interest' (1990, p.195). This can be understood as the physical institutionalization of the developmental state. This group provides central guidance for the economy through planning and direction (Johnson 1987; Amsden 1989; Wade 1990; Sheridan 1993). In post-war Japan this group is typically identified with the Ministry of International Trade and Industry (MITI), the Ministry of Finance (MOF), the Bank of Japan (BOJ) and the Economic Planning Agency (EPA) (Johnson 1982, 1987; Sheridan 1993; Fingleton 1995); in Taiwan in the Council for Economic Planning and Development (CEPD) (Johnson 1987; Wade 1988, 1990) and the Economic Planning Board in South Korea. These bureaucracies are for the most part autonomous from special interests and pursue the goal of developing the state.

In the case of the CDS in East Asia state autonomy is primarily derived from the 'revolutionary' origins of the state élite. As demonstrated when discussing developmental legitimacy, new élites came to power in Japan, Taiwan and South Korea with very weak ties to the existing social formations. In Meiji Japan the old decentralized and highly factional feudal system was swiftly replaced by a bureaucratic system that relied on national, not local connections. Although in the early period (up to the 1890s) this system was dominated by the Satsuma-Choshu groups who had led the Meiji Restoration, by the end of the nineteenth century a meritocratic, examination-based system had been established and was functioning effectively (Beasley 1990, pp.65–9). The traditional conservative groups had little ability to influence the developmental project. The autonomy of the bureaucracies was further strengthened by the American Occupation, which destroyed the power of the Japanese military in politics, carried out a vigorous land reform programme and weakened the other political groups to the extent that they were dependent on bureaucratic help for almost all legislation. The bureaucracies also for the most part escaped the purges and reforms that affected the rest of Japanese society, and what reforms did occur increased the bureaucracies' power and autonomy.

The leaderships of Taiwan also seized the opportunity offered by having weak ties to society. As stated above, the KMT ideology of the 'Three Principles of the People' was a developmental ideology aimed at modernizing China. However, because of the lack of autonomy that the KMT regime had enjoyed on the Chinese mainland in the 1930s and 1940s and the importance of landowners and business groups to the KMT, reform-minded groups had been unable to implement these policies. On Taiwan, however, Chiang had an almost free hand and was able to reorganize the KMT and implement comprehensive land reform on the island with American assistance. The élite groups which had emerged under the Japanese occupation of Taiwan (1895 to 1945) had little ability to influence the KMT's developmental strategy. Many were killed during the disturbances outlined previously and those who remained were either co-opted or marginalized.

In South Korea the picture is more complex. Land reform occurred, although primarily as a result of the devastation of the Korea War that removed the former landed class from South Korea. From the end of the Korean War until 1960 the ROK was governed by Syngman Rhee, and is a classic example of a corrupt and self-serving regime. However, the military coup led by Park Chung-hee saw the emergence of a leadership autonomous from the Korean society in a way that Rhee had never been. It is significant that all three countries underwent some type of land reform. This was vital in breaking down traditional power groups and increasing the relative autonomy of the state over society. In all three cases this was in part aided by the US, but it was not simply externally imposed but very much the product of domestic action.

Technocracy is preferred here to bureaucracy because although the technocrats will typically also be bureaucrats, this is not a necessary factor. The interpenetration of political and bureaucratic élites in political systems dominated by one party or one group has meant that technocrats have become important political figures. This is particularly true in Taiwan since the late 1980s, where the leadership of the KMT has been almost entirely taken over by highly educated former bureaucrats: in 1988 twenty-one out of twenty-four members of the ROC Executive Yuan had received postgraduate education at European, American or Japanese universities, and of that twenty-one, fourteen had doctorates (Tien 1989).

The technocratic élite in the CDS is staffed by the most able and educationally qualified groups in the country. The key to the success of this group is their commitment to national goals rather than self-aggrandizement and their relative autonomy from powerful interest groups within the state (Wade 1988, p.256). The bureaucrats are able to function technocratically because they are insulated from direct political influence and can be seen as ruling rather than reigning (Johnson 1987). As Trimberger has demonstrated, in Japan these bureaucratic élites are loyal to the state and their status and advancement depends on the state (Trimberger 1978).

Developmental states possess skilled and committed bureaucrats who enjoy autonomy from most political and societal pressures and so are able to focus on the developmental project. It is this group, often in informal alliance with business interests and political parties or the military, that steers and guides the plan rational economy. Their legitimacy for this task is derived from their ability to deliver economic development. The technocracies draw up the industrial policies which lie at the heart of plan rationality. Bureaucratic success in achieving economic goals is not one hundred per cent, as Arnold has demonstrated in the case of the Taiwanese motor industry (Arnold 1989), but viewing the developmental process as a whole it is the economic bureaucracies, in alliance with business interests and other political actors, which, in Wade's terms, govern the market. The bureaucracies should not be viewed as 'depoliticized' but highly politicized, with development being the supreme political goal, and other key actors (LDP, KMT, big business) concurring with this.

In Japan this is most clearly seen in the process known as *amakudari*, where retiring bureaucrats go on to take senior positions in Japanese companies. This practice creates an important transmission belt for ideas and strategies between business and the state. The former bureaucrats not only promote the idea of their former ministries; they also put the case for their new employers to the bureaucracies. This cross-fertilization of ideas has been important in enabling the state to avoid isolation from the reality of the economy and also to maintain influence over the decisions of 'private' companies. While this practice has not been prevalent in Taiwan or South Korea, formal and informal interaction between the state technocrats and business has also played a role. Also in Japan a number of bureaucrats have taken up posts in the LDP on retirement. This again has led to the cross-fertilization of ideas and transmission belts for the ideas and issues that concern the electorate to the bureaucracy.

Business organization has been examined as one of the key elements in the success of the CDS, but business organization cannot be examined as an ideal category of the CDS in East Asia because of the important differences in the business structures of the countries concerned. In Japan a dual economy exists, with large industrial groupings (*keiretsu*) centred on banks competing in the global market being served by numerous small businesses. In South Korea the economy is dominated by a small number of large industrial combines (*chaebol*) which resemble the Japanese companies in certain respects, but do not base themselves on small domestic producers to anything like the same extent. Taiwan's domestic structure is very different. Although there are a few large companies (such as Tatung), their size and role in the Taiwanese domestic economy are very different from that in Japan and Korea (Whitely 1990). The Taiwanese economy is dominated by small- and medium-sized enterprises (SMEs) employing under 1000 workers.

The issue of technocracy also highlights the evolutionary nature of the CDS strategy. The economies of the three countries analysed here have all undergone significant 'de-regulation' and 'privatization' in the 1980s and 1990s. However, this has not necessarily led to a weakening of the power of the bureaucracies over the economy. Indeed, Stephen Vogel has demonstrated that de-regulation has in fact increased the ability of certain Japanese bureaucracies to influence the decisions of Japanese companies (Vogel 1994).

Global and regional context

The CDS strategy did not emerge out of a vacuum, and the global and regional context which enabled it to take place was of great importance to the success of this type of development. This section will briefly address the key external factors of the CDS strategy, grouping them into four broad and overlapping categories: (1) colonial heritage; (2) the regional developmental dynamic; (3) the role of the US, and (4) the post-1945 open global trading system.

Japan's colonial heritage is significant because of its absence. Japan was one of the few countries in the world which escaped direct conquest and colonization by a western power as the result of a conjuncture of political and economic factors, most important of which was the greater interest of the imperial powers in the potential of China relative to resource-poor Japan (Norman 1940, pp.43–8). The causes of Japanese imperialism are hotly contested, but by 1910, only fifty years after the opening up of the country, Japan had annexed both Taiwan and Korea. Japanese imperialism had a determinant impact on the subsequent economic trajectories of these two countries, instituting the fundamental dynamics of the North-east Asian political economy that exists today (Cumings 1987; Bernard 1989; Geon 1992). Cumings argues,

> In the 1930s Japan largely withdrew from the world system and pursued, with its colonies, a self-reliant, go-it-alone path to development that not only generated remarkably high industrial growth rates but changed the face of Northeast Asia. In this decade what we might call the 'natural economy' of the region was created; although it was not natural, its rational division of labour and set of possibilities have skewed East Asian development ever since.
>
> (Cumings 1987, p.55)

The colonial heritage thus relates directly to the second key category, the regional developmental dynamic. The colonial period established a transfer of production and technology from Japan to Taiwan and South Korea that continues today. Bernard and Ravenhill (1995) have ably demonstrated that this process is not simply the operation of a unilinear product cycle and that regionalized production networks have emerged, dominated by Japan. This is of great significance to the CDS strategy because it provided important inputs for the Korean and Taiwanese economies that were necessary for them to develop, while also providing outlets for Japanese business. However, one area of the regional dynamic that remains under-researched is the role of the Japanese bureaucracies in guiding this process.[6]

The importance of the United States in providing a global framework within which the CDS strategy was able to operate is the third factor of importance. Since the onset of the cold war in the 1940s the countries addressed in this question, particularly Japan, have played a key role in the strategic thinking of American politicians. As a result, the US provided these countries (especially in the 1950s) with vast amounts of financial and military assistance (Haggard and Cheng 1987). The US government also established formal military ties with Japan, South Korea and Taiwan,[7] providing security guarantees for all three: for Japan this freed capital to be invested in industry, but Taiwan and South Korea have maintained significant military establishments to no obvious detriment to their economic development. Furthermore, the Korean War provided a vital boost to the the Japanese economy that had been devastated by the Second World War, and in much the same way American involvement in Vietnam came at a fortuitous time for Taiwanese and South Korean industrial development (Woo 1991). US advisors were also fundamental in the planning and organization of the post-war land reforms in these countries which, as discussed earlier, were a significant factor in creating state autonomy for the developmental élites.

The fourth international factor of great relevance to the CDS strategy is also based on the role of the US and its cold war considerations: the open trading system that emerged from the Bretton Woods conference. The United States provided free access to its markets for Japanese, Taiwanese and South Korean goods while tolerating (at least up to the 1970s) the strong protectionism of their domestic economies practised by these countries. Indeed, these countries received preferential treatment under the General System of Preferences (GSP) until 1988. As well as maintaining access to the US market, American power also provided an international open trading system from which these countries benefited greatly. The rise of 'new protectionism' in the 1980s and 1990s would have to be regarded as a factor mitigating against the ability of other states to copy this type of developmental strategy.

Assessing the success of the developmental state

Assessing costs and benefits is a difficult and value-laden exercise, and the process of categorizing in these terms will inevitably influence the assessment: the benefit of industrialization (as seen from a business perspective) can also be a cost (if seen from an environmental perspective). Given that assessing costs and benefits is not comparing like with like, the following two sections will range across a broad field of disciplines and levels of analysis to give an overview of ways of understanding the implications of the CDS strategy.

The most obvious benefit of the CDS has been its patent success. The economies of the capitalist countries have been the fastest growing economies of the region in the world since 1945, contrary to the predictions of most commentators in the immediate post-war era. Not only has growth been rapid but income has been distributed far more equitably in these countries than in many other countries, be they developed or developing. These countries have also moved up the product cycle from producing simple goods such as textiles to increasingly complex manufactures such as electronics and computers. The standard of living, level of education and access to health care facilities in these countries have also expanded to levels that bear comparison to any country in Western Europe or North America. In addition, crime levels appear to be lower and the social problems associated with high unemployment and widespread drug abuse have been avoided.

Another important dimension of the success of the CDS strategy has been the increasing political pluralism of these countries. Japan has been a formal democracy since the occupation, but bureaucratic dominance and single-party rule have been the dominant features of Japanese democracy since 1955. However, there has been a gradual increase in pluralism in Japanese politics, especially during the 1980s (Muramatsu and Krauss 1987; Muramatsu 1993). Whether the dramatic events of 1993 will have a significant impact on the nature of Japanese politics is the subject of considerable debate. Taiwan and South Korea have undergone remarkable changes in their political structures. Both countries were run by vicious military regimes for much of the post-war era, but have been undergoing a remarkable process of democratization since the mid-1980s, moving from 'hard' to 'soft' authoritarian regimes, and then on to an increasingly plural democratic system. Although the causes of this democratization cannot be simply placed at the door of economic development, the growth of these countries' economies and the emergence of a middle class have undoubtedly contributed to this process.[8] Although far from the ideal of the western democracy, Japan, Taiwan and South Korea offer important and successful examples of political systems that have become more plural with evolving civil societies and are certainly more democratic and open than the lesser developed countries of the region such as North Korea or Myanmar.

As a strategy of competition in the global economy the CDS succeeded in transforming three primarily agricultural economies into dynamic, advanced industrial economies, and at a speed and on a scale unknown elsewhere in world history. The benefits of the CDS strategy are clearly apparent, especially if compared to the performance of other less developed countries. However, the success has had its price. The next section of the chapter will examine the distinct costs of the strategy.

Authoritarianism has been a key aspect of the CDS strategy. Apart from a vaguely democratic interlude in the 1920s, Japan's political history since 1868 has been marked by control, dominance and authoritarianism. Although Japan has been a formal democracy since the end of the American occupation in 1952 the dominance (until the 1990s at least) of a single political party, and the dominant role of unelected bureaucrats have led many commentators to question how democratic modern Japan actually is (van Wolferen 1989). Taiwan and South Korea have both been dominated by authoritarian military dictatorships until recently and, particularly for South Korea, the stability of this new democracy is far from assured. Labour movements have faced severe difficulties in improving the circumstances of workers because of a combination of both direct oppression and the engineering of social restraints on labour activity. The impact of this state strategy on the people who live in the countries concerned is thus a significant cost of the CDS.

A further cost of the CDS strategy has been considerable environmental degradation (Bello and Rosenfield 1990). All these countries are also deficient in what Sheridan calls 'social capital' (Sheridan 1993, p.219), the infrastructural components that enable a populace to lead fulfilling and enjoyable lives outside the workplace. Finally, the substantial trade surpluses that this CDS strategy has generated for these countries have led to strains on the liberal trading system. In a number of ways the new protectionism of the Clinton administration has evolved in response to, and learning from, the CDS strategy.

The CDS strategy has resulted in unprecedented growth in East Asia, which raises important questions concerning the applicability and suitability of this strategy for other countries in the global economy. The CDS has been outlined according to five ideal types based on evidence from three countries in North-east Asia. This final section addresses the extent to which these could (or should) be replicated by other states, and assesses whether the changing international context, in particular the issue of globalization, has made this strategy redundant.

The blurred distinction between public and private was shown to be the central element underlying the CDS strategy. It emerged as a conjuncture of specific historical, social and political–economic factors, and its replication is hard to envisage. Furthermore, the dominance of the Anglo-American economic discourse in global economic institutions mitigates against this conjuncture occurring again. The state ideology factor is one that could be replicated, but race/ethnicity has been an important underpinning in mobilizing a population behind the developmental project. Given that few countries in the world are as racially and ethnically homogenous as the East Asian states addressed here, it would be more difficult for a state élite with diverse populations to unite a people behind a cause. Furthermore, the stress on discipline and obedience present in 'Confucian culture' which has been exploited by state élites may not be present in other countries.

The success of a country's economy clearly influences the legitimacy of a government in any regime: from western liberal democracies to Stalinist North Korea, keeping the population fed, clothed and employed is a vital consideration. In this sense developmental legitimacy is already present as a factor in all developing countries. However, other forms of legitimacy (legal–rational, charismatic, etc.) can interfere with this process and prevent it from becoming dominant. All regimes want development, but few appear able to deliver it. A key factor in this is that 'plan rationality' is often difficult to replicate. Many revolutionary regimes since 1945 have followed 'plan ideological' developmental strategies (Henderson and Appelbaum 1992, pp. 18–20; Henderson 1993a) which while initially successful have been unable to sustain development. Global financial institutions such as the World Bank and the IMF are dominated by people who contend that market rational/market ideological approach is the only correct course for development, and so use their structural power to influence the developmental strategies that the leaderships of these countries are able to implement. Therefore the main constraints on the emergence of plan rationality are external, and although the World Bank has begun to pay lip-service to the significance of the state in development (World Bank 1993), it is still confined by its neoclassical beliefs in the free and open trading system and what Amsden (1994) calls 'market fundamentalism'. The so-called 'second-tier' countries of Southeast Asia, such as Malaysia and Thailand, are attempting a plan rational approach to engineering development, and their relative success can in part be explained by the pragmatism of these countries' leaderships over the questions of the relative roles of state and market.

The final 'internal' factor, autonomous economic technocracy, is also hard to replicate. Training technocrats is not necessarily difficult, but ensuring that they work for a commonly held 'national' interest rather than towards their own interests or those of their group is much more difficult, as the discussion on neo-patrimonialism in Chapter 9 shows. Drawing up intelligent and coherent policies is one thing; being able to implement those policies is another. This relates to the second vital consideration of autonomy. As demonstrated above, a specific conjuncture of domestic and international factors enabled the ruling élites of these states to achieve sufficient autonomy to implement their specific developmental strategies. The new regimes can be seen as being revolutionary, in that they overturned the pre-existing order and had few restrictive links to their domestic societies; whether other LDCs have the capacity for this kind of revolutionary change can only be gauged from a careful case-by-case examination of the various countries.

A further important consideration that operates between the domestic and international is the historical context within which the CDS strategy first emerged. Japan escaped colonial conquest in the nineteenth century, and thus the attendant distortions of its domestic political economy. Taiwan and Korea were both subject to Japanese colonialism which took a strongly developmental aspect that was perhaps unique and vitally important to the nature of those countries' political economies after 1945.

The CDS strategy, particularly in its post-1945 stage, was able to exist within a strongly favourable international trading environment. The global economic boom that took place in the 1950s and 1960s was founded on the open trading system devised at Bretton Woods and its key institutions such as GATT. American cold war interest in seeing capitalist North-east Asia thrive also provided Japan, Taiwan and South Korea with an amenable and open market for their products and an important source of technology. The USA also provided these regimes with security guarantees and support in international political and economic fora. The emergence of regional blocs and the neo-liberal ideology of the international financial institutions all mitigate against the possibility of states being able to implement this kind of strategy.

Finally, globalization is an important consideration when assessing the ability of a state to follow a CDS-type strategy. Globalization remains a contentious subject (see Chapter 1), with vigorous arguments taking place about its significance and implications, and the ability of the state to cope with these changes is one of the fundamental issues in IR and IPE theory. One point is clear though: the transnationalization of production and the globalization of international finance both have profound implications for the autonomy of individual states to implement certain policies. The state in East Asia has proved remarkably able in coping with the changing international and global environment, and the question now confronting the CDS is whether globalization can be 'managed'.

Conclusion

To summarize, the roots of the CDS in East Asia lie in the transformation of Japan following its opening to the West in the nineteenth century. The creation of market society in Japan and the dominance of German developmental economic ideology led to a blurring of public and private that has been of fundamental importance to political economy in the region, as it was replicated by follower nations. The state used this blurring of public and private to perpetuate a state ideology centred on nationalism that dominated and controlled labour and/or other potentially 'dissident' movements. Successful development became the core source of legitimation for the East Asian regimes, both for domestic and international purposes. The economy was organized around a plan rational system that finely balanced the rigours of the market with goals of the state. This organization and development were primarily in the hands of a group of economic bureaucracies working for a commonly perceived 'national developmental interest', and the autonomy of this bureaucracy was achieved through the utilization of the previous factors. It should be noted that this strategy has been flexible and evolutionary, and a key element to its success has been the foresight and luck of those involved to adapt to changing domestic and international political and economic circumstances.

The CDS strategy has undoubtedly delivered the goods. Japan, Taiwan and South Korea have seen unprecedented growth that has been sustained consistently, while many other countries in the world (developed and developing) have struggled to achieve or maintain economic growth. The negative consequences of this strategy (labour repression, environmental degradation, etc.) have been present historically in all successful developmental strategies and may, unfortunately, be unavoidable. Certain aspects of the CDS strategy, particularly its international aspects, make it an unpromising model for other countries. However, certain elements of this strategy, in particular understanding that the state can play a vital role in generating development, offer valuable lessons for other states.

Notes

1 Nester in particular uses neo-mercantilism in an extreme way that verges on racism: 'Japanese neo-mercantilism is not just a set of nationalist policies, it is a way of life deeply interwoven in Japan's culture, institutions and psychology. ... The idea that Japan is locked in a perpetual trade war with the outside world is the spiritual engine of Japanese neo-mercantilism that single-mindedly drives virtually all Japanese, from the highest manager to the lowest factory worker, to devote themselves to Japan's success' (Nester 1993; p. 91).

2 The CDS explanation of East Asian development has come under criticism, but a number of its key tenets have been taken on board. Attacks on the CDS often fail to take account of the sophistication of the approach and set up the developmental state as a straw man to demolish. This problem is apparent in recent work by Clark and Chan, where they fail to address the sophistication of the state-centric approach in an otherwise useful and informative edited collection (Clark and Chan 1994). The World Bank report on East Asia (World Bank 1993) is interesting in this respect, but should be read in conjunction with the scathing reviews in the special edition of *World Development* (1994, 22 (4), pp. 615–70).

3 It is the failure to adequately deal with the issue of blurring public and private that undermines many of the traditional neoclassical and Marxist interpretations of the CDS. An example is Calder's extensively researched book *Strategic Capitalism* (1993). The book's fundamental flaw is the over-rigid distinction Calder draws between 'public' and 'private'.

4 On this point I disagree with Bracken (1994) that East Asia represents an exception to Hintze's thinking on state organization.

5 This assessment of the 1955-system and the Yoshida Doctrine is derived from Masumi (1988), Pyle (1992) and Kataoka (1992).

6 My own research based on interviews with Japanese bureaucrats and business leaders with regard to Japanese investment in Taiwan indicates that the Japanese bureaucracies have played a significant role in guiding Japanese business to move declining sectors to Taiwan.

7 The formal US security relationship with Taiwan was obviously transformed by Washington's recognition of Beijing in 1979, but the US government has consistently stated its opposition to the use of force in settling the dispute between Taiwan and the PRC.

8 The relationship between economic development and democratization is the subject of considerable debate and is one of the perennial issues in the study of politics and political economy (Rueschmeyer *et al.* 1992). There has been little written on this issue that focuses specifically on Japan, primarily because of the way the contemporary Japanese democratic institutions were

introduced during the occupation period. For Taiwan the principal works are Gold (1986) and Wakabayashi (1992), and for South Korea a good overview is given by Pyo (1993).

5

The Shielders' strategy: the competitive advantage of social democracy

Structural change in the international political economy is fundamentally altering the character of states and the societies that comprise them (Strange 1994a and b). The growing integration of the world market, under the combined impact of the multilateral liberal trading regime and rapid technological change (Chesnais 1994), is presenting states with new opportunities and sacrifices. In this new environment the options for states are often presented in simple dichotomous terms. States should either try and take advantage of the 'liberal trading regime' (Ruggie 1982) by liberalizing their economies, lowering tariffs and other impediments to trade and the flow of capital. Alternatively, they should attempt to stem change by resorting to protectionism and government intervention.

For a while during the 1980s it did seem that a number of European welfare states like Sweden, Finland, Norway, Switzerland, Austria and in different ways Germany, North Italy and possibly France, were successfully resisting the pervading hegemony of neo-liberalism. Such states appeared to present a way of combining economic efficiency without compromising their societal values. They did so by shielding themselves from the disintegrative effects of the international market while remaining competitive and generally committed to an open liberal trading regime. They have been the home of some of the more technologically dynamic, well-managed, competitive and yet socially enlightened firms.

The argument we wish to advance is in principle not very different from that of Katzenstein (1986), namely that the crucial aspect in any 'shielding' strategy is a selective integration into the world economy – what we refer to as economic dualism. Dualism refers to the fact that in certain industrial sectors these states belong to some of the most open economies in the world in terms of (1) the ratio between exports and GNP, and (2) the use and level of import restrictions in relation to both tariff and non-tariff barriers. At the same time other industrial sectors are protected by a whole host of barriers and subsidies. Such protectionism is commonly justified in the name of the strategic interests of national security, the preservation of culture and/or traditional ways of life, and so on.

The competitive advantage of welfare policies

Welfare provisions and other egalitarian measures appear at first glance essentially internal arrangements, introverted, and if anything, oblivious to the demands of an increasingly competitive world market. The social programmes that are associated with welfarism apparently make little sense externally and are expensive in terms of the cost to the individual taxpayer, corporations and government. It is not perhaps surprising then that since the late 1960s the welfarist consensus, and the theoretical assumptions upon which it was based, began to come under vociferous attack from the neo-liberalism of the 'New Right' (Stein and Dorfer 1991).

The rise of neo-liberal politics notwithstanding, for a while it did appear that a number of social democratic regimes had succeeded in competing in the world economy while maintaining a high provision of welfare. Indeed, social democratic states have consistently been among the most affluent in terms of income per capita. While it is true that during the 1980s the rate of economic growth among most of these countries was below the OECD average they nevertheless managed to maintain low levels of unemployment (OECD 1991). In Switzerland, for instance, economic prosperity was sufficient to employ nearly all available Swiss citizens as well as many guest workers (Porter 1990, pp.307).

Such factors led commentators like Lipietz (1987), Porter (1990), Pfaller *et al.* (1991), Albert (1993) and others to argue that rising labour costs and generous state social spending are not necessarily disadvantageous. Such conditions force firms to (1) improve productivity by increasing investment in new technology, and (2) encourage them to concentrate output into increasingly differentiated market segments. Social democratic programmes offer international production something in return for investment, namely political stability, social harmony, a better educated and more productive workforce and a good infrastructure.

According to its advocates social democracy and welfarism offer a number of competitive advantages:

- Universal training and education for all provides a *highly skilled workforce*. For example, in Germany only 20 per cent of the labour force do not possess any form of paper qualification, whereas in France this is a disappointing 42 per cent. Moreover, whereas in the UK the apprenticeship system absorbs a meagre 14 per cent of school leavers, in Germany this figure is almost 50 per cent. Training is also ongoing, with companies being encouraged to provide further training with government subsidies.
- High wages forces companies to adopt *new methods of production management*: the most famous of these has been the Volvo Kalmar factory in Sweden, but similar innovations can be seen in Japanese factory production, namely a break with the 'dehumanizing' factory line associated with Taylorism and Fordism.
- State spending need not be an inefficient use of public resources:

'Knowledge and human capabilities are probably the most important competitive assets of today's highly industrialised nations' (Pfaller *et al.* 1991, p.9). Thus *spending programmes on education, training schemes and research and development can visibly aid competitiveness and efficiency.* Likewise, spending on infrastructure and infrastructural support benefits industry: roads, railways, postal services, telecommunications, etc.

- By guaranteeing incomes that are not fully subject to changing conditions in the market, the shielders are able to *protect their societies from sudden changes.* Moreover social spending can be directed towards achieving the adjustments required to maintain competitiveness whilst cushioning or even avoiding the dislocating effects that allowing the market to direct such changes would entail.
- A more egalitarian society is *a more cohesive and homogenous society*, and a society less plagued by crime, poverty and drugs. The pursuit of full employment will in turn reduce spending on unemployment benefit whilst providing the skills for those areas of the economy with shortages.

As we will argue in the next section, these beneficial factors are not the inadvertent consequences of disparate policies but the outcome of a fairly coordinated and coherent pattern of integration into the world economy. In fact, the shielders' strategy offers a sophisticated, if remarkably uniform, societal model.

Selective integration and domestic compensation

One of the most striking yet consistent features of the shielders' states is that they are also some of the most 'open' economies in the world. The Nordic and Rhine states have consistently supported extensive liberalization in the various GATT rounds. Their record on operating tariff barriers has also been exemplary in comparison to the larger participants in GATT. Average tariff levels, the extent of their usage and the use of non-tariff barriers have all been substantially lower than in the larger advanced industrial countries. In 1975, for example, Sweden's weighted manufacturing import tariff stood at 5.4 per cent compared to an EC rate of 7.5 per cent (Therborn 1991, p.232).

On average, exposure to foreign competition in the shielders measured in terms of export as a percentage of GNP is three times higher than in the larger capitalist states, while in Belgium, that area of the economy which is responsive to international demand is nearly eight times larger than its counterpart share in the USA. Of these countries, Sweden and Finland are the least dependent upon the world market, but Finland's export industry is overwhelmingly dominated by a single good, namely paper and pulp. The Netherlands is essentially a transit economy. Belgium is an important base for re-exports, while Norway is an important seaboard economy of international shipping recently bolstered by oil.

The consequence is that they are more dependent on the world market than most major capitalist states.

And yet, while these states boast some of the more 'open' economies in the world, they also invariably possess some of the most effective protective barriers around their economy. This protectionism has been both explicit and subtle. Explicit protectionism takes the form of high tariffs and quotas in some sectors of the economy, principally agriculture, while the more subtle forms can be seen in specific assistance and/or regulation for firms, or as in the case of Austria the lumping together of all the unprofitable industries into a state holding company. In Austria the OIAG is responsible for 17 per cent of total exports and 15 per cent of all employment (*The Economist* 1989)! Similar state-run conglomerates are to be found in Italy and Spain. In Switzerland protected local monopolies and cartels coupled with high standards and regulations have created the *de facto* protection of telecommunications, brewing and truck manufacture by driving up the price of foreign imports (Porter 1990, p.328).

The dual nature of these economies is best demonstrated in the agricultural and fishing industries of the Scandinavian countries. Both these industries arouse deep passions, and are the most subsidized across the industrialized world. But the level of protection is particularly high in the Nordic countries. The average producer subsidy in the OECD stands at 44 per cent, in Norway this subsidy is 78 per cent, accounting for some 7 per cent of GDP (see Figure 5.1). Swedish agricultural subsidies are often explained in terms of the strategic requirements of Swedish neutrality to be self-sufficient in times of war (Dohlman 1989). In Norway, defenders of the subsidies argue that this assistance is a necessary policy instrument to maintain a settlement distribution in remote areas of the country. The Norwegians claim that this support is justified to maintain a traditional and cultural heritage, Arctic farming, a heritage about which the Finns are also particularly sensitive. In Norway, about half of total subsidies came from direct payments, including deficiency payments to *shelter domestic production from world markets*. In addition to the tax burden on consumers to support these policies, strict import barriers also maintain high prices in the domestic market (*Financial Times*, 26 June 1992).

The continued pursuit of full employment through the provision of temporary wage subsidies and active labour market policies is an additional compensatory mechanism. The Swedish government has been particularly active in this respect, initiating the Swedish *Arbetsmarkands-styrelsen* (National Employment Authority), funded in part by the investment reserve fund; high quality training courses (until recently these accommodated approximately 1 per cent of the labour force; recruitment and wage subsidies up to 50 per cent (for those out of work more than six months), and the so-called 'solidarity policies' which regulate wages and incomes in order to promote social equality and limit the income spread within different economic sectors. Such policies ensured that until recently Sweden had the most successful labour market policy in Europe

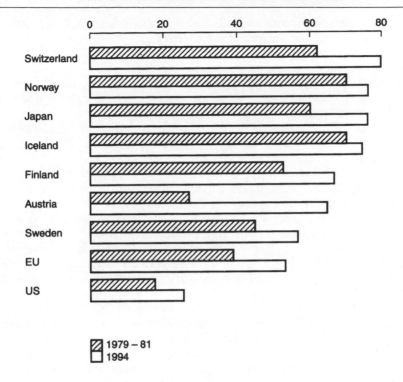

Figure 5.1 Farm subsidies: producer subsidy equivalents as percentage of value of
production
Source: OECD as reported in *The Economist* (1994)

which, although costing 1 per cent of GDP, ensured that less was spent
on unemployment benefits (*The Economist*, 4 October 1991).

The shielders' states are therefore paradoxically some of the most
'open' and yet protected societies in the international political economy.
They achieve this by dualizing their economies and integrating with the
world market (indeed, they are at the forefront of international trade
agreements) while compensating for the regressive impact of unfettered
market forces. The latter is principally achieved by protecting specific
sectors of their economy and by employing the welfare state as a massive
distribution mechanism of the benefits such openness can yield.

Industrial concentration and differentiated markets

Only the most competitive companies can survive in the world economy.
The level of integration into the world market that the shielders are prepared to tolerate has meant that only their most competitive firms could
survive. By compensating for the small size of their home market, many
corporations in these states have gleaned economies of scale from the
world market and consequently have become internationally competitive.

In addition, the rising cost of labour, combined with the implementation of an active labour market policy in cooperation with the trade unions and the employers' federations, has forced inefficient and less profitable firms out of business (Gould 1988). The second common characteristic of the shielders is that they all possess (apart from Austria) unusually concentrated industrial sectors – a point of great political significance and to which we will return.

Industrial concentration in Sweden is particularly striking, with the most open sectors of the economy dominated by a handful of large corporations. With a population of only 8.4 million, Sweden is home to seventeen of the world's largest non-US private corporations. By 1985, for example, 46 per cent of Swedish manufacturing production was sold for export with total exports representing about 35 per cent of GDP. Of these export sales, over 40 per cent are registered by Sweden's twenty largest firms. The most famous and successful of these domestic corporations are Volvo and Saab-Scania, Ericsson, Atlas Copco, SKF and Electrolux. In 1988 Volvo accounted for 12 per cent of Sweden's exports and employed 6 per cent of the country's manufacturing workforce (Wilde 1994a, p.60).

Similarly, in Finland the telecommunications company Nokia emerged from a spree of acquisitions and restructuring in the 1980s to become the world's second largest mobile telephone manufacturer with 17 per cent of world market share, an area in which Finland has no special tradition, while four firms dominate the Finnish paper and pulp industry, a sector responsible for 50 per cent of GNP. An analogous representation can be depicted in the Netherlands with Phillips, KLM and DAF, and in Switzerland with Nestlé, Ciba-Geigy, Hoffman-LaRoche, Lindt and Rolex. For many of these corporations foreign sales account for over 50 per cent of total sales, further reinforcing the necessity of an open economy for economic survival.

Industrial concentration is, however, only one aspect of the unique industrial and manufacturing architecture of the shielders, which have proved particularly adept at identifying market niches. The shielders are in relative terms high spenders on research and development; none the less, their small market size prevents them from competing in the more expensive technologies. Their companies typically focus on niches that do not require a great deal of restructuring, but rather a great deal of imagination. The principal advantage in moving into such market segments is that competition on price becomes less important, with costs being less of an issue. Instead quality, design, portability, fashion, safety, after-sales service and an ability to respond to consumer preferences become the important determinants.

Swedish companies have successfully pursued the exploitation of niche markets. Sweden is the only small country in the OECD to have a domestic car industry with two prosperous car makers: Volvo and Saab-Scania. Volvo, at about the same size as BMW, is Sweden's largest corporation, with its sales in 1987 corresponding to just less than 10 per cent of GDP. In the mid-1970s in the face of mounting international competition, small production capacity and high labour costs, both firms decided to concentrate production in the up-market car class. Although responsible for less than 1.5 per cent of the total world car market, by 1986 these two companies had captured over 10 per cent of the luxury car segment of the world's largest car market in the US, and production volume had risen by 60 per cent (Berggren 1992, pp.60–1). Volvo in particular concentrated on building itself a reputation for being one of the safest cars in its class.

Likewise, when faced with ever-increasing competition from low wage countries in the developing world, many of the shielders are shifting their production into such niche markets. The Swiss were among the first to do this. Indeed, Switzerland gained certain advantages from being the most affluent society in the world. The high standard of living in Switzerland provides a luxury consumer market which acts as a testing ground for such markets in other states (Porter 1990, pp.322–3). The Swiss revived a relatively stagnant watch industry by concentrating on precision instruments (Rolex), and individually tailored fashion watches (Swatch). Likewise, throughout the 1980s the Swiss established a whole host of consultancy firms to sell industrial software tailored to the needs of the individual customer. Italy too has followed this pattern of concentration on fashion design and quality. Today Italy is the world's leading exporter in the textiles industry and has benefited from the internationalization of Italian style (Porter 1990, p.424). Italian designers such as Armani, Versace, Valentino and Bellini are synonymous with *haute couture*.

The question that is often raised is why do companies who inhabit shielder states appear to be better at identifying market niches? Is it the result of the combination of the size of the domestic market with its integration into the world economy that forces firms to innovate, or is it the unique cultural heritage combined with a strong labour movement that force companies located in the shielders to innovate? Porter lays the stress on the structural–logistical conditions. He points out that most of the large Swedish companies can be traced in some way to Sweden's natural resource endowment (1990, p.342). He identifies in particular what he calls 'selective factor disadvantages' such as high wages and benefits, that have forced companies to innovate. Among these he includes: the long winters and cold climate that led to the development of sophisticated technology in energy conservation; the long distances between resources and cities that led to great sophistication in transport and logistics-related industries, and the hard climate and rugged geography which has imposed unusually tough conditions on Swedish mining, transport and manufacturing companies (1990, p.345). Such facts may well be true, however, but as is often the case with abstract structuralist analysis, this does not offer a complete explanation; otherwise countries like Canada, Argentina and Chile, not to mention the Soviet Union (now Russia), should have been in the forefront in these industries.

Institutional economists tend to place the emphasis on 'cultural' dimensions, and in particular the relationship between capital and labour

(Thompson and Sederblad 1994). Berggren, in her study of Volvo, maintains that Swedish industry as a whole has been pursuing alternative methods of production:

> For one, the use of the assembly line . . . was repeatedly questioned. To obtain more flexible work structures and more attractive jobs, many alternatives were tested. . . . Second, the Swedish version of teamwork was marked by a desire to increase the workers' organization autonomy and scope for independent decision making.
>
> (Berggren 1992, pp.6–7)

There appears to be widespread agreement that high wages and social benefits combined with the absence of a large natural market have forced the shielders' companies to innovate. Innovation took place in two principal forms, either by concentrating on high value-added segments of an industry (Bang and Olfson, Rolex, Swatch) or alternatively through the creation of a more innovative company structure (e.g. Benetton, IKEA, Volvo). Comparisons with the 'developmental model' (Johnson 1982) are of interest here. The developmental state strategy can be characterized by the attempt to restructure the entire industrial and manufacturing sectors in the direction of high value-added mass goods, progressing from low value-added industries like textiles and steel to high value-added industries. In comparison, by focusing on differentiated market segments, the shielders have discovered an additional dimension to the international division of labour. They have identified high value-added segments in traditional industries such as textiles, steel, mining and automobiles as well as in high value-added industries like telecommunications.

Targeted industrial policy

Similarly, the shielders have developed their own unique brand of industrial policy designed to assist industry in adapting to changing realities in the international economy. Unlike in larger European states and the US, industrial policies in the shielders have not taken the form of blanket protection against foreign competitors. Rather, their response is characterized by the provision of temporary assistance for individual firms in difficulty as well as support for those firms attempting to regain competitiveness in the world market. In particular, such assistance is targeted towards well-established, large corporations that are perceived to be struggling with unfavourable developments in the international economy.

Industrial policy in the Netherlands, for example, has been most systematic in high technology sectors. To remain competitive in aircraft and satellite communications production, the Dutch government has supported joint ventures. In electronics this support has been focused on Dutch multinationals such as Phillips. Similarly, Sweden, like the Netherlands, developed an industrial policy targeted towards *individual* firms from the 1950s onwards. The relationship built up between government and industry has subsequently been very supportive and has been enhanced by low corporate taxes. However, this support has focused heavily upon established Swedish multinationals rather than on small to medium-sized businesses (Porter 1990, pp.351–2). For instance, while Sweden operates strict anti-trust laws locally they are not applied nationally in order to allow Swedish companies to gain from economies of scale and scope. Consequently in Sweden, only 6 per cent of people are employed in manufacturing work in firms with fewer than twenty employees, while 56 per cent work in firms with over 200 employees. A situation unlike that found in other industrialized states (*The Economist*, 5 November 1994).

Even in Switzerland with its minimal intervention in areas such as telecommunications, brewing and truck manufacture, protected local monopolies and cartels have been sanctioned. Elsewhere government regulations and standards have driven up prices in order to ensure domestic protection for Swiss firms (Porter 1990, p.328). On the whole the main function of this policy has been to assist industry in adapting to the challenge of competitiveness as opposed to offering blanket protection.

Austria's adjustment policy has likewise stressed limited protection, less extensive support for exports and temporary, massive domestic subsidies to protect employment. The latter has been most vividly illustrated with respect to the Austrian steel industry. The industry is dominated by a handful of large nationalized corporations which have generally been allowed to conduct their business largely independent of direct government interference. In particular the industry has enjoyed a high degree of financial autonomy, with Austria's largest steel firm Voest enjoying access to both national and international capital markets. However, in the late 1970s and early 1980s the industry began to suffer *vis-à-vis* its international competitors. This was due, on the one hand, to import competition from low cost producers, but on the other by the government's request that the industry contribute towards the maintenance of full employment. The immediate result of these pressures was falling productivity which dragged the industry into deficit and threatened to make Austria's second largest industrial corporation, the United Speciality Steel Company (VEW), insolvent. By 1980 with combined debts of $1 billion the government stepped in with a massive subsidy to prop up the corporation. It was a decision supported by all the major political parties at both national and provincial level and reflected a shared belief that to allow a corporation as large as the VEW to fail would be disastrous for the economy and for the labour force. Indeed, although assisting the government's policy of full employment had obviously contributed to a deterioration in the corporation and industry's competitiveness, only 10 per cent of Austrian steel workers lost their jobs between 1975 and 1981, compared to one-third across Europe as a whole (Katzenstein 1984, pp.198–216).

A stark example of the differences in industrial policy between the social democracy of the shielders and the neo-liberalism of the 'Anglo-Saxon' states is provided by the recent experiences of the mining and shipbuilding industries. The adverse effects of the recession of 1990 to 1993 were felt particularly in such traditional industries of the advanced capitalist states. In the UK the already exposed and fragile shipbuilding and coal industries were dealt further blows: in the case of the former, by the insolvency of the Swan Hunters yard in the North east, and for the latter when the government announced a far-reaching pit closure programme in 1992. Despite impassioned public campaigns, no substantial government assistance was forthcoming. In Germany, although it was equally recognized that both industries required massive structural changes and reconversions, government subsidies were made available in order to cushion the inevitable impact on jobs and living standards. Cuts were to be made, but unlike in the UK, they were to be phased in gradually in order to preserve social harmony and cohesion.

Among the most common measures to assist industry in the shielders have been policies to encourage investment and to ease investment instabilities. Perhaps the most prominent of such policies has been Sweden's investment reserve. This reserve, which dates back to legislation first drafted in 1938 (Katzenstein 1984, p.48) allows firms to place profits into a special reserve fund in order to avoid taxation. However, during protracted economic difficulties these funds are then released in order to fund specific government-approved projects. This fund has proved particularly valuable; for instance, during the stagflation crisis of the early 1970s it accounted for about 12 per cent of total annual investment. A similar policy has been pursued in Switzerland through the government's procurement programme which has likewise encouraged investment during economic downturns, while in Austria the government has consistently subsidized domestic investment.

Without such policies to encourage sustained investment in plant and machinery, the shielders would not have been able to finance the high wages that their industries command. Thus while labour costs in these states are on average 20 per cent to 23 per cent higher than in Italy, France and Japan, and 32 per cent higher than in the UK, sustained investment has yielded productivity advances that have improved quality and reduced costs sufficiently to allow workers to command such salaries (Therborn 1991, p.234). It is no coincidence, therefore, that the OECD countries which invest the most in such capital goods are Germany, Switzerland and Sweden. Here, investment in research and development amounts to about 3 per cent of GDP. In the United States, although such in investment amounts to an almost equal figure of 2.7 per cent of GDP more than one-third of this investment (1 per cent) is defence-related (Albert 1993, p.140). Consequently labour costs, as Therborn observes with reference to Sweden's manufacturing firms, 'were not mentioned among the ten biggest problems . . . nor did their reduction figure in the most popular competitive strategies' (1991, p.267).

The shielders' emphasis on the firm rather than on the industry as a whole appears therefore to be the key to its efficient industrial policies.

Katzenstein argues that this emerges from a perception that competitive developments occur within rather than between industrial sectors.[1] However, as we demonstrated earlier, most of the shielders are characterized by a high level of industrial concentration. Such concentration generates oligarchic power and thus it should come as no surprise that policy has been targeted towards individual firms rather than industries. This is the way oligarchy operates (Tamburini 1994; Guzzini 1995). This dimension to industrial policy was highly innovatory during the 1960s and 1970s conferring specific advantages on the shielders. However, by the late 1980s such policies had become standard across the OECD (Vickey 1993). As we will demonstrate, the targeted character of the shielders' industrial policy gave companies a very good reason for remaining located in these countries. Once lower wages competitors, or alternatively competitors located within the EU, began adopting similar strategies, such companies had fewer reasons to stay. Between 1985 and 1988, for example, Swedish investment in the EU increased seven-fold, while in neighbouring Finland it quadrupled (*The Economist*, 5 November 1994).

Adaptive politics

The work on 'Nordic' states or the Rhennish model invariably places the emphasis on the unique political culture of these states. Unlike the adversarial political character of Anglo-Saxon democracies, these states are characterized by what may be described as non-conflictory political culture. Explanations as to how this culture emerged are divided, but broadly they stress three principal factors: first, the role the welfare state has played in ameliorating social divisions; second, the distributive policies pursued to achieve this, and third, the recognition that labour should participate in the decision-making process.

The shielders and in particular the societies of Scandinavia are characterized by egalitarianism and equity. Poverty in such states is conspicuous by its absence as are the social ills associated with the underprivileged urban underclass of the US and UK. As Milner argues, 'equality is more than income distributions . . . it is . . . a matter of expectations . . . woven into the inherited political culture' (1994, p.150). As a consequence, transfer payments are used to reduce wage differentials in Sweden to among the lowest in the world (Therborn 1991, p.238). For example, whereas in the United States as much as 17 per cent of the population are on incomes below half average earnings, in Sweden this proportion is just 5 per cent. Wages have effectively become a tool for redistribution. According to Esping-Anderson (1991), the Scandinavian model is characterized by three essential features: (1) the comprehensiveness of the human needs that are satisfied by social policy in comparison with other welfare states; (2) the level of institutionalization of social rights as citizenship rights, and (3) the sense of public solidarity which such institutionalization compels.

The extent of redistribution that takes place in such states is enormous. The welfare state acts not just as a safety net but is centred on the 'public provision of education and care, care for the elderly, for the sick and the handicapped, for the children of working parents' (Therborn 1991, p.236). The extent of transfer payments is so great in Sweden, for example, that they provide about 45 per cent of personal disposable income, with perhaps 65–70 per cent of Swedes dependent on the public sector for their livelihood. Not only are transfers so extensive, they are also among the most generous in the world. Until the Bildt coalition introduced reforms to benefit law, unemployed Swedes could expect to receive 90 per cent of their previous earnings, a figure matched only by Denmark (NOSCO 1993, pp.83–4). Coupled with the narrow wage differentials mentioned earlier, these policies have discouraged the conspicuous consumption associated with the US and UK. Flamboyance and extravagance are not common Nordic traits.

The final factor in this non-conflictory political culture is the social contract between the representatives of industry, labour and government. At the institutional level this is characterized in most of these states by 'co-responsibility' within the power structure and organization of corporations, and coordinated, usually national, wage bargaining (Albert 1993). It is this social contract that is deemed to be the principal cause of the relative harmonious nature of industrial relations in the shielders. Indeed, throughout the post-war period, strikes in the shielders have been uncommon (Katzenstein 1984). The institutional arrangements are intended to offer all parties an opportunity to participate in corporate decision making regardless of whether they are shareholders, employers, executives or trade union officials. For example, in Germany it has been compulsory since 1973 for all firms employing 2000 or more to implement this system of shared decision making, while since 1976 the same firms have been compelled to allocate shareholders and employees an equal number of seats on company supervisory boards (Albert 1993, pp.110–12).

'Co-responsibility' also extends into the wage bargaining nexus within these societies. The shielders are characterized by strong trade union movements, and yet their record in unemployment has been on the whole more impressive. The evidence from both the shielders and Germany appears to suggest that such policies can be as successful as market-driven wage negotiations but, unlike the latter, they are more socially acceptable. This is because in these states, unions and employers have coordinated their wage bargaining either across industries or on a national basis rather than in an uncoordinated manner, as is largely the case in the United Kingdom. For example, in 1993, Volkswagen employees in Germany agreed to reduce their working week and take a pay cut so as not to further penalize the company during the post-unification recession; not to have adopted such a pragmatic approach would have resulted in compulsory redundancies. Likewise in the Netherlands, the economic surge of the 1980s was made possible in part by union acceptance of wage moderation, which bolstered the competitiveness of Dutch industry and reduced inflation to practically nil. Yet what are the causes of this accommodative political culture?

Katzenstein maintains that accommodative political arrangements are a necessity because many of these states are punctuated by deep ethnic, religious and/or linguistic divides. He cites Belgium with its Flemish-speaking Flanders and French-speaking Wallonia and Switzerland with its tripartite ethnic/linguistic division coupled with a Protestant/Catholic divide as the principal examples. Such divisions, Katzenstein continues, necessitated the creation of accommodative politics and in the process generated a culture of bargaining and consensus that ultimately underlies democratic corporatism.

One of the problems with this explanation is the link between corporatism and consociationalism. The emergence of accommodative politics is seen as almost a prerequisite for the emergence of corporatism, yet the divisions found in Belgium and Switzerland are missing in the Scandinavian countries. In contrast to Belgium and Switzerland, and to a lesser extent Austria, the Scandinavian countries are characterized by a homogenous population where linguistic, ethnic and religious cleavages are marginal. Here, others have argued that the religious heritage of Lutheranism perhaps serves as the basis for the underlying egalitarian and consensual nature of Scandinavian politics; however, religion alone cannot be identified as the sole factor of explanation.

We are therefore more persuaded by the argument that the principal cause of this consensual accommodative political culture is the strength of the labour movement in such states. For example, in Sweden the density of trade union membership has consistently been the highest in the world with over 80 per cent of the workforce unionized, a figure only Finland comes close to (Jackson 1982, p.2; Milner 1994, p.173). One of the strengths of trade union organizations in the Nordic countries is that on the whole they are not internally divided between separate coordinating bodies for Protestant, Catholic, communist and socialist unions, and where white-collar and blue-collar organizations are generally cooperative. In countries such as France where such divides exist, this has seriously weakened the labour movement and partly explains the low level of unionization (Jackson 1982, p.4). In addition, in Germany and Sweden unions have also been broadly based on industrial lines in stark contrast to Britain with its craft, industrial and general unions (Owen Smith 1981).

The tradition of co-responsibility can be traced back to truces struck between labour and business during the Depression and war years: Norway's 'Basic Agreement' (1935), Switzerland's *'Paix du travail'* (1937), Sweden's *'Saltsjobaden* Agreement' (1938), the fifth Corporatist chapter of the Dutch constitution of 1938, the 'Social Solidarity Pact' in Belgium (1945); in Austria, labour and industry established an Economic Commission in 1947 to make recommendations to the government for economic development (Jacobs 1973, pp.139–40). Such agreements and the general consensual nature of politics have proved crucial in the post-war open liberal international system, given the dependence of these states upon international markets. All actors have realized that conflicts should be the exception and consensus the norm, with the redefinition of divisive class interests in terms of a more encompassing national interest.

Conservative progressives

As we have seen, the shielders' strategy holds the promise of a socially acceptable 'middle way' between capitalism and socialism. The evidence for such a 'third way' is to be found not only in the remarkable results the shielders' states have achieved, i.e. extended welfare provisions combined with rigorous, effective and wide-ranging redistributive policies, but also in the very economic and political structure of these societies.

While these states may appear in the context of the late twentieth century to pursue 'progressive' policies, that does not mean that they are progressive states. One of the critical questions we pose is *why* diverse countries like the Nordic states, Austria, the Netherlands, Switzerland, and to a lesser extent Germany, pursue egalitarian policies. Katzenstein seeks to explains this by arguing that '[t]hese policies are carried by the conviction that it is important to counter some of the harmful effects of international liberalisation' (1984, p.47). The problem with such an explanation, as we demonstrated in Chapter 2, is that the agency behind such a decision is not identified. Consequently we argue that such characteristic egalitarianism was the product of long political struggle in which a number of key groups, such as farmers or blue-collar organizations, were able to pursue their interests and inadvertently produce both welfarism and the dual-natured economy we described earlier (Wilde 1994a).

If there is a common thread between these societies that explains both the paradoxes they exhibit and the reasons why they appear to represent a 'third way' between capitalism and socialism, it lies in their 'conservative' (with a small 'c'), slightly anachronistic socio-economic structure. As Fehrenbach comments, although with reference to the growth of the banking sector in Switzerland, 'Europe changed and Switzerland did not'. Although Fehrenbach is concerned with the making of the Swiss banking system, in principle his verdict is correct, namely that Switzerland's greatest asset is that it consistently refuses to move with the times – as is best illustrated by the refusal of the Swiss to join the EU (joined now by the Norwegians: in both countries arguments about traditional political cultures swayed the voters). Likewise, Austria's flirtation with the extreme Right, the election of Kurt Waldheim, and Austria's policies towards the disintegrating Yugoslavia (Palan 1992), should dissuade anyone from entertaining the notion that Austria is a progressive society.

Several commentators have identified the common religious heritage of Lutheranism as the source of the welfare culture in the Nordic states. Lutheranism, it is argued, imbued in these cultures both a strong sense of individual responsibility as well as a feeling of responsibility for the welfare of others (Wilson 1979; Milner 1994; *The Economist* 1994).

However, as Milner remarks, world value surveys have found the peoples of Scandinavia to be among the most agnostic in the industrialized world (1994, p.151). This would appear to invalidate our claim that these societies are inherently conservative. On the contrary, Milner continues by arguing that the origins of the cultural commitment to welfarism lies in 'the pre-industrial villages, which though hardly egalitarian, placed rigorous standards of competence and honesty upon the gentry' (1994, p.151).

Wilson (1979) argues that the historical development of the welfare state in Sweden was largely *reactionary* rather than progressive. Midway through the nineteenth century a sudden increase in population growth resulted in the emergence of a large, landless agricultural proletariat. Neither agriculture nor the fledgling manufacturing industry was able to absorb this group which subsequently suffered extremely harsh social conditions (p.2). One solution to this was emigration; for example, between 1870 and 1890 one million Swedes chose to leave the country mainly for the United States, almost one-fifth of the entire population! Those who remained provided a ready supply of cheap labour for new industry and were forced to accept low wages and appalling living conditions (p.4). However, the origins of a more enlightened welfare policy can be found in a much earlier form of industrialization. This had largely taken place in *bruks* (manufacturing workshops), dispersed throughout towns and villages, 'which started their own paternalistic brand of welfare, often providing housing, health care, education and pensions to their workers' (Gould 1988, p.164).

Elsewhere, particularly in Stockholm, the landless proletariat provided fertile ground for a constellation of popular movements. It should thus come as no surprise that the 'Left' in Sweden emerged from a combination of three movements: the temperance movement, the free church movement and the trade union movement (Gould 1988, p.165; Wilson 1979, p.4). While Esping-Anderson distinguishes between the 'conservative' welfare policies of Bismark and the social democratic welfare state common in the Nordic countries (1990), Wilson suggests that 'the social reforms introduced in Germany by Bismarck provided food for thought for Sweden and Swedish employers . . . [who] felt that social insurance might take some of the heat out of the growing conflict between Capital and Labour' (1979, p.6). Certainly the first three decades of this century were ones in which conflicts between labour and capital were severe. Yet at the same time social and political reforms were being introduced: women were given the right to vote in 1921, temperance legislation was passed, the Poor Law was reformed and trade unions introduced unemployment insurance (Gould 1988, p.165).

It was not until as late as 1937, however, that the first foundations of Sweden's welfare state were laid. The victory of the Left in 1932 began an uninterrupted forty-four years in power. However, despite this success in the early years the Social Democrats were reliant upon the support of the Agrarian Party to command a majority in parliament (Gould 1988, p.165). To win this support the Social Democrats made what is known as the 'first historic compromise' in 1937, whereby the Agrarian Party backed legislation to create major work projects for the unemployed in return for agricultural subsidies which formed the basis for the development of the dual-natured economy described earlier. Prior to this compromise the Agrarian Party had actually blocked earlier social legislation, such as the work-based insurance scheme put forward by the Conservative and Liberal parties (Wilson 1979, p.6). Subsequent legislation was introduced to provide subsidies for the unemployed, limited government intervention and welfare policies for the family, 'not that the changes proposed were in any way revolutionary' (Wilson 1979, p.7). It is important to remember that even at the height of support for the Social Democrats, over 90 per cent of industry was in private ownership.

Is there a future for a shielding strategy?

The 'dualist economy' has produced, in the context of the European shielders, a surprising mixture of competitiveness and innovation combined with a commitment to preserve tradition and cultural values. This is the source of the success of these societies. Conversely, the crisis of social democracy and welfare in the 1990s may be interpreted ultimately as the growing incapability of balancing competitiveness with this commitment to preserving 'tradition'. Ironically, it appears that one of the pressures on the shielders emanated from a growing divergence between capital and labour – undermining the very compromise which is at the heart of these societies.

In Wilde's analysis (1994a, 1994b) it was the demands of the labour movement the (LO) for a commitment to the socialization of the means of production through the wage-earner funds that drove a wedge between labour and capital in Sweden (Wilde 1994b, pp.194–5). The progressive forces in Norway and Switzerland, by rejecting EU membership, have begun a similar process in their societies with the big pharmaceutical companies in Switzerland already threatening to migrate over to the French side of the border. Similarly, Kvaener, Norway's third largest company, is reported to be considering moving its headquarters to one of the EU member countries (*European*, 29 December 1994). Economic dualism, which has led to an overdependence on a few giants, has made these societies extremely vulnerable to the decisions of a small number of corporate bosses.

This exposure was exacerbated by the liberalization of the financial markets which was forced upon the governments of many of these countries during the 1980s by growing national debt. Such financial liberalization has facilitated capital migration by the removal of capital controls. Meanwhile, the targeted industrial policies which were once unique to the shielders are now being adopted across the OECD as a whole, with the consequence that firms such as Tetra Pak and IKEA, caught between growing demands from labour and a more attractive

European industrial framework, began a trend by relocating their headquarters to cheaper European neighbours. The direct outflow of capital into the EU, for example, rose from 10 billion Swedish Krona in 1987 to 459 billion Swedish Krona by 1991 (Stein and Dorfer 1991). Today over 50 per cent of the employees of Sweden's manufacturing companies are working in foreign subsidiaries (*The Economist* 1994).

Just as these trends were taking place, the shielders were dealt a number of severe exogenous shocks that in combination have shaken the foundations of their economic strategy. In the Nordic states financial de-regulation from 1985 to 1990 facilitated an inflationary boom; for example, in Finland GNP grew at 3.4 per cent a year during this period, in Sweden 2.2 per cent (OECD surveys). To control inflation Norway, Finland and Sweden pegged their currencies to the ECU. Then the 1990 to 1993 recession hit. Another of the characteristics of economic dualism is, as we have demonstrated, an open domestic economy – consequently recession hits the most open the hardest. The recession was exacerbated by the maintenance of high interest rates which, although provisionally employed to control inflation, were increasingly raised to prevent speculative outflows and maintain exchange rate parities. In addition, economic activity was dealt a further blow by a banking collapse. As a result of such exogenous shocks, between 1991 and 1993 Sweden's GDP contracted by 1.7 per cent a year, Finland's by 4.5 per cent a year, situations neither has experienced since the Great Depression. Caught in this vicious circle of economic woe, unemployment has soared, and with it the budget deficit. With nearly full employment such societies could afford such generous benefits; with mass unemployment this generosity has wreaked havoc with government finances.

Nevertheless, despite such economic misfortunes and the beginnings of a neo-liberal erosion of various areas of the welfarist model, the shielders have proved to be remarkably resilient. Although no longer the shining examples of a 'third way', the Nordic countries have returned to growth, while Austria and Switzerland came out of the recession of the early 1990s remarkably unscathed. In addition, public support for social policies remains high. The Swedish electorate, for example, made it clear in 1994 that the reforms of the conservative coalition of Carl Bildt (1991 to 1994) had gone far enough and promptly returned the Social Democrats to power. Similarly, in Britain despite sixteen years of rule by a Conservative party committed to the free market, the Welfare State remains largely intact. It is clear then that the shielders' strategy has been under attack in recent years. However, the fact that it has survived bears testimony to the desire by large swathes of voters, public servants and other interest groups to maintain a form of integration with the world economy that protects and shields society from the more harmful effects of market forces. Indeed, the strength of such groups within Europe as a whole ensures that social dimensions exist within the European Union as well.

Note

1 '[Unlike France etc] The small European states generally found comprehensive or sectoral planning efforts increasingly inapplicable, simply because of their economic openness . . . the problem was one of selecting the devices of stabilization that were in harmony with their social objectives. But economic openness also inhibited the small European states from relinquishing planning altogether' (Katzenstein 1984, p.63).

6

Hegemony:
power and competitive advantage

So far the discussion in this book has rested on an implicit assumption, namely that the benefits of sharing in an integrated modern economy outweigh the 'natural' predisposition of states for acquisitive and aggressive behaviour. It makes sense for states to restructure themselves and compete economically only as long as the world economy remains integrated. The 'competition state' therefore may only survive as long as states do not seek to revolutionize or destroy the system but merely to manoeuvre within it.

If so many states are already 'embedded' structurally and politically in the liberal trading regime (Ruggie 1982), and if the values of the competitive capitalist economy have been institutionalized to such a degree, then by the same token the entire gamut of power relationships and power games must have changed accordingly. With the exception of Strange's concept of structural power (1987, 1988), current theories of power in the international system overlook this fundamental change. To what extent then can states take advantage of their 'power' in the global competitive game? Does power offer any competitive advantage? Is it still an important concept in the age of the competition state?

In this chapter we analyse the most exclusive competitive strategy in the world economy, the use and *misuse* of hegemonic power. Like all other strategies discussed in this book, hegemony raises a number of specific questions, which makes a 'cost–benefit' analysis extremely complicated and difficult to assess. We are confronted, to begin with, by several competing interpretations of the 'true' function of state power and hegemonic processes: from statist interpretations, some of which stress the problem of 'imperial overstretch', to the transnational school which views hegemony as an institutionalization of transnational class relationships. These varying interpretations complicate our task because they suggest that our principal question, namely whether hegemony offers a competitive advantage, cannot be disentangled from an ancillary question, who gains from hegemonic processes? Is it 'the state'? Is it a class or an alliance of classes? Is it sectoral interests? In addition, there are a number of interpretations of the dynamics of power in the international system. These range from straightforward 'relational' power theories to Susan Strange's concept of structural power. Added to this we suggest the notion of a 'multiplier effect' of power dynamics in a cooperative system. Thus our task is further complicated because it is not only a matter of *whether* hegemony offers an advantage and for whom, but also *how* it is exercised.

Hegemony as a competitive strategy

Hegemony is one of the most fashionable concepts in international relations. Traditionally it has been used to represent the way by which powerful states stamp their authority upon both their environment and other states. Hegemony is therefore taken to be an organic dimension of the behaviour of powerful states in the international system. For neo-realists the emphasis is placed on the beneficial outcome of such power distribution. This new twist to the theory of power politics, in which powerful states are now understood not only to pursue their own 'egotistic' interests but also to provide 'public goods' to their neighbours, has been greeted, not surprisingly, with suspicion as the latest version of a self-serving American ideology (Strange 1987).

A minority of scholars, however, have opted to treat hegemony (whether they employ the term or not) as a controversial and yet specific foreign policy option that is open to a select number of powerful states. The implication of such an analysis is that hegemony is a competitive strategy which states may or may not wish to adopt. Such considerations were implicit in the debate that took place a few years ago among many international relations scholars over the future role of Japan in the international system. Similar considerations permeate a number of key texts exploring American foreign policy, including David Calleo's *The Imperious Economy* (1982), Ricardo Parboni's *The Dollar and Its Rivals* (1981) and Susan Strange's *Casino Capitalism* (1986). These authors take us away from the world of the 'will to power', implicit and explicit in many international relations texts, to the world of policy, interest and choice. In line with their ideas we define hegemony therefore as *a calculated foreign policy instrument which aims at translating a state's powerful position in the international system into a competitive advantage in the global political economy.*

The hegemonic strategy presents us with a number of analytical difficulties. Whereas other strategies discussed in this book are either sectorally driven (e.g. parasitical (Chapter 8), size (Chapter 3)) or represent historic compromises (e.g. the developmental state (Chapter 4); the shielders (Chapter 5)), hegemony by its very nature defines a 'holistic' foreign policy which must dominate all other possible strategies. It is far more complicated in execution, and less identifiable with specific interests. The competitive advantage it provides is almost always obscured, at times intentionally so. It is therefore difficult to determine who are the potential beneficiaries of hegemony. There are at least three, not necessarily contradictory, interpretations of hegemonic practices.

The first of these theories can be found in Paul Kennedy's *The Rise and Fall of the Great Powers* (1988). In this comparative historical study of the European state system, Kennedy reaches the conclusion that previous hegemons lost power because of their tendency to overburden themselves with imperialist responsibilities. Kennedy's theory appears to have been modelled on the Habsburg Empire, whose very size over-extended its capacity for integration. Such over-extension twice resulted in the division of the Empire. On the first occasion, despite the intro-duction of administrative centralization by Charles V, a sequence of European wars eroded the Empire to the point that his successor, Philip II, divided it among his family into a western part, including Spain, Portugal and the Low Countries and the eastern Habsburgs which later became the Austro-Hungarian empire. On the second occasion, the growth of nationalism and defeat in the First World War resulted in the final dissolution of the Empire. Imperial overstretch equally may have been the downfall of Napoleon Bonaparte.

Although the notion of imperial overstretch is less applicable to the British Empire, Parboni (1981), Calleo (1982) and others have argued that US military commitments were at the root of the breakdown of the Bretton Woods System. The imperial overstretch thesis therefore musters impressive historical evidence, and has become a lasting critique of hegemonic policies. Nevertheless, there are three principal problems with Kennedy's interpretation. First, Kennedy's operating assumptions are essentially 'statist' and they do not allow for a 'reformist' hegemonic state which theoretically could be more attentive to the pitfalls of hegemonic designs. Second, Kennedy's presentation is historically deterministic, with the Great Powers presented as if they are driven by forces beyond their control. Finally, it is doubtful whether dynastic politics can serve as a model for modern state policies. Kennedy provides no indications, to use Mann's (1986, 1994) notion, that each of these empires/states is constructed of a diverse combination of power sources and relationships and hence each ultimately possesses different dynamics of development.

A more subtle, and far more persuasive, version of the imperial over-stretch argument was put forward by, among others, Anderson (1974) and Nairn (1978). In their view hegemony (although they do not use the term) fixes class relationships and social structures which feed off, and by implication depend upon, other formations. When hegemons eventually lose power, they do so because they are too inflexible to respond to chang-ing conditions. Consequently, as Anderson observes with respect to Spanish hegemony:

> The very fortune of its early control of the mines of America, with their primitive but lucrative economy of extraction, disinclined it to promote the growth of manufactures or foster the spread of mercantile enterprise within its European empire. (Anderson 1974, p.61)

In a similar vein Nairn asks: Why is it that in Britain the development of modern industry and techniques of production were retarded? The reason, he maintains, are to be found in 'Britain's prior involvement in an older web of external relations, in a system, now archaic, to which capitalists had adapted themselves only too well' (1978, p.5).

Britain's role as the world's banker in the nineteenth century has left the City and financial interests in a predominant place which consequently contributes to the neglect of industry (Nairn 1978; Ingham 1985). American academics similarly point to the deleterious effect that America's predominant place has had in the car industry (Harrison and Bluestone 1988; Dertouzos *et al.* 1989). Whatever the short-term merits of hegemonic policy, long term it is likely to turn sour because social formations are less flexible and adaptable. In this view, therefore, hegemony is an inappropriate competitive strategy, especially in a period of accelerating change such as we are experiencing today.

A second critique, associated with J.A. Hobson and the early élite theorists, maintains that hegemonic practices conform to the egotistic needs of select interests in the country to the detriment of the 'national interest'. 'Although the new imperialism [of the late nineteenth century],' writes Hobson, 'has been bad business for the nation, it has been good business for certain classes and certain trades within the nation' (1988, p.46). 'Some of these trades,' he goes on,

> especially the shipbuilders, boiler making, and gun and ammunition making trades, are conducted by large firms with immense capital, whose heads are well aware of the uses of political influence for trade purposes. These men are Imperialists by conviction; a pushful policy is good for them (p.49). . . . Still more dangerous is the special interest of the financier, the general dealer in investments. (Hobson 1988, p.56)

A distinction then is made between the interests of certain sections of the 'élites', who may well directly gain from hegemonic practices, and the interests of the country as a whole. Similar points are made by Mills (1956) and other critics of the 'military–industrial complex' (Kaldor 1981; Galbraith 1991) of the US. Calleo, for example, argues that the '[h]uge military spending reoriented large sections of the American economy and created numerous symbiotic relationships between business and government around the superpower role' (1994, p.17). While such an argument is grounded in a distinction between the national interest and parochial interests, it none the less reminds us of the likely vociferous domestic criticism of hegemonic practices.

At the same time, the very character of the hegemonic project is disputed. The domestic sources tradition has an advantage over power politics (imperial overstretch), in that it identifies concrete interests behind the hegemonic project rather than some innate or even metaphysical desire for power and prestige. Nevertheless, this tradition still perceives hegemony as an aggressive and powerful foreign policy design pursued by one state (often) to the detriment of other states. A different tradition perceives hegemony as offering an insight into the underlying structural ordering of the world economy. Hegemony may take the form of a powerful state imposing its will on others, but in reality the picture is much more complicated. Hegemony in this representation 'is exercised within a wider social and political constellation of forces . . . [a] "historic bloc"' (Gill and Law 1988, p.93) that comprises not only a national but also a *transnational* coalition of interests (Van der Pijl 1984; Gill 1991; Overbeek and Van der Pijl 1993).

Arguably the most ambitious project in this vein is Kees Van der Pijl's *The Making of an Atlantic Ruling Class* (1984). Van der Pijl documents the transnational coalition of interests evident in the formation of US hegemony, and demonstrates that US hegemony reflected the rise of a new coalition of interests which he defines as a liberal/internationalist transnational class. A Gramscian notion of 'hegemony' has been added to suggest that transnational class alliances are alliances of classes and fractions united by an overarching ideology or concept of control (Overbeek and Van der Pijl 1993).

Following this line of argument, the second difficulty with hegemony is whether the essence of the strategy is the ability to shape the environment of accumulation. In other words, does hegemony imply the ability to shape the 'rules of the game' in favour of one's own *national economy and society*, or, as is often the case, does it refer to the use of state power to shape the environment in line with the strategic interests of a *coalition of transitional classes?* In the case of the first question one would assess, although with great difficulty, the impact hegemonic policies have had on national growth; in the latter, the idea of national economic growth is not particularly relevant. This central ambiguity lies at the heart of the critique of hegemony as a competitive strategy.

Relational and structural power

At the same time there are debates and controversies as to the role and function of power in an international political economy, debates to which we now turn. The conventional image of power is of the strong states or the 'great power' dominating its neighbours, from which it exacts tributes and concessions. Smaller states are reduced to dependencies in the international system and hence do not count in the power games. This image has been modified due to the policies of Great Britain in the nineteenth century, and more so, the United States in the twentieth. Here hegemony works differently or even 'positively'. A state power is employed first and foremost to shape and create a transnational order, in which other smaller and less powerful states are granted a certain autonomy as well as responsibilities. These transnational orders (such as the 'free world', the liberal trading system) are held together by the hegemon. The hegemon's immediate interest is to create both a market and a stable supply of raw materials for its economy. However, in order to do this, the hegemon produces a transnational order with its own rules, rules which in principle all are subject to, but which in return offer others opportunities for growth.

Such arguments can be found, for example, among the work of the 'revisionist' school of the cold war historiography (Kolko and Kolko 1972; Williams 1972; McCormick 1989). This view maintains that at the end of the Second World War, the US pursued a surprisingly coherent set of policies that aimed to establish an international trading system which broadly suited the interests of the dominant sectors of the US economy (Kolko and Kolko 1972). The patterns and institutions of this liberal trading 'regime' were not arrived at spontaneously, but through negotiations at which the US exercised an undue influence because of its sheer power both economically and militarily. Consequently, the immediate beneficiaries of this new order were the very industries which had expanded during the war years.

There are, of course, numerous instances in which the US employed its considerable powers to advance its economic interests and to exact compromises from its allies. Since US industry evolved in a continental environment, the US administration took a number of steps to ensure that the post-war international economic arrangements would create a system not dissimilar to the American market (Kolko and Kolko 1972; Williams 1972; Armstrong et al. 1984; McCormick 1989).[1] The US occupation administration, for instance, reformed the political and social structure of countries under occupation, namely Germany and Japan (Armstrong et al. 1984, p.55). The aim was to restructure these countries to complement America's socio-economic structure and to make them full participants in an American-led world economy. Similarly, as the principal actor in the Bretton Woods conference, by the time serious negotiations were taking place only two competing proposals were on the table. Keynes, reflecting perhaps British concerns, emphasized access to international credit for nations undergoing reconstruction and to a limitation on the ability of the proposed fund to interfere with the domestic economic policies of participant countries. Harry Dexter White's plan, on the other hand, was more concerned with global liquidity. Not surprisingly the American proposal was accepted and, in placing the stress of adjustment on debtor countries, undoubtedly reflected American interests at the time.

Similarly, the Economic Cooperation Administration, the administration of the Marshall Plan, populated by American business and CEOs, was set up with the intention of shaping the European economic environment to benefit American business interests. Although the Marshall plan has been and continues to be widely applauded, it is interesting to note that UN reports on the state of the world economy in 1947 and 1948 never saw the need for such a plan! (*A Survey of The Economic Situation and Prospects of Europe, 1948.*) The international liberal trading system was therefore undoubtedly shaped to service the requirements of American business.

Hegemonic power then can be exercised in three principal ways:

1 Positively: to create a transnational order and produce the rules and laws of this order. The hegemon helps to shape, in effect, a co-operative international system.

2 Negatively: one finds that the hegemon then often disregards the rules when it suits.
3 Structurally: the hegemon gains certain additional advantages accrued from the very fact that it is at the core of the cooperative system it created.

How are these three facets of hegemonic power to be understood? To explore this theme further we employ Susan Strange's notion of relational and structural power. Relational power draws on a Weberian concept of power: '"Power" is the probability that one actor within a social relationship will be in a position to carry out his own will despite resistance' (Weber 1978, p.53). This notion of power, although 'sociologically ambiguous', as Weber notes, places the emphasis (when projected upon states, which is a problematic proposition) on states as entities bent on maximizing their advantage. This view of hegemony stresses the use of state power, or more accurately the dynamics of the projection of state power, in pursuit of economic goals. It corresponds to the second dimension of hegemonic power as defined above.

Strange, however, points out that power relationships operate differently in the international political economy. It is to explain the dynamics of power in this environment that she employs the notion of 'structural power' which she defines as follows:

> the power to choose and to shape the structures of the global political economy within which other states, their political institutions, their economic enterprises, and (not least) their professional people have to operate. This means more than the power to set the agenda of discussion or to design (in American phraseology) the international 'regime' of rules and customs.
>
> (Strange 1987, p.565)

Structural power then can be regarded as the first dimension – the positive aspect – of hegemonic power. In the next section we seek to identify the processes that shape the third dimension of hegemonic power.

A theory of power distribution in a cooperative system

There are a number of 'cooperative' international political systems (or 'regimes'), each characterized by distinctive sets of rules and what may be defined loosely as 'system coherency.' The capitalist world economy may be thought of as one such system. This 'free liberal trading regime' has achieved a degree of formalization, the rules of which are enshrined in clubs such as the IMF and the GATT agreements. The United Nations was supposed to provide the main venue for the political leadership of the system but, as is well documented, the UN proved cumbersome and ineffective in this respect. Other geographically more limited cooperative systems are the formalized and tightly linked European Community (now the European Union), as well as NAFTA, the Maghreb Union and a number of others.

What makes the EU, or the liberal trading system, essentially a coopcrative system is the fact that member states join together on a voluntary basis. They do so in the understanding and belief that they may gain more through cooperation than by 'going it alone'. Since they have joined voluntarily, and hence have a 'stake' in the system, they are likely to avoid behaving in a way that might wreck it. However, although participation in the system may offer some benefits to all members, the likelihood that such benefits will be distributed evenly is slim. Clearly some will gain more than others. Politics in such systems is therefore about the distribution of values and benefits without rocking the boat.

There are a number of loci for power struggles in such political systems. The focus of negotiations among members rapidly shifts from the threat of violence to attempts to play a leading role in defining the rules that govern the system. The one who makes the rules is presumed to benefit in relative terms more than the others. Not surprisingly, therefore, there has been remarkable interest in multilateral venues like the GATT (now the WTO) and the IMF. The 'rules of the game' are ostensibly defined in negotiations at these forums by majority vote. In reality, as Strange informs us, the 'rules' are often predetermined by one's structural power.

To further clarify the dynamics of power in such cooperative systems, we employ the example of the joint-stock company. A joint-stock company is a venture in which a number of shareholders come together in order to raise a project. The earliest modern forms of joint-stock companies were the ventures of the East India Company and its counterparts. (However, there are records suggesting that such enterprises existed as early as the Roman era (Chaudhuri 1965).) The prohibitive expenses and risks involved in sending ships and their crews on long journeys were simply too much to be borne by one individual. Individuals therefore joined forces and bought shares in such ventures. The idea took root and by the end of the nineteenth century the joint-stock companies were a common occurrence, soon to replace the predominance of family-based firms.

In a joint-stock company one buys shares in expectation of profits, which indeed are divided according to one's share. All shareholders are united by one common aim, namely that they would like to see the company profit, and they are likely to cooperate in order to achieve this overall aim. Shareholders are also 'owners' of a portion of the company; they not only have a stake in the profits, they also have a stake in the management of the firm.[2] Management, however, has implications that go beyond profits; managers make decisions about personnel, the future direction of the company, and perhaps more importantly, the formation of strategic alliances with other companies. Owning shares in a company therefore buys not only a legal claim to a portion of the company's earnings, but also certain 'powers' to direct the future conduct of the company. Since the company is part of the economy, or the economy may be thought of as the sum total of economic activity, a share in a company in effect amounts to a share, however negligible, in the economy.

While profits are distributed according to one's share in the venture (or so at least they should), it did not take long to realize that one does not need to own 100 per cent of the shares in a joint-stock company in order to control it. Indeed, in a joint-stock company one only needs to own 51 per cent in order to control the company. That means, of course, that while one gets only 51 per cent of the profits, one is in effect in control of the entire company, effectively doubling one's economic power. If the company in question is valued at two million dollars, a shareholder need only control one million dollars' worth of shares to effectively wield, in terms of representation in the economic world, two million dollars' worth of power. Yet as is well known, in most companies, in particular the large multinational enterprises, one need not even control 51 per cent of the shares in order to control the company. Due to the large pool of very small shareholders, often a bloc vote of 15 per cent or 20 per cent of the voting shares may translate to effective overall control. In such circumstances power can be multiplied several times over. These powers are of no great interest to the small shareholder who is there for the expected return. But for large shareholders, individual and corporate alike, the economic world is about power and influence, and they may aggregate enormous 'economic power' far beyond their net 'worth'. Such power considerations drive the policies of the Deutsche and Dresdner banks in Germany, or the Mediabanca in Italy, which, through a judicious acquisition of voting share, are able between themselves to steer and control the best part of the two countries' economies. Indeed, some studies suggest that even larger economies like the US or Japan are ultimately dominated through a judicious acquisition of share and cross shareholding by five or six power centres (Grou 1983).[3]

The same principles of multiplying power can similarly be stipulated for cooperative political systems. Thus we can conceive of the EU as operating like a joint-stock company. Indeed, the rules of voting and power distribution within the EU are not dissimilar to the principles that govern the joint-stock company. For example, in the EU not all shareholders, in this case states, have the same stake in the venture. They vary greatly in size, from the diminutive Luxembourg with 400,000 people to Germany with a population of over eighty million and the single largest economy. Being the largest economic player within the European Union has proved to be very beneficial to Germany. Powerful as it is alone, Germany is potentially even more powerful because of its leadership of a cooperative system in the international scene. This influence was illustrated very clearly during the ERM crises of 1992 to 1993 and in the proposed European Monetary Union.

Our notion of a 'power multiplier' represents our third dimension to hegemonic power. And as we will see in the next section, it offers the best explanation for the competitive advantage of hegemonic policies.

The application of hegemonic power

In this section we examine the 'multiplier effect' of hegemonic power by assessing whether hegemony conferred upon the United States in the post-war period any specific competitive advantage. One of the more intriguing and illuminating arguments that can be advanced in attempting such an assessment suggests that the United States has from time to time employed its sheer diplomatic and/or economic power to either advance specific sectoral interests, or alternatively, to reduce the costs of factors of production to its industry and hence improve its competitive advantage. Such arguments resonate with the notion that the US government has manipulated the decline of US power in order to advance its economic position, an argument proposed by Parboni (1981), Calleo (1982, 1994), and Strange (1986). To illustrate this thesis we will examine the policy of the United States regarding oil and finance.

Oil policy

America's policy towards oil provides a good example of the exercise of hegemonic power. One of the less well-known and documented consequences of the Marshall Plan, for example, is that it transformed Europe from a coal-based economy, a deposit which Europe has in abundance, to one based on imported oil, a product where American companies were dominant (Armstrong et al. 1984; Yergin 1991).[4] This transformation was not wholly unwelcome to many in Europe at the time. Coal production and productivity in the immediate aftermath of the Second World War were low. In addition, across the Continent communists held pivotal positions within miners' unions threatening disruption on a regular basis. Shifting from coal to oil thus both met the energy demands for recovery while somewhat diffusing the power of organized labour in the coal industry.

The periodic panic during the war years that the US was 'running out of oil' gave rise to a post-war policy of developing and controlling foreign reserves in order to conserve American deposits (Yergin 1991, p.395). This resulted in the rise in the price of petrol worldwide which placed America's European partners in dire straits. In fact, two billion dollars of the Marshall Plan (or almost 20 per cent) were for oil imports. At the same time the ECA blocked plans for European crude oil production (Berberoglu 1992). 'How unfortunate it was,' the British Foreign Secretary Ernest Bevin told the American Ambassador, that 'while the Americans were voting money to help Europe, the rise in oil prices nullified their efforts to a considerable extent' (Yergin 1991, p.424). That particular dispute was settled and the price of oil declined.

Another demonstration of US hegemony in the world market for oil took place in the early 1950s. As British Petroleum, Royal Dutch/Shell and to a lesser extent French companies began to make inroads into Middle Eastern oil production, American companies were in danger of losing franchises. Consequently in 1955, in order to maintain its interests in the Middle East, the US confirmed legislation dating back to 1918 that allowed an American company operating overseas to deduct from its United States income tax what it paid in foreign taxes (Yergin 1991, pp.446–7). The consequences of this allowed US companies to maintain their shares of Middle Eastern oil production on the one hand while bolstering pro-Western governments in the region on the other. It did this by enabling US companies to meet demands from host governments for fifty-fifty agreements, i.e. '[that] various royalties and taxes would be raised to the point at which the government's take would equal the companies' net profits' (Yergin 1991, p.435). Because such increased taxes in the host country would be ultimately deductible from the companies' US tax bills, the overall tax burden for the US oil companies would remain flat. However, the revenue to the host country would increase markedly, allowing government expenditure to rise and/or debt to be financed. Both episodes capture well the way the US has used its powers to advance both *its* strategic interests using oil as well as the strategic interests of its oil companies.

Perhaps the greatest illustration of the use or abuse of America's hegemonic power in the world oil markets surrounds the events leading up to and following the oil crisis of 1973. While the oil crisis is often presented as an unfortunate set of events, it appears in retrospect to have been almost an inevitable outcome of a number of American policy decisions. The charge has been made that the United States in fact engineered a rise in oil prices in order to gain a competitive advantage over its allies. Until 1970, the US was nearly 90 per cent self-sufficient in oil (Parboni 1981, p.51). However, fears about declining domestic oil deposits combined with concerns that European and Japanese competitors were gaining a competitive advantage from Middle Eastern oil. Such fears linked with the broader concern about the loss of American competitiveness that had led the Nixon administration to retreat unilaterally from the Bretton Woods agreement.

In response to such fears the US changed its oil policy and began importing Middle Eastern oil in large quantities. Demand for oil had risen dramatically in the early 1970s to the point that the US could no longer meet its own demand. As a consequence Nixon first froze oil prices within a broad anti-inflationary policy, and second he abolished the quota system that had guaranteed and managed domestic supplies and instead replaced it with a two-tier pricing system. Almost immediately, US oil companies began importing on a massive scale. Oil imports initially shot up from 3.2 million barrels a day in 1970 to 4.5 million barrels in 1972 and 6.2 million barrels a day in 1973. As a result of the two-tier pricing system introduced in 1973, oil extracted from wells that were already functioning in 1972 had to be sold at a price no higher than $1.35 more than the prevailing market price on 15 May 1973 – about $3 a barrel. Oil produced by wells that had been functioning after 1972 was exempted from this control as was imported oil. The imposition of a ceiling on 'old oil' discouraged extraction from existing wells, particularly following the tripling of the price of oil by OPEC. US producers found it more advantageous to leave the oil in the ground than to sell it at a price of one-third of the world market rate.

In such a fevered market the world price for oil began to rise, markedly shifting the world oil market from a buyers' to a sellers' market. However, at a stroke the devaluation of the dollar reduced foreign dollar holdings worldwide, subsequently reducing the receipts due to the oil-producing states. This decision led the Kuwaiti Oil Minister to ask,

> What is the point of producing more oil and selling it in exchange for an unguaranteed paper currency? . . .Why produce the oil which is my bread and butter and strength and exchange it for a sum of money whose value will fall next year by such-and-such percent?
>
> (quoted in Yergin 1991, p.595)

Indeed, the devaluation of the receipts of the oil-producing states only further encouraged them to act unilaterally to ensure that the price of oil and hence their receipts remained high.

Two separate charges are made against the US with respect to the oil crisis. The first charge is that notwithstanding the 'lead' the US took in resisting OPEC, the US in effect engineered the crisis that gave OPEC such powers. This charge is based primarily on the evidence of two secret State Department studies, both of which were written by James Akins. The first was commissioned in early 1970 and the second was produced in April 1973, which predicted the coming oil crisis and pro-posed a number of solutions. At the same time the 1970 Shultz Report commissioned by the President which came to similar conclusions was also shelved (Yergin 1991, p.588). This charge is addressed indirectly by Yergin, whose argument seems to be that the competitive lobbying of various interests (the majors vs. the independents, the petrochemical companies vs. the oil industry) lay at the roots of American policy and so the broader implications were frankly ignored.

The second charge is that the US took advantage of the oil crisis to improve its competitive advantage *vis-à-vis* its 'allies' (Parboni 1981). Following the tripling of the price of oil in 1973 by OPEC, the two-tier pricing system, introduced in the same year by Nixon, ensured that the average cost of oil in the US was a good 40 per cent below world market levels. This enhanced American competitiveness, particularly in those industries that required large inputs of energy or petroleum derivatives. Similarly, higher oil prices rendered both alternative energy sources economical[5] as well as encouraging new exploration, particularly in Alaska and the North Sea. This increase in US competitiveness was further exacerbated by the fact that imported oil from the Middle East accounted for a much larger portion of the total oil supply in Europe and Japan than in the US. Parboni reads into these decisions a clear American policy of taking advantage of the crisis to improve competitiveness by reducing the relative cost of oil to its own industries. And indeed, for a short while American companies were able to take advantage of this relative cost advantage in oil to improve their competitive advantage. What seems to be in little doubt is that the oil companies gained:

> Within the industry the most important division is between the oil companies and the rest. Whereas the bulk of the industry faced higher costs and squeeze on profits, the oil companies had a profit bonanza.
>   (Armstrong *et al.* 1984, p.309; see also Halliday 1983, p.183)

American energy policies therefore reveal an intricate and fascinating story. As these two incidents demonstrate, American oil policy represents a combination of the first and second dimensions of hegemonic powers. The US initially used the dependence of its allies to shape their economies to suit American interests. Subsequently, the US used its diplomatic and economic power specifically to strengthen the hand of American industry *vis-à-vis* foreign rivals.

Finance

Finance has possibly been the central instrument used by the US to advance its strategic interests. Specifically, two forms of power are used in the financial markets.

Seigniorage

As the only currency guaranteed free convertibility into gold or other currencies during the early period of the Bretton Woods system, the US dollar soon became the 'key currency' of the international monetary system. This was partly due to the monetary position of the US dollar but it was also due to the conditions of structural disequilibrium between Europe and the US. Outside Germany the level of industrial output in Europe had been virtually restored by the last quarter of 1946. However, the European countries experienced a huge balance of payments deficit.

This unique position that the dollar enjoyed bestowed upon the US specific advantages, or 'seigniorage'. Parboni (1981) defines seigniorage as 'the privileges accruing to the country whose money serves as the major international means of payment. The country that holds seigniorage is able to increase the international money supply by printing more of its own currency, (1981, p.37). There is much controversy over whether the dominant position of the dollar was a planned US policy or merely an accidental development. The US dollar, in Triffin's words,

> had unwittingly acquired the positioned 'privilege' of being used overwhelmingly as the universally acceptable 'parallel' currency against which every other country sold or redeemed its own national currency in the exchange markets.
>   (Triffin quoted in Angel 1991, p.13)

De Gaulle, on the other hand, was convinced that the US used its privileged position to export inflation to Europe, effectively making other countries creditors against their will (Calleo 1982, p.65).

Whatever the initial causes, there is no doubt that in time the US was able to exploit its seigniorage to its advantage. As the French economist Jacques Rueff explained,[6] under the Bretton Woods agreement, when the US was in deficit, instead of receiving gold, central banks received US treasury bonds. This resulted in a corresponding increase in the respective national currency relative to the dollar, thus contributing to inflation among its allies. However, the US did not have to reduce its own money supply in response to a growing external deficit; the treasury instruments were simply added to the debt. The unique position of the dollar afforded the US three principal benefits. First, the US was able to evade to some extent the monetary constraints that other countries were experiencing and in effect maintain a level of government demand above its own means. Second, American industry did not suffer a competitive loss as a result of the inflationary pressure which was generated. Because of the US government's ability to 'export' inflation, American industries' principal competitors experienced similar levels of inflation in their own economies. Third, the US was able to finance increased military spending for the Vietnam War as well as President Johnson's 'Great Society' programme without raising domestic taxation. Instead, the US simply expanded its budget deficit, consequently passing the subsequent inflationary pressures to its allies. This spending was thus in effect paid for involuntarily by America's allies. These spending programmes fed two of America's strategic industries: defence, including the automobile and aerospace industries, and the pharmaceutical industry. As we will see, these industries hold a commanding position in the world market. American allies were therefore indirectly contributing to sustaining a number of their principal competitor's industries.

Such examples vividly demonstrate how power can be augmented in a cooperative system. Not only did the US have the strongest economy in the world but, by virtue of the unique place of the dollar, its currency in effect served as the global currency. American policies in the 1950s and early 1960s may have been prudent (Parboni 1981; Strange 1987, 1994b) but once US industry began to lose ground to its competitors, the US began to employ the benefits of being a hegemon to the detriment of others in the system. None the less, it must not be forgotten that by occupying this hegemonic position the US also incurred a number of penalties. Currently, two-thirds of the dollars in the world reside outside the territorial control of the US. The Federal government's control over its money supply has been consequently diminished.

As Calleo (1994) observes, in the long run seigniorage proved detrimental to the US. Furthermore, the notion of structural power suggests that once a country achieves a certain weight in the international economy, its activities are likely to have significant outcomes for others. For example, Japanese economic power is becoming an important determinant for world economic fortunes. Recent events have vividly revealed the extent to which Japanese governmental decisions can have global repercussions.[7] During the 1980s the US ran up an enormous budget deficit which was largely financed by the purchase of treasury bonds by Japanese investors rather than by domestic savings. This world has been turned on its head by recent events. In early 1994 the Japanese government sought to stimulate its own economy. To achieve this aim the government turned to Japan's financial institutions to provide 15.2 trillion yen. Almost overnight, Japanese banks stopped using available liquidity to repay borrowing facilities and instead purchased Japanese government bonds. This has had three serious effects for the international financial system:

1 The dollar went into free fall against the yen, damaging the prospects of Japanese recovery.
2 The Federal reserve had to increase interest rates, threatening the US recovery from the recession of the early 1990s.
3 As a result American investors had to pull out from the budding 'emerging markets' whose stock markets and currencies suffered immediate downturns.

Manipulation of the cost of money

The cost of money is central in the current competitive economic conditions. A country where money is cheaper offers a clear advantage to its companies. Can hegemony keep the cost of money low? Roy Allen (1994) has recently put forward an argument which implies that the US employed its hegemonic position to reduce the cost of money for its own companies.

Allen notes that at the beginning of the 1980s high interest rates in international markets were in US dollars, whereas the Japanese yen and German mark maintained relatively lower rates. That divergence gave an incentive to US companies to borrow in the world capital markets. But as financial markets were rapidly de-regulated and integrated, the dollar share of international lending fell between 1983 and 1988 from 72 per cent to 53 per cent. Over the same period the yen's share rose from 3 per cent to 10 per cent while the deutschmark's share rose from 5 per cent to 10 per cent (1994, p.12). Allen argues that as interest rates in the major currencies moved closer together during this period, US companies gained a *relative* advantage as money became cheaper for them, compared to their European and Japanese counterparts. Allen interprets America's policy commitment to international financial de-regulation as a tactical manoeuvre which offered specific advantages to US industry.

International financial de-regulation undoubtedly played a leading role in US foreign policy in the early 1980s (Livingston 1992). The Joint Japan–US Ad Hoc Group and the Finance Ministry[8] may be a case in point. In the early 1980s, rather than face the consequences of the burgeoning government budget and trade deficits and the growing indebtedness to Japanese investors, US policy aimed at 'liberalizing' the Japanese financial market to stimulate a parallel expansion of the Japanese economy. The hope was that an expanding Japanese economy would suck in (American) imports rather than increase Japanese production and exports. The recommendation of the Japan–US Ad Hoc Group helped accelerate the liberalization of the Japanese financial market, which in turn did stimulate the expansion of short-term financial markets, contributing to the Japanese bubble economy in the late 1980s.

This is not to say that Japan has lost as a consequence. In spite of this uninvited Anglo-Saxon type of boom-and-bust cycle which naturally raised significant, but ultimately over-represented, opposing voices, Japanese business on the whole took advantage of higher capitalization and began to borrow heavily in the Euromarkets to finance their expansion in East Asia. (It is estimated that half of the Japanese expansion was financed by such borrowing.) Furthermore, the new ways by which Japanese companies had begun financing their operations from the mid-1980s is significant. Although the average Japanese company has proved to be more successful than its western counterparts, Japanese managers have been more constrained than their western colleagues. However, in the late 1980s, as the Japanese expanded the horizons of their financial operations, it is argued that this industrial control structure has begun to unravel (Groenewegen 1993). As a result, Japanese managers have gained a new and cherished measure of independence.

Financial hegemony distinctly illustrates how structural power can be wielded effectively. Because of the unique and continuing role of the US dollar as a global currency, the US has had the ability to effectively determine and influence the monetary policies of its competitors. As we have tried to illustrate there are clear examples of American policy decisions that have sought to take advantage of this to the benefit of the US economy and American corporations.

Conclusion: assessing the advantages of hegemony

Few would deny that the US has not enjoyed an unprecedented degree of hegemony in the post-Second World War world. Yet has the *US economy* or *US capital* gained an advantage as a result? The evidence for making a positive conclusion is ambiguous at best. Consider the following three facts alone:

- Since 1945 the US economy has lost absolute ground to other advanced countries.
- The US post-war growth rate has been slower than *most* of America's competitors, although US productivity is still considered to be the highest in the world.
- Although American companies were able to take advantage of the creation of an open liberal international economic order and to expand internationally, they have lost ground to non-American multinationals over the past few decades.

We can interpret these facts in a number of ways:

First, they provide the necessary proof that hegemony does not provide any long-term competitive advantage. It suggests that (1) the US failed to translate its overwhelming power into a 'competitive advantage', and (2) other states took advantage of the system the US helped put in place more successfully than the US. This interpretation is favoured by economists, who believe that state intervention in any shape or form is unlikely to have any long-term beneficial outcome.

Second, an alternative interpretation is that the US *mishandled* its hegemony (Calleo 1982, 1994; Dertouzos *et al.* 1989). The US experience does not offer sufficient information about the competitive advantage of hegemonic practices because the US was simply a bad hegemon. Indeed, Calleo points out that the character of the US political system prevents it from advancing any long-term goals. The mishandling of America's hegemonic position was inevitable because of the structural limitations of the US political system (1982, 1994): the USA was incapable, in this view, of becoming an efficient hegemon. The performance of the US economy cannot therefore be taken as conclusive evidence of the advantages of hegemony.

A third interpretation suggests that the other two arguments over-simplify the facts because they are grounded in one major assumption, namely that provided with the right environment, US companies would have done better than others. This assumes that the international economic system was uniformly liberal, which we well know was not the case. Certain countries, particularly Japan and the four NIEs (as was demonstrated in Chapter 4) were allowed to favour their own industries thorough protectionism and privileged access to the US market. The other interpretations also overlook micro-economic developments, such as the innovative practices of German, Japanese and other companies. Indeed, there is considerable literature which emphasizes micro-economic decisions over both macro-economic and macro-political decisions. The famous MIT commission, for example, (Dertouzos *et al.* 1989) stressed the behavioural weaknesses of American business. Essentially in this interpretation hegemony and indeed other competitive policies are not particularly useful. Such an interpretation, however, poses a very difficult question, namely how would US companies have fared in the world economy *without* US hegemony? Clearly such a question is hypothetical and hence inherently difficult to answer.

A fourth interpretation argues that raw national data are misleading. This rests on two mutually supportive arguments. The first is that US hegemony was not employed to advance US national interests, but to advance certain coalitions of interests. Therefore, if one is to assess US hegemony, one needs to examine the performance of certain industries. A study by the Parisian institute CEDETIM (1978) states that 'American domination is a strategic domination, they dominate strategic industries and banks' (our translation). Of the strategic interests they argue that American domination is most marked in the following sectors:

oil
automobiles
petrochemicals
pharmaceuticals
telecommunications
electronics
computer technology
aerospace
banking

We have already discussed how US power and hegemony helped to ensure its continuing dominance in two of these strategic industries, and it is interesting to note that US companies largely maintained their dominant position in these industries throughout the post-war period. Indeed, in some cases, specifically telecommunications, aerospace and computer technology, the US has increased its domination since 1978. This may be the first real indication that US hegemonic practices may have had their intentional consequences.

This last observation links well with Parboni's thesis (corroborated by Strange (1986) and Calleo (1982)) that the US had 'managed' what appears to be a decline to achieve tactical concessions from its allies. The decline of the US economy was accompanied by a wave of internationalization of US business abroad. Thus, while the US economy appears to have lost in relative position, US business, in particular the strategic sectors identified above, have been able to maintain that position. Taking into account the earnings of American affiliates worldwide, Allen (1994) concludes on that basis that the US overall balance of trade went into deficit only in the early 1990s.

Hegemony offers, however, an additional specific advantage in the age of globalization, an advantage which is not illustrated in the various economic data that is available. Structural power, as Strange observes, is the power to shape the environment. This implies that the environment of accumulation is shaped and synchronized by the hegemon. As is well known, national economies go through rhythmic cycles of growth and decline or stagnation. These cycles are unavoidable, but only the hegemon has the unique ability to determine (to the extent that it is possible to determine) the pace and rhythms of these cycles. In determining the pace of reflation and deflation for its own economy the hegemon will subsequently determine the economic fortunes of others as well. This was vividly demonstrated in Europe during the recession of the early 1990s. Faced with recession, Europe required the stimulus of lower interest rates to promote recovery. This was not forthcoming, however, because Germany had other economic considerations due to reunification. The inflationary consequences of Chancellor Kohl's decision to convert the East German currency to Deutschmarks at a rate of one for one, coupled with increased spending on upgrading obsolete East German infrastructure, meant that Germany maintained a tight anti-inflation policy. The consequence of this for the rest of the European Continent was that high

German interest rates were maintained. Consequently because of the pivotal role of the Deutschmark in the ERM, this meant that European interest rates had to remain equally high, thus plunging the rest of Europe into a deeper recession.

Among the strategies identified in this book, hegemony is the nearest to the developmental state in that both require a broad societal support. They are costly strategies that hinge on coherence and management skill of the government. In an increasingly integrated world market such societal support dwindles very easily. We will hazard a guess therefore that the sort of hegemonic ambitions harboured by the United States between the 1940s and 1970s are a thing of the past. It will be difficult to reproduce the same set of circumstances and broad support. Instead, hegemony is increasingly exercised around the third dimension of power we have identified, the multiplier effect. German or American hegemony, in the EU and NAFTA respectively, is qualitatively different: it is less costly and perhaps brings with it greater advantages. To conclude, what we are perhaps witnessing is a situation in which hegemony is becoming closely entwined with the strategy of size.

Notes

1   Europeans had already adopted and improved American techniques in steel, petrochemical and automobile industries during the 1920s and 1930s. Subsequently their American counterparts were calling for an 'isolationist' foreign policy. However, following European devastation at the end of the war, they saw their chance of penetrating European markets and took their place at the forefront of support for *laissez-faire* economics. See Lauderbaugh (1980).
2   'Management is that body of men [and increasingly women] who, in law, have formally assumed the duties of exercising domination over the corporate business and assets' (Grou 1983, p.10).
3   At the beginning of the twentieth century, J.P. Morgan, through his bank, J.P. Morgan and Co, created and then controlled through amalgamation General Electric, American Radiator, International Harvester, AT&T, the Pullman company and US Steel. AT&T had more assets than twenty-one states in the Union (Quigley 1966, p.30), while the amalgamation of US Steel produced the first one billion dollar company. Individuals like J.P. Morgan, the Rockerfellers or the Rothschilds, were certainly fabulously rich, but through the facility of the joint-stock company they amassed untold power, far more than their not inconsiderable personal wealth would have warranted.
4   'Yet, despite all the controversies, the fundamental fact was that the Marshall Plan made possible and pushed a far-reaching transition in Europe – the change from a coal-based economy toward one based on imported oil' (Yergin 1991, p.424).
5   Parboni remarks that in the alternative energy domain the US possesses reserves well above those of all the other industrialized countries both in relative and absolute terms (1981, p.55).
6   For a detailed discussion see Parboni 1981; Calleo 1982, 1994.

7   The following draws on the analysis by Thierry Naudin: 'Fiscal fault lines trigger financial earthquake', *European*, 29 December 1994.

8   Report of the Joint Japan–US Ad Hoc Group and the Finance Ministry 'Present Status of the Prospects for the deregulation of Finance and Internationalisation of the Yen', 1984.

7

Downward mobility: repression and exploitation as a strategy of development

> If by wise policy or blind luck, a country has managed to control its population growth, provide social insurance, high wages, reasonable working hours or other benefits to its working class . . . should it allow these benefits to be competed down to the world average by unregulated trade? This levelling of wages will be overwhelmingly downward due to the vast number and rapid growth rate of underemployed populations in the world.
> (Daly, H & Goodard, R 1992, cited in Goldsmith, J 1995, pp. 157–8)

In 1988, the American Federation of Labor and Congress of Industrial Organisations (AFL-CIO) petitioned the US Congress to remove the preferential trade privileges that Malaysia enjoyed under the General System of Preferences. At issue was the fact that the Malaysian government had consistently refused to allow workers employed in the electronics industry to form trade unions (Jomo 1993, p.10). Although the petition was rejected, such images of the repression of human rights and the exploitation of workforces by developing world countries persist. From the five million children working in Thailand's unregulated factories (Schaffer 1995) to girls working for less than nine US cents per hour for transnationals in Bangladesh (Chomsky 1991, p.239), the image portrayed by developing country industrialization is one reminiscent of Victorian-style sweat shops, or what Lipietz calls 'bloody Taylorisation' (1987, p.76).[1]

Traditionally, the finger of blame has been pointed at the nefarious activities of transnational capitalists seeking to maximize surplus value by exploiting Third World workforces. Increasingly, however, it seems that governments in a number of these countries have been deliberately attracting such capital by using policy instruments to 'trade down' long-term environmental or social goals for a short-term quick economic fix. Such policies have included the absence of stringent labour and environmental legislation, the repression of trade union activities and authoritarianism.

However, even where environmental and labour legislation exists it is not always implemented, sometimes deliberately in order to affect industrial location decisions. Indeed, this kind of often explicit official neglect lies behind the exploitation of child labour despite international commitments to eliminate it. The International Labour Organization, for example, estimates that nearly 200 million children under the age of 15 are employed worldwide with over 50 per cent of these in Asia. Such exploitation occurs principally because 'a lack of enforcement mechanisms make a sham of regulations intended to protect children' (Schaffer 1995).

Similarly, some states today are now specializing in 'pollution' on behalf of more advanced countries. Only this year in China a Beijing-based trading company imported dangerous chemical waste from South Korea under the pretext of it being fuel oil. On the arrival of the waste in the port of Nanjing the cargo was seized and the port closed for 150 days while the authorities decided on a course of action (Zhang and Lin 1995).

Among the most exploited of all Third World workers are young women who dominate the famous export processing zones scattered across these states. Lipietz cites a Malaysian investment brochure promoting such facts:

> Oriental women are world famous for their manual dexterity. They have small hands, and they work quickly and very carefully. Who would be better qualified by both nature and tradition to contribute to the efficiency of an assembly line? . . . Wage rates in Malaysia are amongst the lowest in the region, and women workers can be employed for about US$1.50 a day.
>
> (Lipietz 1987, p.75)

Such activities generate rising profits for the transnational corporations involved while securing employment and limited accumulation within the host state. However, as most goods are then re-exported to the First World the costs are spread, as one of the principal losses is employment in the advanced world. Faced with growing unemployment in labour-intensive industries and pressures from human rights groups to act against such appalling conditions, the general response from the First World has been increasing protection. This reveals the inherent vulnerability of the promotion of downward mobility as a strategy of development, dependent on the markets of advanced countries on the one hand and faced with increasing competition from a near inexhaustible reserve army of Third World labour on the other.

This chapter examines in closer detail the phenomenon of downward mobility as a strategy of development. In particular it addresses the wider issue of Third World industrialization and argues that the exploitation of labour and the environment are not the sole characteristics of such development strategies. Indeed, central to the growing number of industrializing states in the developing world is both the changing nature of the international division of labour and the relationship between host governments and foreign capital. Each of these issues is first addressed, an overall history of the strategy presented and the costs and benefits of the strategy appraised. The conclusion assesses the effectiveness of the strategy for development and highlights the inherent risks that accompany it.

The end of the old Third World: towards a new international division of labour

Interpretations of North–South relations still remain, for the most part, attached to a division of the world into exporters of manufactured goods and exporters of primary products. Such interpretations fail to see that the 'old' Third World has broken down into at least three if not four distinct groups of states: the downwardly mobile, the parasitical (see Chapter 8), those not in the game (Chapter 9) and a select few which can be classed as developmental states (as discussed in Chapter 4). While some commentators have remarked on growing industrialization in the developing world, most merely characterize this as a threat to the developed world because of the massive pool of cheap labour that is a feature of such states. Such observations, however, invariably fail to see that cheap labour only forms part of a complex strategy of development. Labour may indeed be abundant but across the 'old' Third World governments are repressing trade union activity and allowing labour and environmental legislation to be flouted in order to provide a competitive advantage in a new international division of labour.

Under the assumptions on which the 'old' international division of labour was based, the South exported raw materials to the North from which they earned the revenue to pay for imports of manufactured goods. According to this framework, the South's economic position in the world economy was hindered by a dependence upon the North that at its simplest assumed three factors:[2]

• First, adverse terms of trade for products from the South. If we hold to this division of the world economy clear statistical evidence reveals that commodity prices have been declining throughout this century, and particularly sharply in the early 1980s when levels fell to their lowest since the Second World War (World Bank 1983). This trend has continued into the 1990s with recent figures showing a decline in most non-fuel commodity indices. For example, food prices fell by 7 per cent in 1991 and by an additional 2 per cent in 1992.
• Second, a dependence of the South on the North for finance and technology for development.
• Third, the dependence of Southern industrialization and development on the North as an engine of growth for the world economy.

However, during the past two decades the export composition of the South has fundamentally changed, so much so that it challenges the existing perception of North–South relations. Whereas in the early 1950s manufactured goods accounted for less than 5 per cent of the total exports from the South, today such goods account for between 60 per cent and 70 per cent. The value of these exports had risen from a negligible amount to approximately US $250 billion by 1990 (Wood 1994, p.1), accounting for a share of 22 per cent of world exports of manufactures, up from 5 per cent in 1970. Taking new weights in purchasing power parities instead of market exchange rates, the IMF has estimated that the rich industrial economies of the North today only account for 56 per cent of global production, down from a pre-revised ratio of 73 per cent.[3] Suddenly the 'old' international division of labour no longer looks realistic.

Many commentators on the Left argue that such 'developments' are not as radical as they first appear. While manufactures may indeed be shifting from the core to the periphery they are not fundamentally altering the division of labour. They maintain that the new industries of the South are the old declining industries of the core. By using the easily transferred technology of such old industries a number of states are able to take advantage of low wages to capture a segment of the world market and elevate themselves to semiperipheral status (Shannon 1990).

Although the composition of the developing world's exports has fluctuated with the price of oil, the share of manufactures in non-fuel exports had risen steadily to 71 per cent by 1989 (see Table 7.1). As Gereffi notes,

> between 1980 and 1986 the number of Third World countries . . . that exported goods worth $1 billion or more increased from 27 to 49. This expansion of Third World export capacity, particularly for manufactured goods, embraces such a diverse array of countries that it appears to be part of a general restructuring in the world economy.
>
> (Gereffi 1992, p.86)

While the North and South are consequently now specializing in the production of different sorts of manufactured goods (Wood 1994, p.3), the divisions within the developing world between manufactured goods producers and primary exporters is in many cases as sharp as the old international division of labour between North and South. For example, this new shift in production is most marked in the countries of East and South Asia but less marked in Latin America. For example, in the latter,

Table 7.1 Composition of North–South merchandise trade, 1955–1989

South's exports to North	1955 (%)	1970 (%)	1980 (%)	1989 (%)
Primary and processed primary:	94.8	84.1	84.1	45.3
Fuels	20.4	33.1	66.4	24.8
Manufactures	5.0	15.6	15.2	53.3
Total manufactures as % of non-fuel exports	6.3	23.4	45.1	70.9

Source: Wood 1994, p.2.

manufactures represent about one-quarter of total exports and primary commodities one-third, while in sub-Saharan Africa, although manufactures have been increasing in recent years from 7.4 per cent in 1980 to 8.0 per cent in 1990, their share in the total exports of the region is still tiny by comparison with primary commodity exports – around 45 per cent to 50 per cent (World Economic Survey 1995).

These divergences within the developing world are mirrored by divergences in the growth rates of these countries. While between 1980 and 1989 the developing world as a whole grew at 4.3 per cent, this figure was as a high as 8 per cent for East Asia and as low as 1 per cent for sub-Saharan Africa. However, there are a number of important exporters outside East Asia, including Brazil ($51.2 billion worth of exports), Mexico ($43.9 billion) and India ($38 billion). Whereas before the developing world supplied the advanced industrial countries with primary products and semi-processed goods, now the former increasingly supply the latter with manufactured and processed goods. As a consequence, rhetoric that calls for structural transformations in the world economy to remove the causes of inequality is becoming increasingly less common and accurate.

From import substitution to export orientation

Like all other strategies this one was evolutionary in nature and it took time to understand that clear policy decisions were involved in its emergence. Most prominent writers believe that the late 1960s to early 1970s is the most significant period. Prior to that there existed the traditional dichotomy of a small number of core countries importing raw materials and foodstuffs from a large periphery which in return bought manufacturing and luxury goods, i.e. the old international division of labour. However, from the early 1970s onwards this old division broke down as manufacturing exports from the developing world continued to increase.

Central to the strategy of downward mobility is the acceptance that foreign direct investment and capital are essential as engines of growth and development. This acceptance has invariably occurred following a shift in economic policy towards export-orientated industrialization. Prior to such a switch many developing countries had followed the example of the larger Latin American countries such as Brazil and Mexico in the pursuit of a policy of import-substituting industrialization begun during the Depression years. In the 1950s and early 1960s this policy received official sanction when economists in the Economic Commission for Latin America (ECLA), and specifically the first Secretary-General of the United Nations Conference on Trade and development (UNCTAD) Raul Prebisch, 'set forth the structuralist argument that the world economy was biased against the development efforts of the less developed countries' (Gilpin 1987, p.275). To enable them to break free from their peripheral position in the world economy

Prebisch advocated rapid industrialization which was to be achieved by adopting ISI. The rationale for such action was that Latin America had experienced a spurt in economic growth during the Depression years because it had been cut off from the West (Frank 1967). Thus economic protectionism and national planning should be used to reduce the dependency of the less developed countries on the world economy.

Economic protectionism would be used to protect a nation's infant industries so that a diversified industrial structure could be nurtured and developed while reducing the dependency on foreign capital. By pricing foreign goods out of the market it was hoped that domestic production would be encouraged. Indeed, tariff levels on imported consumer goods in Brazil in the 1960s averaged over 300 per cent (Dicken 1992, p.178). The problem, however, was that ISI soon faltered; while such protection encouraged domestic production, dependence on imported *capital* goods increased to feed industrialization. Outside the larger economies such as Brazil and Mexico, the small size of the domestic economy meant that economies of scale could not be reaped and thus prices for the domestically produced goods remained high.

Ironically, around the same time ISI was receiving official sanction a number of smaller developing countries in East Asia began to shift policy towards a more export-oriented industrial strategy. Initially in the post-war period both Taiwan and South Korea had pursued similar ISI programmes in textiles, cement, flat glass, etc. Although such industries had been protected by a wall of tariffs and overvalued currencies, the small size of the domestic market in these states had led to an earlier realization that import substitution alone could not lead to rapid industrialization and thus ISI faltered as early as 1958 to 1959 in Taiwan and 1960 to 1962 in South Korea (Cumings 1984, p.68). The switch to export-led industrialization was encouraged by US aid officials and was not fraught with the political and social consequences that such moves faced elsewhere in the developing world. ISI in East Asia had been much shorter than in Latin America and had not led to the creation of a strong industrial working-class movement as was characteristic of Argentina and Brazil under Peron and Vargaz. Furthermore, labour had been excluded by the military governments in Taiwan and Korea in the 1950s and thus '[t]he political sequence of inclusion followed by exclusion, as the "easy" phase ended and export-led development began, was absent' (Cumings 1984, p.70).

In 1960 and 1961 respectively Taiwan and South Korea implemented a comprehensive reform package that fundamentally altered their industrialization strategy. This involved: the devaluation of their currencies in order to lower the price of their exports on the world market; the lowering of tariff barriers that had protected nascent industries, tax holidays, exemptions and incentives to encourage firms to export; monopoly rights; transportation subsidies, and the creation of export processing zones (Kaoshiung, Taiwan in 1965; Masan, Korea in 1969). As Cumings, Wade and others note, such reforms enhanced these states' comparative advantage in cheap, semi-skilled labour so that 'Taiwan and the ROK became suppliers of labour to an increasingly far-flung division of production' (Cumings 1984, p.71).

The success of these policies is well documented and hotly debated. The role these states played in the United States Grand Area strategy against Communism and the argument of 'development by invitation' (Cumings 1984, p.68) are stressed by underdevelopment theorists who argue that the development of these states is exceptional. Such arguments will not be considered here. However, whether or not the NIEs' development is exceptional, their export-led industrialization strategy has served as a model that other developing states have sought to emulate: Singapore in 1967 with the Economic Expansion Act (Haggard and Cheng 1987, p.105); Malaysia in 1969 with the launching of the New Economic Plan; Sri Lanka's Economic Liberalization Plan begun in 1978; Mexico's relaxation of its rules on foreign investment in the 1980s and its much earlier Border Industrialization Plan that created the infamous Maquiliadoras, and the Doi Moi reforms in Vietnam begun in 1986, to cite but a few.

The shift in policy to export-oriented industrialization was facilitated by favourable external developments: the liberalization of world trade during the 1960s following the Dillon and Kennedy rounds of GATT; the compression of space and time through new technologies in communication and transport, and the global spread of transnational corporations. Several scholars argue that the most significant of these exogenous factors was the latter. Indeed, Lipietz (1987), Armstrong *et al.* (1984) and Itoh (1990) have argued that this expansion of transnational capital was fundamental in the emergence of a new international division of labour, and that the reasons for such a global shift lie at the heart of the crisis of Fordism in the advanced industrial countries.

The crisis of Fordism and the expansion of transnational capital

According to this thesis, productivity gains began to fall off in most branches of industrial activity from the second half of the 1960s (Lipietz 1992, p.14). Nevertheless, wages continued to increase in real terms while the costs of fixed capital similarly continued to rise. Under such conditions the rate of profits began to fall. This slow down in the rate of profits reflected a more general paradox at the heart of the Fordist labour process model. So long as young people and women as well as migrants from the countryside and the Third World were entering the workforce, discipline was maintained. However, as time passed, better education, greater self-awareness among workers and a widespread desire for work satisfaction and dignity led to increasingly open revolt against the denial of personality at the heart of the Taylorist division of the workforce into those who designed and those who performed tasks. Such revolts gave rise to a general left-wing upsurge culminating in the 1968 riots in France. However, by the 1970s this radicalism had fizzled out as growing unemployment and the threat of redundancy restored worker discipline. None the less, productivity continued to be low and profits depressed.

To recover their profitability, multinational corporations (MNCs) expanded their global operations. By forging links with certain countries in the developing world (particularly the NIEs) MNCs sought both to take advantage of lower wages in the developing world and hence increase profits, but also to release themselves from the economic quandary described above. These two cost-push factors combined with a number of developments to create an additional cost-pull factor.

- A number of Third World countries had labour forces which were sufficiently cheap *and* educated and in addition a sufficiently sophisticated infrastructure to handle low-tech high volume production. Such states were primarily found in Latin America (Brazil, Argentina, Chile) and in the newly industrializing economies of Asia (Taiwan, South Korea, Singapore). These conditions had been partly created during ISI-led development which, while having failed to generate sustained economic growth, had none the less created a modern industrial infrastructure.
- Reduction of transportation costs, especially before the oil crisis.
- Changes in GATT – the extension of GATT rules, and in particular the granting of the Generalized System of Preferences to developing world countries.
- US policy encouraged development as a buffer against the spread of Communism, particularly in Asia.
- Improvements in real-time communication meant that control could be more easily exercised over the foreign subsidiary from the central headquarters.
- The growth of the international financial markets – the Euromarkets, etc. – meant that the ability and ease of financing relocation were augmented.
- The adoption by a number of developing countries of policies explicitly designed to attract foreign capital by reducing the very costs they were seeking to minimize. As mentioned above, this stems from the adoption of export-oriented industrialization by a number of developing countries during the late 1960s and early 1970s.
- To summarize: the evolution of the strategy of downward mobility was clearly facilitated by the internationalization of capital. As a consequence a number of states in the 1960s adopted a series of policies designed to attract this capital and incorporate it into their development strategy. While an acquiescent and cheap labour force was an important part in such policies, of equal importance was the provision of a whole range of incentives, infrastructural support and export-oriented industrialization.

The strategy in practice

Central to the growth of manufacturing in the developing world has thus been the attraction of foreign capital and in particular multinational corporations. Indeed today, multinational corporations employ approximately seven million people in developing countries (Dicken 1992). This strategy has long been attacked by dependency theorists who have continually stressed its negative consequences (cf. Frank 1967; Cardoso 1974; Cardoso and Faletto 1979). These have included: the tendency for foreign investment to adversely affect the industrial structure of the host economy by raising industrial concentration; the danger that foreign corporations would saturate the local market thereby destroying local manufacturers; that by absorbing local talents foreign capital would 'crowd out' domestic entrepreneurialism; that profit outflows would generally exceed new capital inflows, and that capital intensive technology would eliminate jobs. Ultimately it was claimed that in most developing countries the state was too weak *vis-à-vis* foreign corporations. As a consequence such states were unable 'to establish rules for foreign investment or profit remittance, and . . . are compelled to provide incentives for foreign investors' (Stallings and Kaufman 1990, p.57).

In contrast, neoclassical economists, echoing the sentiments of early modernization theorists, have stressed the importance of the MNC as an 'engine' for development. By attracting foreign corporations new employment opportunities will be realized, technology transfer will occur, backward linkages will be forged with local suppliers and foreign markets opened. Such diffusion and linkages will allow developing states to move beyond being mere export platforms through (1) more skill- and technology-intensive production in component parts supply, and (2) the development of domestic producers of manufactured goods. The central problem for developing states is therefore 'to devise policies that will encourage a greater flow of foreign resources and at the same time ensure that it makes the maximum contribution to the achievement of development objectives' (Chowdhury and Islam 1993, p.108). Consequently, a number of policies have been adopted across the developing world with the explicit goal of managing foreign capital as effectively as possible to provide the maximum contribution to the host economy. However, this is not to say that such states have broken free of a 'dependence' on exogenous actors. Foreign capital needs to find productive outlets and is itself therefore dependent to some extent on the 'state' – whether for its market, its labour force, etc. Hence the relationship between foreign capital and developing states is problematic. The key to a successful development strategy therefore rests on how this dependent relationship is *managed*. First, the developing state has to attract foreign capital. This has invariably been achieved in downwardly mobile states through the repression of organized labour in order to drive down wage costs. However, once the capital has been induced policies have been adopted to tie this capital into the host economy. Principal ways in which this has been achieved have been through the use of export processing zones and local content requirements.

Repressing labour

The most enduring image in the West of the newly emerging economies in the developing world is of Victorian-style sweat shops where working conditions and wages are intolerable by western standards. Such conditions, however, are not merely natural, as Bello comments:

> Perhaps the key contribution made by East Asian governments to the creation of an attractive climate for foreign investors was the repressive control of the working class, which drove the wages of workers below the market value of labour.
>
> (Bello 1992, p.42)

In South Korea, for example, the Hee regime systematically demobilized labour between 1962 and 1979. Strikes and independent trade unions were outlawed; a state ideology identifying production objectives with the struggle against Communism was promoted (see Chapter 4), and a sophisticated internal security apparatus was created to monitor labour and repress it when and where necessary. To quote from Bello again,

> The KCIA [Korean Central Intelligence Agency] labour-control program involved not only infiltrating factories with hundreds of agents but also making the government-controlled union leadership an adjutant of the state . . . KCIA agents regularly attended meetings of the central committees of the national unions and regularly intervened in elections to get candidates of their choice elected.
>
> (Bello 1992, p.43)

In addition to these measures the Korean intelligence forces resorted to mass imprisonment, torture and assassination.

A similar situation can be found in the so-called 'second-wave/tier' of newly industrializing countries/economies. In Malaysia, for example, in the early phase of industrialization there were no unions established in the free trade zones in order to attract foreign investment. This proved to be 'a major plus factor that helped attract large American electronics firms to Malaysia' (R. Rasiah quoted in Jomo 1993, p.130). Although unionization grew throughout the 1980s, the electronics industry remained largely free from unionization as late as 1988. Indeed, while Japanese firms have allowed the creation of in-house unions broadly in line with the situation in mainland Japan, American firms have stubbornly resisted any worker representation; indeed, '[n]ine managing directors of American component firms in the . . . FTZs . . . stressed that their presence in Malaysia would be seriously undermined if unions were allowed in their firms' (Jomo 1993, p.131).

However, labour is not only directly repressed by government action. Labour is increasingly being indirectly repressed by the failure, as mentioned earlier, of governments to enforce social legislation. This lack of law enforcement may in some cases be the result of insufficient government funds to provide the necessary regulatory authorities; however, in other cases it is nothing less than a conscious decision taken by central and/or local authorities in order to provide additional incentives to capital. As Demaio reports, 'In the Tijuana maquiladoras, it is standard procedure to assign difficult and dangerous work tasks to pregnant women so that they will quit before the companies are obligated to pay maternity benefits' (Demaio 1995). Similar evidence may be found of official compliance with respect to child labour. In Bangladesh, for example, the myriad regulations to improve the status of children are confusing and frustrated by a lack of enforcement. Similarly in Nepal there are an estimated three million children working in agriculture, carpets, garment and handicraft industries despite a minimum legal employment age of 14.[4]

Export processing zones

Once capital has been attracted by cheap labour and other financial sweeteners, states attempt to manage this capital to their best advantage. Export processing zones were largely devised as a means of providing outlets for such activity while protecting the domestic economy at large from the vicissitudes associated with the penetration of emerging markets by multinationals. An EPZ can therefore be defined as

> a relatively small, geographically spread area within a country, the purpose of which is to attract export-orientated industries, by offering them especially favourable investment and trade conditions as compared with the remainder of the host country. In particular, the EPZs provide for the importation of goods to be used in the production of exports on a duty free basis.
>
> (UNIDO 1986, p.6, cited in Dicken 1992, p.182)

EPZs are therefore little more than export enclaves within which special economic privileges apply. In addition to incentives and inducements often provided by the host country, EPZs are usually exempt from certain kinds of legislation that apply in the country as a whole, such as restrictions on foreign ownership or local content requirements. The most common of such exceptions, however, is that EPZs generally allow the duty-free entry of goods for re-export (Haggard and Cheng 1987, p.91). Furthermore, within the zone the host government provides the physical infrastructure and services necessary for manufacturing activity: roads, power supplies, transport facilities and low-cost or rented buildings (Dicken 1992, pp.182–3).

It is estimated that globally some 1.3 million workers were employed across 116 EPZs in 1988. The overwhelming majority of these zones were located in the Caribbean (48 per cent) and East Asia (42 per cent). However, over 60 per cent of those employed in EPZs globally are concentrated in Asia, where the majority of such zones are located in Singapore and Hong Kong (see Table 7.2). Almost all of today's EPZs were established, as a conscious strategy after 1971. Before the mid-1960s

Table 7.2 Location of East Asian EPZs and employment therein[5]

Country	No. of EPZs	Employees
Singapore	22	217,000
Hong Kong	14	89,000
Malaysia	11	109,796
Taiwan	4	80,469
Philippines	3	39,000
South Korea	3	21,910
Sri Lanka	3	77,011
Indonesia	2	N/A
Thailand	1	N/A

there were only three EPZs – Kaoshiung in Taiwan, one in India and another in Puerto Rico.

As mentioned earlier, the failure of ISI led to a conscious decision to shift to export-led industrialization in a number of East Asian countries in the 1960s. In Malaysia, for example, by 1968 unemployment was running at 10 per cent with capital-intensive manufacturing costly, inefficient and dependent on protective tariffs (Sivalingham 1994, p.4). Similar situations had been reached or were being reached across many Third World states. In an endeavour to generate jobs and exports, export-oriented growth was championed and EPZs were seen as a way in which this goal could be achieved without the domination by foreign firms of the domestic market. In South Korea, for example, the idea of setting up EPZs

> originated from two sources ... One was a report by officials of the Federation of Korean Industries (FKI) who had visited Japanese industrial facilities in 1963. The other was a request from Korean residents living in Japan for the establishment of a special export zone on the south east coastal area.
>
> (Oh, Won Sun, 1994, p.2)

EPZs have until recently been conspicuous by their absence in the development strategies of the overwhelming majority of South American states. The exception to this rule has been Mexico which during the 1970s and 1980s introduced the largest ever EPZ strategy. In 1965 the Mexican government introduced its border industrialization programme which, according to Dicken, was a conscious strategy to 'siphon off some of the offshore investment by United States TNCs which was flowing to Asian countries in an attempt to reduce costs' (1992, p.184). Between 1965 and 1988 the number of Maquiladora plants along the northern border with the US increased from twelve to 1,383 and the workforce from 4000 to over 310,000. In addition, the Mexican government expanded this zone of special economic activity to non-border locations, which by 1988 employed an additional 77,000. Within these Maquiladora plants the Mexican government waived its duties on the import of materials and components imported from the US as long as the end-products were re-exported. The proliferation of EPZs is of course continuing as more and more developing states attempt to follow the path of export-led industrialization. However, EPZs for the most part with the exception of Singapore, Hong Kong and a number of Caribbean islands, generally employ only a small proportion of the state's workforce.

Local content requirements

However, export incentives and labour costs are not the only concern of foreign investors. In the automobile industry, for example, transport costs, the relatively low share of the cost of labour and the need for at least a semi-skilled labour force mean that the opportunities for the use of export processing zones are very limited. Equally important in the automobile industry is *market share*. One of the principal problems for developing countries in the past has been the fear that opening their markets to foreign produced goods will lead to the saturation of their markets by these goods, leading in turn to the destruction of indigenous industry and the domination of their economy in vital sectors by MNCs. Again the 1970s marks a turning point in this standard view of the relationship between transnational capital and the developing world.

The new model of developing country–MNC relationships over market access can be traced back to the 1972 Preferential Interest Decree made between Spain and the Ford Motor Company (Lipietz 1987). This deal combined elements of both import substitution and export-led growth. By the late 1960s Spain had a relatively semi-skilled labour force, was in close proximity to the large consumer market of Western Europe, was developing its own sizeable domestic middle-class market and had an authoritarian regime to hold down wages and hence labour costs. The principal difficulty for Ford was that most peripheral countries demanded in line with standard ISI formula that as many local inputs as possible be used in the production process. However, although the home market was often attractive as a potential emerging market it was rare that it was sufficient in size to make the local inputs both efficient and competitive. However, relocation was necessary to prevent the loss of the emerging market altogether. Faced with these problems in Spain the result was a famous compromise which laid the foundations for new forms of relocation.

The result was neither pure ISI for an inadequate local base nor the sole use of the country for re-exporting, but a combination of the two. Spain provided an expanding market even though working-class consumption was low (Lipietz 1987, p. 104). As a result, Spain accepted a lower level of integration into the domestic economy in exchange for a clear commitment that Ford's plants would be used to re-export certain components on a mass scale. In response to a reduction in the minimum rate of integration from 95 per cent to 66 per cent, Ford agreed to re-export two-thirds of its total output and to increase its sales in Spain by no more than 10 per cent. In addition, major facilities for importing machine tools were also granted (ibid., p. 105). Consequently further US companies, in particular General Motors, followed suit. Renault followed the same example in Portugal, and in return for establishing four vehicle and engine plants which provided 13,000 jobs, the Portuguese government extended a degree of protection that saw Renault's share of the local market rise from 12 per cent to between 30–40 per cent. On the other hand, approximately 225,000 engines built in Portugal were re-exported (ibid., p. 105).

Encouraging local content to be incorporated in manufactured goods is a principal means of encouraging foreign capital to forge backward linkages with the host economy. Similarly, although EPZs only employ a small number of the total workforce, if the promotion of EPZs by the state is accompanied by a national strategy that seeks to tie this investment into the broader economy, the significance of the EPZ is much greater.

Backward linkages are defined as employment indirectly generated by the foreign subsidiary among its local suppliers. Such suppliers provide the subsidiary with raw materials, parts, components, services, etc. Such linkages have a more positive effect on the host economy since it creates intrafirm linkages which allow a degree of technology transfer. When placing orders with indigenous suppliers for such goods, stringent specifications have to be met which in addition raise technical expertise. The sourcing of such materials locally may lead to the emergence of new domestic firms to meet the demand created, thus increasing the pool of local entrepreneurs, expanding the activities of supplying firms and creating additional employment. While such linkages are encouraged, linkages between foreign corporations and the host economy are more often 'forward'. Forward linkages can be defined as employment-generated by the MNE subsidiary among its local customers (e.g. distributors, service agents). These linkages are less beneficial, generating employment that does not enhance the industrial capacity of the state in question. While it too may create additional jobs, these will typically be in service industries such as cleaning, security, etc.

Backward linkages as already illustrated can be actively promoted by the state in question by insisting that the foreign subsidiary utilize a certain level of locally sourced materials and components. Such local content policies have become increasingly common across both the developed and developing world. To quote the ILO,

> government intervention in the sourcing choices of MNEs appears to have been the single most powerful determinant for the creation of local linkages of MNEs. . . .Without such government intervention it is likely that despite market pressure local MNE linkages would be much less than they are today in various countries and industries.
>
> (Lee 1981, p.94)

Examples of such local content agreements include not only the famous Ford Law with Franco's Spain but also the auto component requirements in the NAFTA text and EU directives. The ability to insist on such deals, however, ultimately depends on the bargaining power of the state and the extent to which the local suppliers can offer the necessary skills and quality. Here the larger and more industrialized developing states tend to be the most successful. Among the factors that enhance the bargaining power of the developing states are: (1) the proximity of the state to a major export market of the TNC; (2) the skills of the labour force, and (3) the costs of the labour force. The ideal location from the TNC's point of view is thus a state which has a sufficient labour pool to allow the labour force to be reproduced cheaply, is close to large markets and provides skilled workers. Clearly some states fit this bill better than others. Spain was thus an obvious target in the 1970s as US and later European TNCs sought to increase their competitiveness within the massive European market, similarly Mexico *vis-à-vis* the US, and Singapore, Taiwan and ROK *vis-à-vis* Japan. Less attractive are states on the 'outer' periphery such as Nigeria, Kenya and Tanzania.

Continued dependence or the way forward: assessing downward mobility

As was noted earlier, the impact of this strategy hinges on the role of foreign investment. In terms of the jobs created by this strategy the impact has been small, but in terms of its contribution to total manufactured exports, foreign investment and especially export processing zones have made a impressive impact. For example, Sri Lanka launched its economic liberalization in 1978 after decades of protectionism. At the heart of this policy was the promotion of export-led industrialization using EPZs as the means for attracting foreign investment. To this end the strategy has been successful. EPZs' share of manufactured goods rose from 8.8 per cent in 1980 to 44 per cent in 1991, while the zones have attracted considerable foreign capital up from 208 million rupees in 1978 to 3016 million rupees in 1991 (Abeywardene *et al.* 1994, p. 8). Similarly in Malaysia, EPZs' share of exports rose from 1 per cent in 1972 to 57.5 per cent in 1990, while total foreign investment rose from $94 million to $4073 million in 1991 (Sivalingham 1994, pp 1–6).

In addition, in a number of cases local small and medium-sized firms have become engaged in subcontracting activities with the multinational investors. In Asia it is argued that this has had more to do with the appreciation that has increased the costs of inputs from Japan (ibid., p.31) than any success the Malaysian government may have had in encouraging such linkages. Nevertheless, a number of these have been significant. For example, INTEL has developed its own Vendor Development Programme which has generated significant growth in its local vendor partners. Similarly in Sri Lanka, the value of local purchases of raw materials and capital goods has increased from zero between 1978 and 1980 to 1,210 million rupees by 1991. None the less, despite such an increase, 95 per cent of the purchases of capital goods

and raw materials in the EPZs are still imported (Abeywardene *et al.*
1994, p. 18).

One of the successes of 'local content' policies is the Malaysian Proton
project. Prior to 1980 local content in the automobile industry in Malaysia
averaged only 8 per cent (Jayasankaran 1993, p.273). This was largely
because the proliferation of foreign cars and models had prevented local
component part suppliers from gaining economies of scale. However,
in 1980 the then deputy Prime Minister Mahathir ordered the Malaysian
Industrial Development Agency to carry out feasibility studies for
a Made-in-Malaysia car. The result was that Mahathir concluded an
agreement with Mitsubushi to create the Proton.

The agreement was similar in character to the Ford agreement
discussed earlier. Mitsubushi was keen to accept Mahathir's request
because it believed the Proton 'represented an opportunity to increase its
share in one of ASEAN's most rapidly growing auto markets, from 8% in
1982 to a possible 60% by 1986' (Jayasankaran 1993, p.276). In addition
the capital outlay was low because the Proton did not fundamentally
differ from the existing Mitsubushi Lancer Fiore. On the Malaysian side
the first Proton produced had a local content of 36 per cent with
Mitsubushi committed to increasing this by 1989 to 65 per cent while
reducing the content of Japanese imported parts from 55 per cent to 20
per cent. In addition the Proton's share of the Malaysian market grew
rapidly from 47 per cent in 1986 to 73 per cent by 1988, principally
because the government exempted the Proton Saga from the 40 per cent
import tariff. Since its initial success domestically the Malaysian government has promoted the export of Proton both within the Asia-Pacific
region as well as to the UK.

However, while EOI is transforming the external image of many states
in the developing world, the direct impact upon lives is, with a few
exceptions, marginal. Export processing zones, while not the only
manifestation of the strategy of downward mobility, may have become
the nucleus for EOI but although employment in these zones has
increased, their workforce as a proportion of the total is still minimal. In
Sri Lanka only 10 per cent of the industrial workforce can be found
in such zones, falling to a paltry 1 per cent in the nation at large. In
Malaysia they account for 8.5 per cent of manufacturing employment
and 1.7 per cent of total employment, while in Korea their effect is even
more marginal, with Masan and Iri EPZs responsible for a mere 0.6 per
cent of all jobs in the manufacturing sector.

Another common feature of industrialization in the Third World, and
in particular within export processing zones has been the predominance
of women in the labour force (see Table 7.3). The simple reason for
this was that for both foreign multinationals and local subcontractors
women could be hired at wage levels below their male counterparts. For
example, in Taiwan, wages for female workers were actually fixed at
10–20 per cent below male wages in the EPZs. In addition to the wage
discrimination many managers of firms in EPZs argue that female
workers are more docile and less unruly and possess greater manual

Table 7.3 The predominance of young female workers in EPZs (%)

Country	Women in EPZs	Women in non-EPZs	Women in specified age groups
Hong Kong	60	49.3	85 (20–30)
India	80	9.5	83 (<26)
Indonesia	90	47.9	83 (<26)
ROK	75	37.5	85 (20–30)
Malaysia	85	32.9	(av. 21.7)
Philippines	74	48.1	88 (<29)
Singapore	60	44.3	78 (<26)
Sri Lanka	88	17.1	83 (<26)
Mexico	77	24.5	78 (<26)
Jamaica	95	19.0	(average early 20s)
Tunisia	90	48.1	70 (<25)

Source: Adapted from Dicken 1992, p.186.

dexterity than their male counterparts (Bello 1992, p.44). Such women are frequently housed in squalid dormitory conditions and often subject to sexual harassment both within the workplace and in their dormitories.

Although foreign firms have contributed substantially to foreign exchange earnings, especially in the EPZs, the linkages between such firms and the domestic economy have remained for the most part weak. In Malaysia, apart from rubber products, the overwhelming proportion of raw material and capital goods for industries in the EPZs are imported, ranging from 96–93.7 per cent for scientific and electrical/electronic goods to 62 per cent in the textile and garments industry. A similar position is found in Sri Lanka where, as mentioned earlier, between 1978 and 1991 95 per cent of all raw material and capital goods purchased by firms in the EPZs were imported. One of the main reasons for this lack of forward and/or backward linkages is that most EPZs allow for duty-free imports to firms located in the EPZs as an incentive for location.

As expected, the vast majority of technology transferred to such states is mainly by wholly foreign-owned firms and joint venture multinationals. Most of this technology, particularly in the electronics industry, is bundled or packaged. This means that it is protected by a whole host of trademarks and patents. Where transfer does occur it is usually limited to contracts between foreign and local firms such as in the produce of designer garments under licence (e.g. Nike shoes, Yves St Laurent shirts, etc). Few firms arc willing to locate their R&D facilities in such overseas operations with these activities taking place in the parent company of the foreign affiliate. There have been a number of attempts to alter this situation by the creation of science and technology parks, for example, in Taiwan and South Korea, and by encouraging the participation of universities in R&D. However, in the case of the latter these facilities have generally been utilized by local firms operating within the EPZs.

Without such backward linkages and technology transfer there is a real danger that EPZs will remain isolated enclaves of economic activity. Without technology diffusing into the local economy, foreign enterprises will find the gap in corporate cultures and skills too great for enhanced cooperation. It also leaves the international position of the EPZs very fragile.

In addition it has not only been labour that has suffered as a consequence of the growth policies associated with this strategy. Environmental degradation has become a serious problem. Across the 'old' Third World, industrial pollution and waste are reaching dangerous levels. In Taiwan unregulated dumping of toxic waste has resulted in a situation where pollution levels in all the lower reaches of Taiwan's major rivers are critical. In the Philippines Manila's water systems are polluted while in Thailand river-borne pollution is affecting both marine life and drinking-water supplies. Bello describes a similar situation in the republic of Korea:

> No tale is more terrifying than the experience of the 10 million people who draw their supplies from the Nakdong river. . . . In April 1991 they were told . . . that the funny smell . . . in their tap water was caused by the surreptitious dumping of some 325 tons of waste phenol, a . . . cancer-causing chemical by a subsidiary of Doosan, a Korean conglomerate that has joint ventures with Coca-Cola, Kentucky Fried Chicken and Nestle.
> (Bello 1992, pp.59–60)

In a similar vein sulphur dioxide levels in Seoul's air are among the highest in the world while in Taiwan asthma cases have increased fourfold in the last decade (ibid.). These environmental costs are not an accidental by-product of industrialization, however. Most states have environmental legislation and/or regulatory bodies; the problem is that bureaucrats and politicians are disinclined to enforce such laws for fear of capital flight, a fear that is ever more real as the number of states offering similar concessions and sweeteners to foreign investors increases.

Global implications

Klaus Schwab, President of the World Economic Forum, argues that revolutions in technology now allow for a flow of capital across borders on an unprecedented scale. Consequently why should firms manufacture products in Germany when educated labour can be hired for a fraction of the cost in Asia? For example, while it costs $25 an hour to employ a production worker in Germany (including non-wage costs such as social security contributions) and $16 an hour in the United States, such workers can be hired for only $5 in South Korea, $2.40 in Mexico, $1.40 in Poland and 50 cents or less in China, India or

Indonesia. For example, Fila, an Italian sportswear manufacturer, now only produces 10 per cent of its output in Italy. The rest has been shifted to subcontractors in Asia.

In the advanced industrialized world higher wages have been justified by higher productivity. However, as trade barriers have been lowered and transport and communications have become cheaper and better, the technology which supports that productivity is being transferred more speedily across borders. Many Third World countries are now getting hold of intermediate low-technology goods and achieving a level of competitiveness that few developed states can match without social dislocation and costs. According to economic theory, when developing world productivity catches up so too should wage rates. However, where such labour is repressed and wages held down, productivity could increase at low wages, producing the developed world's nightmare of a cheap, skilled and efficient labour force. For example, the recent White Paper on growth, competitiveness and employment, published by the European Commission in 1993, argued that among four reasons for increasing unemployment in Europe the most important factor has been competition from newly industrializing countries whose cost levels are too low to compete with (cited in Krugman 1994). Sir James Goldsmith, addressing the Senate Committee on GATT implementation, summed up this nightmare:

> Global free trade will shatter the way in which value-added is shared between capital and labour. Value-added is the increase of value obtained when you convert raw materials into a manufactured product. In mature societies, we have been able to develop a general agreement as to how it should be shared. That agreement has been reached through generations of political debate, elections, strikes. . . .Overnight that agreement will be destroyed by the arrival of huge populations willing to undercut the salaries earned by our workforces. The social divisions that this will cause will be deeper than anything ever envisaged by Marx.
>
> (Goldsmith 1995, pp. 184–5)

Is there any evidence to support such prophecies of doom? Are TNCs leaving the developed world in droves to seek the greater profits that this growing pool of cheap and (semi-)skilled labour in the developing world offers? Globally, the United Nations Conference on Trade and Development estimates that multinational corporations employ 73 million workers. Of these, the overwhelming majority, 61 million, are employed in the developed world. Nevertheless, there does appear to be a trend, however small, of growing employment in the developing world at the expense of their counterparts in the developed world. Between 1977 and 1989 US multinationals cut their manufacturing employment in Europe by 23 per cent while increasing their employment in developing countries by 6 per cent. However, the UNCTAD report concludes that the proportion of FDI that represents a straight swop between developed and developing countries is small. UNCTAD make this conclusion because a large proportion of the total foreign investment in the developing world is located in the mining or service sector where jobs cannot by their nature be exported. However, they do identify that in a few industries, notably textiles and electronics, job relocation is higher.

The fortunes of the textile industry in the past few decades perhaps illustrate the future relationship between the developed and developing world in this 'new' international division of labour. As O'Connor notes, 'The volumes of textiles and garments traded internationally today are enormous. As of 1987 they were the fourth and fifth largest commodity grouping in terms of total imports by market economies (after crude petroleum, passenger cars and office machinery)'. Together these industries contributed approximately $220 billion to world trade in 1990 divided almost equally between textiles and clothing. Although of the $97 billion trade in textiles in 1989 only one-quarter was accounted for by the developing world, this figure was 43 per cent in the clothing industry, which made the developing world the leading export suppliers (see Table 7.4).

While imports to the OECD countries in the textile and clothing industry from developing countries have increased, the textile industry in particular is heavily protected. Nevertheless, these countries have made inroads into the developed world's market share, in particular in the clothing industry. This should not be surprising given that the labour-intensive nature of the industry favours the low labour costs of the developing world (see Table 7.4).

Table 7.4 Comparison of average hourly labour costs in spinning and weaving, 1990

Country	Total costs $	Ratio to US cost %
USA	10.02	100
Japan	13.92	139
FRG	16.46	164
France	12.82	127
Taiwan	4.56	46
South Korea	3.22	32
Hong Kong	3.05	30
Mexico	2.21	22
Brazil	1.97	20
Turkey	1.82	18
Malaysia	0.86	9
Philippines	0.67	7
Pakistan	0.39	4
China	0.37	4
Indonesia	0.25	2
Sri Lanka	0.24	2

Source: O'Connor in Jomo, 1993, p.241.

The OECD's response to such low-wage competition has typically been protectionism. In the textile industry imports from the developing world began to face quota restrictions from the late 1950s. As domestic interests in the United States came under pressure from cheap imports from first Japan and later the NIEs, a series of voluntary export restraints (VERs) were agreed between the US and Japan (O'Connor 1993, pp.246–51). These measures were soon copied by European importers and since 1961 the quota levels have been set under the broad framework of the Multi-fibre Agreement which has been renewed on three separate occasions. With each renewal the restrictions on developing country textiles have increased. Although there has been strong pressure for the liberalization of trade in textiles both within the European Union and the United States powerful lobby groups continue to resist demands from developing countries for such quota levels to be removed. Nevertheless, despite such restrictions the developing world has continued to make inroads into the developed world's share of the world market in textiles although these inroads would undoubtedly have been much larger if the quotas had not been in place.

Textiles are not the only industry in which the developing world has seen the rise of 'neo' protectionism. VERs and orderly market agreements (OMAs) are in place in the automobile, steel, footwear, machine tool and electronics industries. Not surprisingly the chief targets of such measures have been Japan and the NIEs. In addition to VERs and OMAs the 1970s and 1980s have seen the proliferation of a whole host of other non-tariff barriers, the most common of which have been stringent health and safety requirements. The scale of this protectionism should not be dismissed. The World Development Report, for example, estimated in 1991 that over 40 per cent of First World imports are subject to some form of restriction. The growth of such protectionism on developing world imports culminated in 1988 when the United States removed the trade privileges granted to the NIEs under the General System of Preferences.

The cataclysmic predictions of Goldsmith and others are strongly dismissed by supporters of free trade however. Krugman, for example, dismisses them for a number of reasons. First, he argues that there are few examples in economic history of a country increasing its productivity without a concomitant increase in wages. Even in South Korea which has had a particularly repressive labour regime, wages have risen to the extent that some 'worry that wages may have risen too much . . . to compete in low-technology goods' (Goldsmith, J., 1995, p.191). Second, as productivity and wages rise so the prices of those goods being exported from the developing world also increase, reducing their cost-competitiveness relative to their competitors. In such circumstances, the threat to the West comes not from cheap wages but from rising prices for imported goods which lower real wages! In addition, improving productivity should follow through into a widening current account surplus which should eventually cause an appreciation of the currency which would then translate into higher effective wages, and thus higher effective costs. Krugman's third contention is that the scale of relocation in the developing world is exaggerated. During the 1980s the debt crisis actually transferred more in interest payments from the developing world to the North than the South received in investment. Thus all these cataclysmic predictions are based on activity between 1990 and 1993 when investment in developing countries hit a new peak of $100 billion. While this appears to be a significant sum this figure should be set against a combined investment figure for the US, Europe and Japan of $3.5 trillion. Thus the investment figure in the developing world represents a paltry 3 per cent of total investment (Krugman 1994, p.119).

Whatever the facts about industrialization in the developing world, rising protectionism in the First World has not been the only response. Increasingly in Britain and the United States the threat of cheap labour in the developing world has been used as a justification for attacking wages and employment protection. The UK's opt-out from the Social Chapter of the Maastricht Treaty on the grounds that it would destroy Britain's international competitiveness and jobs is perhaps the best illustration of this policy. However, it is more pervasive than this. The Welfare State is under attack in both these countries and the justification of its besiegers is that the social costs borne by employers are discouraging the creation of new jobs; government expenditure is stifling the economy and so forth.

Currently, Britain proudly boasts that its labour costs[6] are among the lowest in the European Union and that one of the fruits of this policy has been that the UK has attracted the lion's share of Japanese investment in Europe, 38 per cent of Japanese investment in Europe up to 1990 and 61 per cent in 1991. Similarly in the United States, real hourly and weekly wage rates since 1973, adjusted for inflation, have fallen by 13.4 per cent and 19.2 per cent respectively. Such policies are inherently flawed. Allowing real wage rates to fall will not alleviate the challenge from developing country industrialization. As Goldsmith argues,

> Imagine that we were able to reduce at a stroke social charges and taxation so as to diminish the cost of labour by a full third. All it would mean is that instead of being able to employ 47 Vietnamese or 47 Filipinos for the price of one Frenchman, you could employ only 31.
>
> (Goldsmith 1995, p.191)

Such policies are likely to only lead to an already growing gap in wages between those in high value-added skilled labour and those in low value-added unskilled employment. Although the scale of this gap is disputed, Wood (1994) concludes that trade with the developing world has already reduced demand for unskilled labour by 20 per cent between 1960 and 1990 and that this is revealed in the wage differentials between skilled and unskilled workers in the US and Britain. Therefore to reduce further social security legislation on such workers is liable to only further widen these disparities. Such actions could subsequently lead to falling purchasing power and hence demand in the economy on the one hand and growing social tensions on the other.

Conclusion

The trend towards the increasing role and importance of the 'old' Third World in international production began in the late 1960s and early 1970s. Its 'rediscovery' by academics and columnists in the 1990s has more to do with the intervention of the debt crisis during the 1980s which reversed much of the trend. However, since 1989 foreign investment has returned to the developing world *en masse*. Granted such investment is concentrated in the newly industrializing economies of East Asia, particularly the so-called second-tier NIEs (Malaysia, Thailand and Indonesia), though the growing importance of China, India and Sri Lanka is also recognized. However, perhaps one interesting point can be made about the debt crisis, namely the vulnerability of the developing world to economic factors outside their control. While debt servicing problems are a thing of the past for many countries, in sub-Saharan Africa and Latin America this problem is still severe. Sustained world economic growth is vital, and the key to this is perceived as export-orientated industrialization.

Few governments in the developing world today refuse to accept that in order to industrialize, foreign capital is vital. This strategy is testimony to this recognition and, some may say, to the continuing dependency of the developing world upon the core states of the industrialized world. What is different in the 1990s from the 1960s and 1970s when the theories of dependency and dependent development were formulated is that there is no longer a credible alternative to dependent capitalism. As Patrick Chabal (1994) comments, the point today is about the management of that dependent relationship, not whether it exists nor whether it is good or bad. However, while many East Asian specialists and world system analysts will argue about the extent to which industrialization has enhanced the autonomy of these states in the 'world system', one cannot deny the fact that a number of states have and others are improving living standards and their economies at rates that would have been hard to imagine thirty years ago. While the detrimental effects of TNC activity in the developing world are well documented, many states have consciously sought to incorporate TNCs into a national strategy which manages the level of penetration that foreign investment has in their economy. Export processing zones, local content requirement deals and joint ventures can all be seen as methods of preventing foreign affiliates from flooding the domestic market with superior goods and thus destroying indigenous industrialization. TNCs are harnessed using a variety of tax holidays, duty-free clauses and cheap labour enticements. This has its costs: labour is often repressed, women exploited and the environment degraded. But what is the alternative? Those states that have held out against the realities of global capitalism have not been success stories, while South Korea, Taiwan and others have.

There are three main threats to what Lipietz has called 'peripheral Fordism'. First, international investors are fickle characters. The slightest change in policy or in the political situation of a developing country can lead to a massive flight of capital to relocate elsewhere. In Malaysia for example, between 1974 and 1975 foreign investment fell by nearly 62 per cent as a result of the Industrial Coordination Act which required all local and foreign manufacturing companies with more than seventy-five employees to invite Bumiputras to acquire a 30 per cent stake in their company and to ensure that 30 per cent of their full-time staff were Malays (Sivalingham 1994, p.7). Similarly in Sri Lanka, a sharp drop in investment in 1983 is attributable to ethnic and civil unrest (Abeywardene *et al.* 1994, p.7) while in more recent memory we can cite the massive flight of capital out of Mexico following the Chiapas revolt and subsequent peso crisis.

Second, with an ever increasing number of developing countries embarking on similar export-oriented development programmes, exploiting their comparative advantage in labour, the battle for foreign investment becomes increasingly fierce. The danger therefore is that

> in the case of EPZs [for example] ... competitive outbidding between sites tends to gradually erode the potential for recovering some of the incurred capital expenses by the government. Indeed in view of the increasing number of EPZ areas, EPZ authorities tend to offer more and more fiscal incentives to enterprises in order to secure new investments and prevent the relocation of existing plants.
>
> (Maex 1983, quoted in Dicken 1992, p.391).

This danger is heightened by the very international capital that the strategy seeks to attract. In taking advantage of the increased mobility of transnational corporations, these states are vulnerable to this mobility. As Chomsky describes,

> In China's Guangdong province, hailed as one of the miracles of capitalist success ... when the government found that, *'the factory of a leading toy manufacturer was engaged in labour law violation – such as 14 hour workdays and seven-day workweeks – it approached the managers and asked them to respect the law. The managers refused, and said if they were unable to operate the way they wanted they would close their Chinese factories and move to Thailand'* – where there are no such unreasonable demands.
>
> (Chomsky 1991, p.239)

The final threat to this strategy is from growing protectionism in the First World. While cheap labour and other financial attractions may yield increased profits for multinationals, the cost is often felt in factory closures and redundancies in the North. Faced with pressures both from trade unions and domestic manufacturers many states have responded by introducing new forms of protection against developing world producers. This threat is perhaps the most real to these states. For example, the Clinton presidency announced that from 1 July 1995 some 140 products exported from thirty-five developing countries would no longer receive duty-free treatment in the United States.[7] The ending of the duty-free access was justified because of concern about the negative impact upon US producers. Such challenges from 'above' and 'below' bear testimony to the short-term gains associated with downward mobility. Unless the downwardly mobile state can diversify and reduce its dependency upon exogenous factors, its development strategy runs the risk of stalling, perhaps plunging the state into the ranks of those 'not in the game'.

Notes

1 'Taylorisation' here refers to the fragmentation of the production process that took place in the industrialized world around the turn of the century. This process is said to have been inspired by Taylor's *The Scientific Principles of Management*. Under Taylorism the workforce was fragmented and the jobs assigned were often repetitive; however, there was little if any automation. Lipietz here refers to the transfer of limited segments of TNC production that are mostly not automated, particularly textiles (sewing machines and single operators) and electronics (microscopes and tweezers).

2 The following list is adapted from Lewis (1978), *The Evolution of the International Economic Order*, p.3.

3 See *The Economist*, 'War of the worlds', 1 October 1994.

4 Cited in Schaffer, J., 'Child labor remains global problem of huge proportions', *USIA East Asia Pacific Wireless File*, 22 May 1995.

5 The Chinese Special Economic Zones are excluded from consideration here, principally because the rules and regulations concerning SEZs are far more comprehensive than those that usually govern EPZs. EPZs are essentially export platforms, largely designed to control foreign capital by excluding that capital from the domestic market. By contrast, the SEZs are also designed to attract foreign capital in order to provide for the considerable domestic Chinese market while withholding such capital blanket access.

6 In 1990 if wage costs and non-wage costs, such as employers' social security contributions, are taken together, Britain's labour costs were 12 per cent below the European Union average.

7 Reported by United States Information Agency, *East Asia Pacific Wireless File*, 31 May 1995, 'US ends duty free access for some developing goods' by Jon Schaffer.

8

The Parasites: tax havens and
off-shore finance

Lord Palmerston . . . once lamented that Queen Victoria's colonies were
multiplying so fast he had to 'keep looking the damned places up on the
map'. Today's international investor, banker and fund manager could be
forgiven for echoing that sentiment, as they survey the world's offshore
financial centres.
(Peagam 1989, Special supplement to *Euromoney: Treasure Islands*, p.4)

Every tax avoider is a special case and needs a particular kind of haven.
(Doggart 1990, p.11)

In one memorable passage in his well-known text on international
relations theory, Kenneth Waltz reiterates the view that the state is the unit
of action in international politics, even in the case of some that 'may be
nearly washed up as economic entities' (Waltz 1979, p.94). In so doing,
he expressed perhaps a common perception among international relations
scholars that many states in the world are not worth dwelling upon because
of their lack of power. Among such 'washed up' communities, arguably
none are more insignificant than the archipelago of the tax haven micro-
states now surrounding all the major trading blocs. This Lilliputian world
of parasitical states is dominated by 'giants' such as Switzerland,
Luxembourg, the Cayman Islands and the Bahamas. In fact, Switzerland
adheres so strictly to neutrality to have exited elegantly from the pages of
most international relations books: the Swiss are the perennial observers
in this game of international politics – observers and suspected thieves
(Naylor 1987). Luxembourg, with an army of 600, about half of which
serve in the orchestra, is not an impressive power. Most of the others are
small tourist resorts, whose dot-size indication on the map exaggerates
their true territorial size in the world. One such example is Gibraltar,
whose 'socialist' prime minister, formerly a cook on the QEII liner, aspires
to make the Rock into one of the major European financial centres
(Duggan 1991). To give another example, the idyllic Bahamas owes its
existence to the Miami mob which established it as an off-shore financial
post (Naylor 1987).

When the modern planners of the post-war order conferred upon
states the rights of self-determination and sovereign equality, they were
meant to serve as the moral foundations of a more democratic and
equitable international system. Little did they anticipate that sovereignty

would become, in the age of mass consumption, just another commodity to be bought and sold by the highest bidder. There is now a new category of state to which sovereignty appears to have become little more than an excuse to implement laws that are implicitly aimed at attracting business from their neighbours.

There are many types of 'parasitical' strategies. The most well known and the one that has had the greatest impact is undoubtedly the tax haven. Although during the 1980s off-shore financing and tax havens became all the rage the phenomenon has a much longer history. Tax havens have now gained widespread acceptance and are discussed openly in the pages of the popular press as an option for pension purposes and tax avoidance. Even the British Rail gazette, *Inter-City* (Dibben 1993), has opted to cheer up its grumpy passengers with an information sheet describing the pros and cons of tax havens.

With over forty states offering a variety of facilities for tax havens and off-shore banking, the tax haven model has proved, at least numerically, to be one of the most popular state strategies in the modern global political economy (see Table 8.1). Indeed, the strategy has yielded a new political and economic map, with each of the major and minor trading blocs now surrounded by an archipelago of small tax havens/resorts: NAFTA by the Caribbean and Central American havens; the EU by the old European havens and the British isles; Japan by the Pacific islands, Malaysia and Thailand; China has Hong Kong; India, Sri Lanka; the Gulf has Bahrain; Nigeria, Liberia; and the fear of political instability in post-apartheid South Africa has already stimulated a potential haven in the 'Marxist' regime of the Seychelles.

The sheer amount of money that goes through the tax havens is nothing less than staggering: the nine havens of the Caribbean hold bank deposits totalling in excess of $400 billion; they are home to roughly half of the world's captive insurance companies, and nearly 14 per cent of the world's merchant shipping. The Caymans and the Bahamas rank among the world's leading international banking centres in terms of size, while Barbados and the Caymans have become two of the world's leading off-shore insurance centres (see Tables 8.2 and 8.3). Yet even these figures underrate the extent of the phenomenon. According to some estimates, 'as much as half of the world's stock of money either resides in, or is passing through, tax havens' (Kochen 1991, p.73).

It is obvious therefore that the tax havens play an important and growing role in the global political economy. Can this strategy be considered a success? Is this the ideal strategy for small states? And what are the wider implications of such a strategy on the global political economy? These questions will be discussed later in this chapter.

Which states can be classified as tax havens?

It is not easy to define a 'tax haven'. As the Gordon Report to the US Treasury Department states, 'there is no single, clear, objective test which

Table 8.1 Worldwide list of tax havens

Land mass	Coastal	Islands
Andorra	Costa Rica	Anguilla
Campiogne	Gibraltar	Antigua and Nevis
Liechtenstein	Hong Kong	Aruba
Luxembourg	Lebanon	Bahrain
Switzerland	Liberia	Barbados
Vatican	Monaco	Bermuda
	Nicaragua	British Virgin Islands
	Panama	Cayman Islands
	Puerto Rico	Cook islands
	Thailand	Cyprus
	UAE	Guernsey
		Isle of Man
		Jersey
		Luban (Malaysia)
		Malta
		Montserrat
		Nauru
		Netherland Antilles
		Philippines
		Seychelles
		Sri Lanka
		Turks & Caicos
		Vanuatu
		United Kingdom
		US Virgin Islands

Sources: Doggart 1990; Grundy 1987; Johns and Le Marchant 1993; Peagam 1989.

permits the identification of a country as a tax haven' (OECD 1987, p.21). The complexity of modern taxation laws and regulations represents the main problem. In one form or another, practically every country in the world offers some sort of haven from taxation and regulation for residents of other countries, even if governments have not gone out to attract business purposefully on the basis of such special rules. What distinguishes tax havens, however, is that they explicitly aim to take advantage of a competitive position created by offering reduced regulation or capital tax. We therefore favour Johns' subjective definition of tax havens as

> economies which have made a deliberate attempt to attract thereto international trade-oriented activities by minimization of taxes and the reduction or elimination of other restrictions on business operations, such that, within the jurisdiction of the centre, aggregated economic activity is substantially geared to the special global invisible needs of external enterprises and investors.
>
> (Johns 1983, p.20)

Table 8.2 The world's leading capital insurance centres

1.	Bermuda	1,178
2.	Cayman Islands	370
3.	Guernsey	170
4.	Vermont (USA)	146
5.	Barbados	142
6.	Isle of Man	73
7.	Luxembourg	66
8.	Bahamas	38
9.	Singapore	33
10.	Colorado (USA)	33

Source: Captive Insurance company directory (as cited in Peagam 1989), Trillinghas publication. Figures represent registered companies.

Table 8.3 The world's leading international banking centres (1990)

Rank		Total foreign liabilities ($ billion)	Type
1.	UK	1,073	Spontaneous
2.	Japan	659.4 (off-shore *)	IBF
3.	US	584.4 (of which New York IBF $332.7*)	
4.	Hong Kong	438.3	Spontaneous
5.	Singapore	335.6	IBF
6.	France	269.8	on-shore
7.	Cayman Islands	233.2 (end 1987)	tax haven
8.	Switzerland	225.0	tax haven
9.	Luxembourg	191.5	tax haven
10.	Belgium	176.6	on-shore
11.	Bahamas	158.9	tax haven

* IMF mid-1988
Source: Hanzawa 1991, p.284.

Because of these difficulties there are diverging interpretations as to which states may be considered tax havens. Currently the most inclusive list would probably be as shown in Table 8.1.

Further complications arise because it is not easy to distinguish, in either theory or practice, between tax havens and off-shore financial centres. Off-shore financing and tax havens have both evolved as strategies aimed specifically at the financial sector. The two strategies are related and yet distinct from each other. Off-shore financing can be defined as 'markets where operators are permitted to raise funds from non-residents and invest or lend that money to non-residents free from regulations and taxes' (Hanzawa 1991, p.284). Off-shore financing need not necessarily take place physically 'off-shore'. When a bank located in one country raises funds in another and then lends that money to clients in a third country's markets instead of using it domestically, that bank is engaged in 'off-shore' activities. These activities are not only free from the regulation of the country in which the bank resides, but are subject to no mandatory regulations whatsoever. An off-shore financial market can therefore be created if books for foreign-to-foreign accounts are kept separate from books for domestic financial and capital transactions.

The off-shore markets are generally classified into three types: spontaneous off-shore sites, such as the UK and Hong Kong; International Banking Facilities (IBF) such as New York and Tokyo, and the tax havens. The London off-shore market arose spontaneously because of stringent exchange controls and the strict separation between the books. In 1979 the Thatcher government abolished foreign exchange controls and in so doing opened up the way for residents to raise and invest foreign currency. Since that time London has been considered an off-shore financial centre.

An IBF is a more stringent type of off-shore market, in which companies must apply for a licence and varied amounts of regulation and restriction are permitted. The New York IBF emerged towards the end of the 1970s as the result of a prolonged and complicated battle between the US Treasury, the Swiss and a number of Caribbean tax havens. With the active encouragement of the New York banking community, particularly Citibank and Chase, the US came to the conclusion that 'if you can't beat them, join them'. A swift volte-face took place, culminating in the establishment of the New York off-shore market, the New York International Banking Facilities (IBF) on 1 December 1980. In turn, the creation of the New York IBF spawned the creation of the Tokyo and Singaporian IBFs and so the effects of off-shorization were spread much wider.

In reality every off-shore market can operate in one form or another as a tax haven, but the tax haven proper may be identified as the least restrictive category. Some distinguish between tax havens and off-shore financial centres by placing the stress on the lack of proper financial back-up in the former. Tax havens are inhabited by 'letterbox' or 'brass plate' companies which exist only on paper, with the real activity taking place in proper financial centres. (For example, there are some 25,000-plus letterbox companies registered in Liechtenstein.)

The 'classic' tax haven has either minimal or no direct taxes, and it generally lacks the facilities of a large-scale financial centre (Hampton 1994, p.237). For instance, whereas the City of London directly employs about 250,000 people, the number of lawyers specializing in financial matters in the Cayman Islands, currently the seventh largest financial centre in the world, can be measured in tens. The famous global banks that stand side by side on its seven-mile stretch or 'high street', are little more than rooms with fax machines and computers, relaying orders that are sent from London or New York. The Cayman Islands are thus mere 'paper tigers' of financial centres.

In their defence, it may be said that every tax haven is an aspiring off-shore financial centre. Unfortunately the sheer number of existing and aspiring havens, their location, educational and infrastructural support mitigates against many ever achieving such ambitions. Bearing these distinctions in mind, what makes a good tax haven? The requirements are varied but should generally include the following:

- An effective bank secrecy law, whereby bank or state officials are barred by law from disclosing the origins, character and name of holders of funds.
- There must be few, preferably no restrictions and regulations concerning financial transactions.
- There must be tax and other financial incentives to minimize the cost of transactions (e.g. low licensing fees and so on).
- The secrecy of transaction must be protected.
- The territory must possess political and economic stablity.
- It should either be supported by a large international financial market or alternatively be equipped with sophisticated information-exchange facilities and/or be within easy reach of a major financial centre.
- The territory's name should not be tainted by scandals, laundering or drug money, for then taxing authorities would not recognize it as legitimate.
- It is also desirable that the market has agreements with major countries to avoid double taxation/regulation (e.g. Monaco has a customs union with France and via France with the EU).

A tax haven can therefore be recognized by legislative and commercial measures taken to attract capital into a state's geographical territory.

Relics of a bygone age? A short history of the tax havens

The tax haven is a peculiarly twentieth-century phenomenon, and can be interpreted as a strategy, in the sense that we use the term in this book, only since the collapse of the Bretton Woods system. Like all other modern strategies, it began its career inauspiciously. However, perhaps ironically, its origins lie in the refusal to change in times of otherwise great transformation. The tax havens are not only one of the contributors to the rise of the 'new medievalism', as some observers opt to describe the 1990s, but their origins are rooted in a conception of the role of the state and individual which, if not itself medieval, is at least pre-Baroquean. In Europe for example, the majority of tax havens are the surviving dukedoms and fiefdoms of a bygone age, while in Asia and the Middle East these territories were the domain of pirates and smugglers.

As the European states were embarking in the 1930s on a course which led them progressively towards increasing taxation and regulation (the rise of the Keynesian or Fordist state), they came into conflict with more conservative Switzerland. As Fehrenbach comments, 'The great flood of gold to Switzerland began in 1920. It began because Europe changed and

Switzerland did not' (1966, p.20). What Switzerland supposedly refused to change was its attitude towards taxation and relationships between its citizens and the state, all centred around banking secrecy laws.

Bank secrecy is a very old principle indeed. It 'was written into Roman law as the *actio iniuriarum*, and in Germanic civil law as the *lex Visigothorum*, or the laws of the Visigoths' (Fehrenbach 1966, p.74). However, the opening of private affairs to outsiders is a recent innovation which began the career of the tax havens. Fehrenbach maintains that Switzerland was the first country to introduce such laws. The Swiss Banking Law of 1934 was 'the first time in history the principle of bank secrecy was put under the official protection of the penal law' (Fehrenbach 1966, p.73). The second innovative aspect of Swiss banking law was that it gave foreign nationals the protection of Swiss criminal law. Swiss bank secrecy law thus became the cornerstone of the tax haven strategy. Therefore any self-respecting tax haven must possess a credible bank secrecy law which bars bank officials from revealing the identity and transactions of their customers – even to their own government.

Bank secrecy laws were soon copied by other long-serving havens such as Beirut, the Bahamas, Tangiers, Liechtenstein and Montevideo. Soon a steady supply of bank deposits with dubious origins flowed into these havens. As an additional measure, the Swiss also allowed numbered accounts, permitting a situation whereby only one or two officials in the bank know the identity of the holder – which in many cases may be different from the ultimate recipent. Thus Switzerland became the bench-mark haven and any newcomer had to 'up the stakes'. For example, Luxembourg took the principle of numbered accounts one step further, allowing only one bank official to know the identity of a holder, while in Austria the principle has been taken to its logical conclusion with the identity of the holder merely being an untraceable number.

In spite of the obvious harm that Swiss banking laws were inflicting on their neighbours, the Swiss have fought to maintain their laws under the cover of their 'independent spirit'. Individualism and an independent spirit, the cynic would say, have yielded tangible rewards in Switzerland's case. Swiss independence and the country's call for 'sovereign equality' have naturally led it into a number of conflicts, particularly with another state which raised the concept of independence, sovereign equality and individualism to a state religion, namely the United States.

The most celebrated battle between the two countries took place in the aftermath of the Second World War. At one stage the American treasury threatened to bar any American company from conducting business with Swiss banks and from allowing Swiss banks to invest in the USA; but the Swiss weathered the storm (Fehrenbach 1966; Naylor 1987). None the less, in the late 1980s, following a series of highly publicized scandals and rumours (particularly the allegation that the former president of the Philippines, Ferdinand Marcos, had deposited over $4 billion of his country's money in Swiss accounts, as well as the Lugano banking scandal), the Swiss began to give up this struggle. In an unprecedented move, they volunteered to provide information.

However, this new willingness to cooperate with tax authorities was, in fact, a shrewd move on the part of the Swiss, because the proliferation of tax havens had made the strategy less lucrative than in the past. Furthermore, with the proliferation of tax havens a hierarchy has emerged, within which Switzerland would like to occupy the upper crest as the most solid, least tainted haven. Indeed, the secret of a successful tax haven is discretion. Switzerland has increasingly sought to attract the 'right' clientele, or at least by appearing to attract the right clientele to defuse much of the criticism that has been directed towards it. Thus in the tax haven business there has been an element of 'quality' competition in a rather similar way to the competition we have seen in the automobile industry during the 1980s. As national and international measures against money laundering have improved (Gilmore 1992), the least tainted, most discrete and preferred tax havens have offered a better chance of tax avoidance. Switzerland is – and would like to remain – apart from the 'blacklisted' countries whose investments are not recognized by tax authorities.

Due to the success of the Swiss package of legislation, the three big Swiss banks (Crédit Suisse, UBS and Swiss Bank Corporation) have become some of the biggest players in the world of investment financing. The irony of Swiss financing is of a world turned upside down. In their overriding desire to de-criminalize and legitimize their holdings, launderers, tax evaders and drug-dealers rarely play the financial markets, their accounts being more like long-term deposits. This has been in stark contrast to the traditional American and British bankers who have turned in greater numbers to speculation. The Swiss banking system is old-fashioned, aristocratic and very different from the American and British bankers harassed by their shareholders. While American and British banks exposed themselves heavily in the then lucrative business of petrodollar recycling, ending up by the early 1980s with enormous debts on their books offering no prospect for remittance, the Swiss have maintained discrete investment in the advanced countries.

The exposure felt by some American and British banks was accentuated by many corporations beginning to find they were able to borrow at lower rates of interest in the financial markets themselves. Subsequently these banks began shifting their operations to non-traditional (i.e. not borrowing and lending) operations such as mergers and acquisitions, exchange rate and other speculative activities, or disintermediation in financial jargon.

The significance of Switzerland also manifests itself in the relationship between advanced and Third World countries. In the late 1950s the big Swiss banks decided to minimize their exposure to Third World investment. As a result, Switzerland has become, in the words of one of its apologists, a major 'clearing house for the passage of money from the unstable, undeveloped "third world" back into the relative freedom and stability of the industrial regions' (Fehrenbach 1966, p.133). As Naylor wryly comments:

the foreign assets controlled in various ways and forms by the Swiss banks [in 1982] total more than $350 billion, approximately equal to the net foreign debt of the world's developing countries – a coincidence pregnant with implications.

(Naylor 1987, p.232)

With such colossal and growing investment portfolios on their books, the vast majority of which are earmarked for the First World, the advanced countries have been careful not to alienate the tax havens. This has been most evident in the case of the United States where policy makers, faced with an ever increasing budget deficit, have been unable to afford the cost of lost investment that would inevitably follow any international crackdown. This must have been one of the considerations which led US authorities to soften their opposition to the tax havens.

Regulation, de-regulation and the proliferation of tax havens

Despite the example set by the old European havens it is only in the last two decades that the tax haven strategy has become increasingly popular. It has undergone, as Johns and Le Marchant (1993) note, a revolution. Why is this? There are four interrelated theories explaining the proliferation in the number of tax havens.

1   The first theory suggests that the growth of the tax haven has been the direct result of increasing taxation and regulation in the OECD countries since the Second World War (Fehrenbach 1966; Johns 1983; Peagam 1989). As Peagam notes, 'It is no coincidence . . . that banking, insurance and ship registration are three of the main pillars of offshore business; they are among the most heavily regulated industries in developed countries (1989, p.6).

The Caribbean tax havens, for instance, have certainly benefited enormously from the attempts by the American states to regulate their banks and other multinational enterprises. A number of key American policy decisions are often mentioned to account for this evolution including the Voluntary Foreign Credit Restraint Program (VFCRP) in 1965 (abolished in 1974) to limit the size of foreign loans extended from the US; the Foreign Direct Investment Program (mandatory since 1968) which attempted to control the export of capital from American business corporations abroad, and the infamous Tax Equalization Act of 1963 which taxed repatriated American money. These measures were intended to increase regulation and control of US financial actors but had precisely the opposite effect, further stimulating American business interest in the Caribbean as a way of overcoming such controls.

Besides its common-sense appeal, this theory does receive some indirect support. An OECD report into tax evasion mentions a study of business attitudes conveyed by the Business and Industry Advisory Committee (BIAC) to the OECD. The BIAC tried to argue that the dash to the tax havens was not prompted by tax evasion:

Much of the use of tax havens is not motivated by the desire to pay no, or little, tax so much as an economic necessity to reduce costs, including taxes, to a bearable level in circumstances where the laws of countries are unco-ordinated, and even the laws of individual countries are inconsistent.

(Quoted in OECD 1987, p.37)

However, in attempting to argue this they only confirm the theory. The BIAC regards taxation and regulation as costs which they are legitimately trying to avoid in order to increase their profits. This theory has the advantage of explaining the differences in tax havens which, by catering to different customers, prompt specialization and expertise. It also explains why, broadly speaking, the havens can be distinguished according to the types of taxation from which they are seeking to provide a haven: personal taxation, corporation taxation and indirect taxation.

(a) Personal taxation: this tends to work only for the very rich, the so-called 'high net worth' individuals. As Margaret Dibben wryly notes, 'The small investor never could evade tax and, even if you travel to your offshore haven and spend the money on local pleasures, the taxman will still expect his dues' (1993, p.27). During the 1980s, Morgan Guarantee's private banking offices were reputed to deal only with clients with a minimum net worth of $5 million (Peagam 1989), other banks settled for $500,000 or less. However, a recent report in the *Financial Times* claimed that as a result of the 1991 to 1993 recession this figure had fallen to $100,000. Clearly then the main beneficiaries of the tax havens are the very rich. Nevertheless, the size of this group is often underestimated. A survey by Citicorp, for example, estimated that in 1990 there were 8 million people in the world with wealth of US$ 1 million or more to invest (reported in Johns and Le Marchant 1993, p.24).

(b) Nevertheless, for most havens it is evasion from corporate taxation and regulation that reaps the greatest rewards. Sometimes, going off-shore can also allow diversification into activities not permitted at home. Off-shore centres are often used for the purpose of avoiding foreign exchange and capital controls, restrictions on foreign investment and other domestic constraints (such as the prohibition of interest payments in some Muslim countries). The tax havens have been absolutely central to global financial de-regulation.

(c) The final type of parasitical behaviour noted here is related to extensions of indirect taxation such as VAT. For example, the lower rates of VAT in havens such as Andorra and Luxembourg are testimony to the attempt to draw upon the tax base of neighbouring states.

2 The second theory maintains that the growth of the modern tax haven should be considered within the wider framework of the transnationalization of the economy. The tax havens are seen as fulfilling an important if not critical function in the modern global political economy. Johns and Le Marchant (1993) voice a widespread opinion, particularly prevalent in business circles, that states have been slow to respond to the needs of transnational commerce, imposing a myriad

unnecessary restrictions which have forced business to find other outlets:

> the arrivist offshore centres of international finance and investment contributed to the radical restructuring of the geography of global finance, and indeed, in many respects acted as *agent provocateurs* for the promotion and expansion of the boundless financial services.
>
> (Johns and Le Marchant 1993, p.xi)

The advantage of this theory is the stress it places on the functional and organic role played by tax havens. They are not seen as an aberration, but as central to the modern global political economy. The tax havens are the grease, smoothing the transformation of the world economy from national to global.

3   Naylor (1987) contends that the immediate cause of the expansion of tax havens is corruption and crime. Essentially there are two types of tax havens: the 'old' ones such as Switzerland, Liechtenstein and the Channel Islands which are historical freaks, and the new tax ones which are, usually, small islands whose governments have been corrupted by organized crime.

> The turning point in the modern history of peekaboo finance in the Caribbean came in 1959, when Fidel Castro unseated one of Meyer Lansky's principal business associates and closed the syndicate casinos and drug-trafficking facilities. (Naylor 1987, pp.39–40)

That gave the cue for the emergence of the Bahamas as a 'financial centre'. Meyer Lansky, the infamous mafia boss based in Miami, was, according to Naylor, the driving force behind the Caribbean and Pacific havens. Indeed, for Naylor, practically every new centre of 'flight capital' was the product of corrupt financiers.

4   Finally there is our own theory, namely that tax havens are an instance of a particular state strategy that has evolved with the globalization of the world economy. As we will argue in the next section, in terms of direct receipts from financial activity, the tax haven strategy may be considered a failure. Yet the strategy appears far more successful if it is 'sold' as a 'package' aimed at attracting finance, tourism and construction.

Is the tax haven a useful state strategy?

The answer is more complicated than one would imagine. To begin with, a distinction must be made between two groups of tax havens. The first group contains the four substantial tax havens – Switzerland, Luxembourg, Singapore and Hong Kong – which possess full banking facilities and are major players in the world of international finance. In the second are most of the other centres which are unable to stand on their own, being little more than dependencies of the larger off-shore financial centres (i.e. London, New York, Tokyo, Honk Kong and Singapore).

Hampton, in his assessment of the applicability of replicating the development of off-shore financial centres (1994), argues that the tax haven strategy yields a number of direct and indirect benefits (pp.244–5). Among the direct benefits he cites are: increased government revenue (off-shore activities in Jersey generated 88 per cent of government revenue in 1990), and local expenditure by banks and their salaried workers and wage employment by off-shore companies (e.g. 20 per cent of the workforce of the Caymans are employed by such companies). Similarly the tax haven strategy can also produce a series of indirect benefits such as: an improvement of the states' own financial system; greater access to international capital markets, and the internationalization of the local economy which should attract greater foreign direct investment.

Any attempt to assess the net economic impact of off-shore financial activities on the tax haven's GNPs can, at best, provide little more than a rough estimate. The very nature of the strategy itself – shrouded as it is in secrecy – makes this especially difficult. Nevertheless, it is remarkable to note, with the exception of the historic havens, just how little 'going off-shore' appears to directly contribute to GNP. While the *Europa Year Book* (1992, p.2945) estimates that off-shore activities generate about 22 per cent of Bermuda's GNP, Peagam (1989) estimates that for the Caribbean havens as a whole such activities generate on average somewhere in the region of 4–10 per cent of GNP (although this underestimates the spin-off business this generates to construction and tourism).

On this basis, the fact that the tax haven strategy has been so widely copied appears surprising. It is an extremely volatile strategy which places a country or territory at the extreme end of dependency on outsiders, where the speed of capital movement from one haven to another is measured in days or weeks rather than months or years. As a strategy it brings marginal revenues, it can lead the state into international disrepute, it is the haunt of gangsters, drug dealers and international criminals, and its effect on international financial markets can wreak havoc with the domestic economic policies of advanced countries (cf. Black Wednesday and the UK's departure from the ERM in October 1992). Given these risks and consequences one must surely ask, why become a tax haven?

Whatever the difficulty in assessing the impact of off-shore finance upon such economies, seasoned tax havens such as the Bahamas and Bermuda had attained, as early as 1970, a standard of living comparable to advanced industrial countries. During the 1970s and 1980s the next generation of havens, the Cayman Islands and both the British and US Virgin Islands also achieved this bench-mark (see Table 8.4). In addition, other tax havens such as Anguilla and Aruba have experienced some of the fastest growth rates in the world. For example, in 1988 Anguilla had a growth rate of 8.8 per cent while Aruba grew at 10 per cent in 1990 (CIA 1991). Such statistics tend to lend support to the argument that the tax haven strategy is not about off-shore finance alone but that it works as a package combining finance, tourism and construction.

Successful tax havens are therefore those which also use their facilities

Table 8.4 Comparison of the GNP per capitas of Tax Haven and non Tax-Haven small island states

Country	GNP per capita [1]	Tax haven
Anguilla[2]	$6,800 (1991)	Yes
Antigua & Barbuda	$5,800	No
Aruba[2]	$17,400	Yes
Bahamas	$17,400	Yes
Barbados	$16,500	No
Bermuda[2]	$27,100 (1992)	Yes
BVI[2]	$10,600 (1991)	Yes
Cayman Islands[2]	$23,000 (1991)	Yes
Cuba	$1,250	No
Dominica	$2,100 (1992)	No
Dominican Republic	$3,000	No
Grenada	$3,000 (1992)	No
Guadeloupe[2]	$8,400 (1991)	No
Haiti	$800	No
Jamaica	$3,200 (1992)	No
Martinique[2]	$9,500 (1991)	No
Montserrat[2]	$4,300 (1992)	No
Neths Antilles[2]	$9,700	Yes
Puerto Rico[3]	$7,100 (1992)	No
St Kitts & Nevis	$4,000 (1992)	No
St Lucia	$3,000	No
St Vincent	$2,000 (1992)	No
Trinidad & Tobago	$8,000	No
Turks & Caicos[1]	$6,000 (1992)	Yes

Notes: [1] 1993 unless stated.
[2] Has not achieved formal independence.
[3] Commonwealth with the United States.
Source: The CIA World Factbook 1994 On Line (http://www.odci.gov/).

as a form of tourist attraction (bearing in mind that tourism is about to become the largest single global industry) and it is hardly surprising that the better of the Caribbean tax havens are also home to some of the most luxurious tourist centres. Both the tourist and financial industries require a similar infrastructure: good communications and transportation and links with one of the large trading blocs. Yet the link goes beyond mere coincidence. In many cases the clients that the havens attract are 'high net worth' individuals, individuals with money not only to invest but also to spend – and where better to combine business and pleasure than the Caribbean?

No doubt off-shore activities generate extra cash, but political and economic stability is also crucial to the success of the off-shore strategy. The Bahamas, for instance, lost a lot of business in the 1970s as a result of negative publicity concerning alleged drug-trafficking and corruption.

Consequently the Bahamas slipped from being the third largest international financial centre to the eleventh. The requirement for political and economic stablity means that in practice the best tax havens are dependencies of larger states. Liechtenstein is dependent on Switzerland, Monaco on France; the US Virgin Islands on the US and the Dutch Antilles on the Netherlands. The UK has a string of attached havens: the Channel Islands, Gibraltar, the Cayman Islands, the British Virgin Islands, Turks and Caicos, Anguilla, Montserrat and Hong Kong. The dependent nature of these territories suggests a level of support for tax havens which is rarely expressed openly. As Michael Bradley, Governor of the Turks and Caicos Islands observes:

> The UK encourages dependent territories to become economically self-sufficient. . . . It is quite content that they develop as offshore financial centres on the basis that they will be responsibly managed, supervised and run with tight and efficient controls.
>
> (Peagam 1989, p.5)

For instance, the UK commissioned Coopers & Lybrand to carry out a review of off-shore regulation in several British territories, 'presumably', writes Peagam, 'with a view to enhancing their competitiveness' (1989, p.5). Indeed there is evidence to suggest that much of the necessary financial legislation was in fact laid down by the British authorities in order to encourage these island states to become effectively self-financing (Hampton 1994, pp.241–2).

There is of course another explanation for the popularity of the strategy. After all, by definition parasitical strategies are relatively painless. Therefore the question many of these small states are facing is not how successful a strategy the tax haven is, but why not use it? Contrary to traditional theories of international relations, where the emphasis is placed on the egotistic pursuit of self-interest, the fact is that since the 1970s the atmosphere of international affairs has changed for the worse. The Bretton Woods system has collapsed and the US has signalled that it puts its own interests first. The world has become once again a dog-eat-dog world of each to their own. In this light what else can small states possibly do, confronted in most cases with little manufacturing infrastructure and economies over-reliant on tropical crop agriculture?

Nevertheless, the tax haven's days may be numbered. It is ironic that the very ease with which tax havens can be set up, and the logic that drives practically every mini-state towards the off-shore markets, may signal their demise. The tax haven strategy clearly already suffers from the effects of 'crowding'. For instance, surrounding the EU there are a growing number of aspiring havens to add to those already in existence. To add to the more traditional havens of the Channel Islands, the Isle of Man, Liechtenstein, Luxembourg, Monaco, San Marino and Switzerland, there is now Andorra, Cyprus, Gibraltar, Hungary, Malta and Trieste. All these havens want to be all things to all tax avoiders. With too many tax havens around offering progressively less regulatory or taxing regimes, the strategy is running itself into the ground.

More significantly, the strategy is suffering from a classic scissor effect. Since the early 1980s the growing momentum of liberalization and de-regulation has progressively eroded the distinction between off-shore and on-shore. In addition, concern with tax avoidance and money laundering has led, particularly in the past five years, to a considerable tightening of loopholes and to concerted international efforts and initiatives led by the United Nations, the EU and the United States to combat tax avoidance and money laundering.

It appears that the main goal of this international effort is to combat and abolish strict bank secrecy laws. A report to the OECD countries on taxation and the abuse of bank secrecy (derestricted 1985) 'urges governments of the Council of Europe member states to abolish unduly strict rules on bank secrecy' (OECD 1987, p.108). The report calls for sweeping improvements in international cooperation. Significantly, four countries did not adhere to the text of this report and its suggestions: Austria, Luxembourg, Switzerland and Portugal (the latter lined up Madeira as a tax haven). The Financial Action Task Force set up by the G7, which includes other OECD countries and coordinates with Caribbean states, African and Asian task forces, states that 'Many of the current difficulties in international cooperation in drug money laundering cases are directly or indirectly linked with a strict application of bank secrecy' (Gilmore 1992, p.xi).

Similarly, the 1988 UN Convention Against Illicit Traffic in Narcotic Drugs and Psychotropic Substances has made a number of strong recommendations. As Stewart observes,

> The Convention is one of the most detailed and far-reaching instruments ever adopted in the field of international criminal law and, if widely adopted and effectively implemented, will be a major force in harmonizing national laws and enforcement actions around the world.
>
> (Gilmore 1992, p.xi)

The gathering storms only attest to the vulnerability of a strategy, the parasitical nature of which condemns it as the ultimate form of dependency.

Global effect

The tax havens have become in effect nothing less than the cornerstone of the process of globalization and in many respects have acted as catalysts for the expansion of financial service activities. Today a global wholesale financial market has emerged whose net worth is estimated in excess of US$5 trillion. This is a pool of liquidity residing 'off-shore' which responds most sensitively to domestic regulation and policies, and which has been one of the key restructuring agents in the global political economy. This 'wholesale' market depends critically on the tax havens (an estimated half of the global stock of capital resides in or goes through tax havens) which appear to have had four major interdependent effects on today's international political economy.

1 De-regulation

Liberalization of the financial markets was encouraged and provoked either directly or indirectly by an expansion of the 'off-shore' market. Off-shore centres are often used to avoid foreign exchange and capital controls, restrictions on foreign investment and other domestic constraints. The Business and Industry Advisory Committee (BIAC) survey, Doggart (1990), Johns (1983) and Johns and Le Marchant (1993) confirm that tax havens have helped maintain pressure on governments to minimize corporate taxation and regulation. Furthermore, the growth of off-shore financial centres and tax havens has forced regulatory authorities to reassess their position and relax regulations at home. As Duggan observes:

> Banking authorities around the world attempted in the late 1960s and 1970s to regulate the new international capital market . . . but they failed. There has always been some offshore centre which had few regulatory scruples and which therefore attracted the international financiers. Eventually instead of continuing their unequal struggle, the supervisors decide to repeal their own regulations and bring the financial markets back home.
>
> (Duggan 1991, pp.9–10)

The problem is that tax havens not only act as *agents provocateurs* for the promotion and expansion of the boundless financial service activities (Johns and Le Marchant 1993, p.xi) but they also contribute to a general lowering of standards of regulation in financial markets. As Johns comments:

> Given that some countries adopt a permissive regulatory environment and others a stringent one, gaps and differentials arise in national systems of regulation. These differences can lead to perverse competition in regulatory laxity and a gravitation by some institutions to the least regulated financial centres.
>
> (Johns 1983, p.6)

The tax havens therefore played an important role in what Susan Strange has called 'Casino Capitalism' (Strange 1986).

2 Tax avoidance

As its name suggests, the tax haven strategy is primarily about tax avoidance. Tax havens have both a direct impact as facilitators of tax avoidance and evasion and a more profound deterrent effect on taxing authorities. Capital flight is often invoked as the main cause for the growing shift from direct to indirect taxation. It is also suggested as a reason for decreasing marginal taxation as well as reducing corporate taxation.

There are two sources of guesses and estimates of the extent of the phenomenon. The OECD study itself relies on two studies: the Gordon Report to the American Treasury which dealt with the nine-year period to 1979 in respect of American taxpayers, and the subsequent Tax Havens in the Caribbean Basin Report which confirmed and updated the Gordon Report. Statistically it is estimated that between 1968 and 1978 banking deposits in tax havens escalated from US$11 billion to US$385 billion. Clearly no withholding tax was paid on these deposits. Furthermore, by 1978 gross dividends, interest and other income payments to tax haven residents from sources in the United States constituted 42 per cent of such payments to non-resident recipients (OECD 1987, p.27). It is also noted that the closing of certain loopholes (F-type regulation) has increased the amount of income made liable to tax. In the United States Subpart F increased corporation tax by US$14 billion between 1978 and 1982 (OECD 1987, p.42). German statistics show that between its introduction in 1972 and 1979 a similar type of clause increased tax revenues substantially. More interestingly, the additional tax appears to have peaked in 1973 and then subsided rapidly. One of the possible explanations put forward by Germany is that 'The introduction of the law itself may have led to the dissolution of some intermediary companies' (OECD 1987, p.43).

3 Capital flight and market discipline

Hand in hand with the 'off-shorization' of the world's financial markets has emerged the damaging phenomenon of capital flight. Although like the havens themselves this is not strictly speaking 'new', the extent to which it has led to the disciplining of national governments is remarkable. Where in the past governments had a number of fiscal and monetary tools at their disposal to prevent the sudden outflow of capital and currency from their market, the revolution in communications means that today the rapid flow of 'hot money' can wreak havoc upon national economic policy and management overnight. The net result of this phenomenon is that a certain discipline has been imposed upon states by the market. Ideology and rash promises have been replaced by harsh realities. Today, any significant change in economic policy has to be conducted with one eye always firmly on the international money market. States which do not subject their monetary and financial policies to such orthodoxy are likely to experience a sudden and acute shortage of capital.

For example, the anti-imperialist and anti-American rhetoric of many Latin-American regimes in the 1980s contributed to a massive flight of capital into the tax havens. It has been estimated that as much as 40–50 per cent of Latin-American debt is residing in the havens (Naylor 1987). The change of heart and policies in recent years, both domestically and internationally, has been rewarded handsomely by massive inward investment. Again much of this appears to be of Latin-American origin (reported in the *Atlantic Outlook* 1992, No. 33). Very often, on closer examination, the so-called 'discipline of the market' turns out to have less to do with the celebrated interdependence of states, but in our opinion more with the proliferation of tax havens and off-shore markets that offer an instant alternative to costly national regimes. The tax havens were instrumental in imposing a disciplinary regime upon recalcitrant states.

4 Centre and periphery

Finally, the tax havens play a significant if largely unrecognized role in the relationship between the developing and the developed world, chanelling capital from the Third World into the advanced countries. As Peagam notes,

> today, the greatest need for a safe haven is probably felt by the more affluent citizens of developing countries. Having accumulated some liquid capital, their principal goal is to preserve and protect their savings, often from rampant inflation, corruption and government incompetence at home.
>
> (Peagam 1989, p.7)

Conservative estimates 'guess' that about 30 per cent of Third World debt has found its way into the tax havens. By 1981 five of the havens considered by the Caribbean Task Force Report (the Bahamas, Bermuda, Liberia, the Dutch Antilles and Panama) had approximately 14.3 per cent of the total estimated investment stock which had flowed from OECD to all developing countries, although the economies of these five havens accounted for less than 0.3 per cent of the total GNP of all developing countries (reported in OECD 1987, p.28). With current Third World debt standing at US$1.6 trillion, that would imply a net inflow of US$500 billion into the tax havens. However, where do the tax havens invest all this money? Basing his views on the Swiss experience, Fehrenbach explains:

> Swiss banks take money from every part of the unstable developed world – the 'poor nations' or 'lower half' – but they rarely squander it or speculate with it. They invest it prudently and cautiously in the rich Atlantic world.
>
> (Fehrenbach 1966, p.126)

This is arguably the most pitiful of all aspects of Third World plight. In the 1960s and 1970s this plight prompted the real prospect of Third World solidarity. Today, however, the phenomenon of the tax haven is testimony to the acceptance among some of that group that economic success is to be achieved whatever the costs. If success can only be achieved through the exploitation of a particular niche in the world economy these states care not what the consequences of their actions might be to Third World solidarity, or to the world economy at large. Such states effectively function as parasites in the international system.

9

Not in the game?

> There are a large number of states in the world that are for all intents and purposes going nowhere, and do not look like they will ever be going anywhere. It is not so much that they do not wish to pursue strategies of development but that they are incapable of doing so.
>
> (Jackson 1993, p.23)

There are several dozen nations, the majority of which lie in Sub-Saharan Africa, on the verge of national collapse (United Nations Development Programme 1991, 1992; World Development reports 1990, 1992). Some are being torn apart by ethnic tensions, while others are dependent for their survival on foreign aid (Jackson and Rosberg 1986). Across the Third World the human cost of this collapse has been staggering. The number of refugees since 1989 increasing by more than nine million (World Development Report 1990). Many of these 'failing' nations have few natural resources. But even countries like Zaire and Nigeria, which are in possession of substantial natural resources, suffer from the constant fluctuations in world commodity prices. This group of states can be classified in our terms as being out of the competitive game in the global political economy. They represent the last areas of the world to be 'conquered' by neo-liberalism – they are the 'new' Third World of the age of globalization.

This chapter examines the category of states that fail for one reason or another to mount any coherent strategy of competition in the global economy. We will argue that on the balance of the evidence, the character of their domestic political system, as expounded in the theory of 'neo-Patrimonialism' (Bayart 1993; Clapham 1985), offers the best explanation for this failure. This is, of course, not to say that the ultimate cause of the deleterious situation is not to be found, at least in part, in the relationship between these countries and the global environment. We find the theories of neo-imperialism and dependency at least partially convincing. However, as the world economy is moving into a new phase, new opportunities open up while others are closed more firmly than ever. In the new conditions of globalization, the main structural impediment that renders these countries wholly unable to participate is their political system. Therefore unless there is fundamental reform or revolutionary change the plight of these countries is likely to remain forlorn, reinforcing their peripheral nature in the global political economy.

Identifying the non-competitive states in the global political economy

How do we begin to define a category to which those states who fail (or appear to fail) to join the new global competitive game belong? Do such states share similar attributes? These questions are far more difficult than they may at first appear. Some of the major texts such as Jackson's *Quasi States* (1993) do not list exhaustively those states which fall into this classification, while others, such as dependency theorists, seem to confine all Third World countries to a single group described as the periphery – a group which in our characterization contains varied strategies of competition, from the developmental state, to flexible labour, and from parasitical behaviour to those which are entirely excluded from the competitive game.

Perhaps we can ask the question differently: what are the absolutely necessary conditions that place certain states in the global competitive game, and yet ostracize others? One of the principal factors is that broadly speaking, competitive states are able and willing to provide a favourable climate for international investment. Of the many factors that determine what exactly makes a favourable investment climate ultimately the issue comes down to the ease by which profits can be repatriated. This is the basic question that the entire financial risk industry seeks to answer (Sinclair 1994). International investment is after all about profit. No one would invest unless they could see a reasonable prospect of getting a return on their investment.

The term 'repatriation of profits' contains a number of separate conditions, all of which must be fulfilled:

1 Profits can be repatriated only if there are legal mechanisms for re-patriation, namely that business is permitted to repatriate profits. For example, most communist states place(d) severe restrictions on repatriation.
2 Security from 'nationalization', from looting, from bandits. Countries besieged by civil wars, banditry, etc. are unlikely to attract a great inflow of capital.

Once these two elementary conditions are fulfilled, then others must be applied as well:

3 Monetary stability, high inflation and convertibility difficulties are likely to impede repatriation of profits as well as planning of costs, etc.
4 Taxation/regulatory environment. High taxation or an extremely severe regulatory environment makes business unattractive.

Ultimately, all these conditions hinge on the *political stability* of a regime.

Without evidence of political stability, none can be remotely guaranteed. Thus political stability must be seen as the quid pro quo of investment.

Using such criteria, which states can we surmise as being structurally excluded from the global competitive game? It was widely considered that the former communist states of Eastern Europe and the Soviet Union were excluded from the capitalist competitive game because they were attempting to construct, in their own ideology, a socio-economic system that was an antithesis to modern capitalism. However, as writers such as Hobsbaum (1995), Halliday (1992) and Frank (1994b) have argued, the efforts in such states were directed more towards 'catching up' with the West. While this was partly achieved during the 1950s and early 1960s, such states only managed to avoid falling behind during the 1970s by accumulating foreign debt. During the 1970s, far from pursuing isolationism and economic autarky, several Eastern Europe countries, namely Hungary, Poland and Yugoslavia, went into severe debt in an attempt to modernize their economies and compete with their western counterparts in intermediate technologies: white goods, cars (Lada, Yugo (Zastava), Polski). Indeed, their economic strategies were not dissimilar to those of Spain, Portugal and Greece; they were competing for the same turf, so to speak. In particular they attempted to remain competitive by sucking in foreign technology and investment, attracted by monetary and political stability, which they paid for by exporting 'derivative manufactures' (Frank 1994b) back to the West. By the end of the 1980s the consequences of this policy had left a scale of debt which had reached approximately $350 billion. Frank (1994a, 1994b) maintains that this debt burden provided the singular most important cause of the 1989 revolutions.

Whether or not Frank is correct is debatable (see Denemark 1994; Hausner 1994; Nove 1994). The point, however, is that communist countries, or centrally planned economies can, at least in principle, participate in a global competitive environment. They possess a number of advantages over many of their 'capitalist' brethren, advantages that can be exploited. First and foremost, although it proved rather illusionary in the late 1980s, they appeared to possess stable political regimes. Ideology apart, this made countries like Poland or Hungary, as indeed China today, rather attractive to capital. They simply had to change their policies towards foreign direct investment. In fact their 'domestic' socio-economic conditions were deemed an advantage (for example, it was thought the government would ensure repayment). This, as we will see, is not at all the case with those countries that are 'structurally' excluded from the competitive game. This is the reason why centrally planned economies are often compared with the authoritarian regimes of certain developmental states. Second, due to their egalitarian ideology, these states have developed an advanced national education system, thus generating the mass of skilled labour appropriate for modern technology. Many East–West tie-ups were intended specifically to exploit a cheaper pool of engineers and technicians.

The second group of states which appear to be most vividly not in the game are those states ravaged by civil wars. In such states legitimate political authority invariably collapses, and with it comes a descent into monetary instability and spiralling inflation. Clearly such circumstances provide a huge disadvantage to most business and investment. However, such conditions allow some businesses to thrive. In particular the illicit trade in drugs and both the licit and illicit trade in arms. The Lebanese lira appreciated *vis-à-vis* the dollar during the Lebanese civil war! For such 'merchants of death' their economic activity thrives in the conditions of anarchy unleashed by civil war.[1]

Such activities, however, are not solely the preserve of narcotic and armament entrepreneurs or war/druglords. Sampson (1977), for example, observes that the small arms traders account for a tiny proportion of the world's arms trade. The majority of such trade is conducted by western governments as legitimate and lucrative export industries. Similarly, Naylor (1987) has revealed the extent to which narco-politics permeates states as diverse as Bolivia, Columbia, Peru, Burma, Thailand, Afghanistan, Jamaica and others. These countries are certainly on the margins of the global competitive game, but they possess the infrastructure and the knowledge base to exploit certain unpleasant niches in the global economic market. Furthermore, the restoration of a legitimate and stable political system is often accompanied by a rapid return to the global competitive game in legitimate industries. Civil wars as such do not define those states that are excluded from the global competitive game.

So if neither of these groups of states can be classified as being non-competitive, which states can? The United Nations General Assembly has attempted to classify such states as least developed countries or LLDCs. LLDCs are considered to suffer from one or more of a number of constraints: a GNP per capita of $300 or less; land-locked; remote insularity; desertification and exposure to natural disasters. The current list of such states is shown in Table 9.1.

Table 9.1 States currently defined as LLDCs

Afghanistan	Bangladesh	Bhutan	Botswana
Burkina Faso	Burundi	Cape Verdi	CAR[1]
Chad	Comoros	Djibouti	Equatic Guinea
Ethiopia	Gambia	Guinea-Bissau	Haiti
Laos	Lesotho	Malawi	Maldives
Mali	Mauritania	Mozambique	Myanmar
Nepal	Niger	Rwanda	Samoa
Sao Tome and Principe	Sierra Leone	Somalia	Sudan
Tanzania	Togo	Uganda	Vanuatu
Yemen			

Note: [1] Central African Republic

This categorization, however, simply tells us that these states are extremely poor. Looking at the statistics, there is no particular indication why, for instance, they would not be able to join the band of states adopting a strategy of downward mobility by exploiting their very evident cheap labour forces. Indeed, it might be argued that they have an advantage over the others in that they can offer even cheaper labour than many of those states currently championing downward mobility as a strategy. Such constraints alone therefore are not the root cause of these states' lack of competitiveness. Most of them are not simply poor, they are also structurally inhibited from joining the global competitive game. How is this so? We define, therefore, those states that are currently excluded from the global competitive game as states whose *domestic socio-economic situation, rather than their given policies, structurally discourages meaningful long-term investment, domestic and foreign, in their economies.*

Non-competitive states in academic discourse

Dependency theories

Dependency theory emerged in the 1960s from attempts to rethink the Economic Commission for Latin America (ECLA) analysis in the light of the failure of its import substitution industrialization (ISI) strategy for development in Latin America. It also offered an alternative to the ahistorical and apolitical assumptions of modernization approaches. Dependency theory's central argument was that the poor conditions in the Third World or the lack of development and industrialization do not merely place them in the category of undeveloped, i.e. those who are potentially at least about to develop and join their advanced brethren, but underdeveloped, i.e. structurally inhibited from development by their link with the global capitalist system.

For dependency theorists the evidence from a number of case studies, mainly by Latin-American economists, appears to suggest that the cause of the Third World's poverty lay in its relations with the 'core' capitalist world. These relations were therefore the source of the problem, not the solution! Instead of creating the conditions for capital accumulation and growth, capitalist penetration of the peripheral countries had created economies which were dependent and incapable of self-sustained autonomous development. Frank (1967) employed the metaphor of a chain of exploitative relations to explicate the structural dynamics of how the process of underdevelopment occurs. On a world scale this was expressed as a relationship between the 'core' First World and the peripheral Third World. This relationship also characterized the relationship in the peripheral country between the relatively advanced capital city and the backward surrounding countryside. Capitalist development does occur in the peripheral state but it is in economic enclaves controlled by a foreign or comprador bourgeoisie. Profits from this enclave are not reinvested in the native economy but repatriated and/or exported. Frank and others thus concluded that the integration of peripheral countries into the world economy, far from encouraging and promoting their development, had actually led to their progressive underdevelopment.

Fanon (1965, 1967), Rodney (1972) and others went on to identify the ruling classes in the periphery as the instruments of the capitalists of the core. It was in the interest of such groups to maintain the system of underdevelopment because they alone were the sole indigenous beneficiaries of the system, usually controlling the economic activity in the 'developed' enclave. Maintaining such a system, however, meant the continuance of widespread poverty and thus political systems in the periphery were for the most part characterized as repressive and militaristic. Samir Amin (1974) demonstrated that the economic hegemony of the comprador bourgeoisie depended on their political hegemony, as in most post-colonial societies access to the state ensured access to the levers of the economy. Such political dependence in the peripheral country ensured that those without access to the state were deprived of the political means to share in the economic profits of dependent capitalism. Class struggle was therefore not played out at a national level but internationally, as the primary social cleavage in the periphery was between the class that opposed both the core and dependent capitalists, and the classes that the system exploited.

Dependency theory was modified and refined in the 1970s and 1980s with reference to a new wave of case studies. These diverged sharply from the earlier 'impossibility of development'. The notion of 'dependent development' stressed that structural dependence on foreign capital and external market does necessarily constrain and distort the peripheral economy, but that it is not *incompatible* with development in the more industrialized countries of the periphery: Brazil, Chile, South Korea, etc. Thus development is possible but it is dependent on foreign bank loans, MNC domination, etc.

The question is whether dependency theory is appropriate to understand that particular specific group which is now excluded from the competitive game. The answer is probably no. And the reasons, on the face of it, are that dependency in fact never provided any sufficient theoretical foundations to differentiate among states within the 'Third World'. It is precisely the theoretical level of analysis, the notion of structural peripheralization at the core of the theory, which militates against such differentiation! To Lipietz the problem lies deeper, in that dependency theory took the central aspect of the international division of labour that predominated in the period between the 1920s and the 1970s, and universalized it into a law of capitalist development. Capitalism, however, failed, as always, to conform to some pre-ordained systems outcome and indeed since the 1970s we have seen widespread industrialization in a great number of 'Third World' countries.[2]

Quasi states

While dependency and world systems theory sought explanation for the 'non-competitiveness' of African states in the structural relations of global capitalism, the broadly realist work of Robert Jackson and Carl Roseberg (1986; Jackson 1993) argued that such states represent an anomaly of the post-war definition of international law and sovereignty. Indeed, as a result of this anomaly such states remain like a balloon floating in the air with no connections to the ground.

The one thing that all these states have in common is that their claim to be formal states rests upon external and not internal legitimacy – with the exceptions of Ethiopia, Burundi, Liberia and Rwanda. Their borders, their national culture/character is one which in comparison with European states is false. Jackson defines this as negative sovereignty. Negative sovereignty, he asserts, derives from legalism – Grotius, Mill, Berlin, etc. – and is characterized by freedom from outside interference. Positive sovereignty, as derived from Rousseau, Kant and Marx, is a substantive condition, one that rests on the ability of the state to provide political goods for its citizens. It exists as a social contract between government and the people. According to Jackson, the nineteenth century was characterized by the ideas of positive liberty and sovereignty. It was the duty of the colonial powers to construct, educate and build up its colonies to the point where they would be able to govern themselves – the notion of the 'white man's burden'. Outside intervention was deemed acceptable to improve the fate of minorities and of unacceptable governments (cf. the debates in the British Liberal Party to support the freedom of the Balkan peoples from Ottoman rule). Colonialism was not just about extraction but, in its own terms, civilizing.

In 1945 the concept of sovereign equality of states and the principle of national self-determination were enshrined in the United Nations Charter. Almost without a fight the former European colonial powers set free their colonies which became states. Yet they did not possess the attributes we commonly associate with modern states. Many of these countries had artificial boundaries which divided ethnic/tribal peoples and there was little if any sense of a national identity. They had inadequate infrastructures, poor communications and an entrenched élite. In such circumstances many of these states were illegitimate domestically, but because they had sovereign equality before the international community they had external legitimacy. Internal order had to be enforced, national identities created. Indeed, to expect such states to consolidate overnight what it had taken Europe and the US centuries to achieve was optimistic at the least. The state in Africa has generally proved unable to articulate, implement and enforce commands, laws, policies and regulations over the people within its national territory. Its existence has not met with an empirical definition based on ability to rule but rather a juridical recognition in international law.

The maintenance of the state, and thus its ability to achieve its goals insofar as it can do at all, depend on its access to the outside world, both for military and for economic help. The more artificial and threatened it is, the greater the need for external support. This support comes both from developed states and fellow Third World states, all of which have a general interest in maintaining the global state structure. In the case of Africa, the Organisation of African Unity (OAU) has found it necessary to articulate explicit rules of respect for the territorial integrity of its members and for non-intervention in internal affairs. Such rules in turn can only be policed by the developed world, either through arms supplies to indigenous governments or, in extreme cases, through direct military intervention – for example, the UN control of Cambodia prior to the recent elections, French interventions in West Africa, and the Senegalese in the Gambia. Intervention, which can be easily condemned as a derogation of the sovereign independence of Third World states, may ultimately be the means through which the state system can be maintained in the face of the weakness of such states themselves (Clapham 1985, p.185).

If such states are not internally constituted, in other words, if they have not developed from the indigenous African society but are implants without internal legitimacy, how have such regimes maintained their existence? Africa is not the only continent in the world where such 'Quasi states' exist or have existed. South Korea and Taiwan in Asia and East Germany in Europe, for example, faced similar problems of being artificial creations – though unlike in Africa these were the product of the cold war. Here domestic legitimacy has been based upon economic legitimacy; in other words, upon the ability of the state in question to deliver rapid, successful development and in particular a development which exceeded that of its political rival: namely North Korea, the PRC and West Germany respectively. In the case of East Germany the ending of the cold war and the stagnation of the economy throughout the 1980s contributed towards the dissolution of the state.

However, in Africa legitimacy based upon economic development has been largely illusive. Given this fact the question still remains as to how such states have maintained their existence. The problem with Jackson, and indeed the various IR/IPE literature is that their argument more or less stops there. They merely point to the deleterious role that foreign forces play in shaping the domestic conditions. They have little to say about the nature of these conditions; in particular there is a failure to recognize that these African states, and more generally the non-competitive states, represent a genuine autochthonous political system.

Neo-patrimonialism and the swollen African state

We now return to the question, why have such unstable states maintained their existence? We will argue that these states fail to participate in the global competitive game simply because the dominant constellation of power within them is operating to survive – to maintain the existing regime. Governance in such states, argue Jackson and Roseberg, 'is more a matter of seamanship and less one of navigation – that is staying afloat rather than going somewhere' (Jackson and Roseberg 1982, p.18). This has given rise to a particular African state phenomenon that has been referred to as neo-patrimonalism (Clapham 1985, 1986).

In the struggle for decolonization a 'historic bloc' emerged which consisted of the existing native colonial élites, the educated intellectual groups which were necessary to initially 'mobilize' the subordinate classes in the anti-colonial struggle, and established regional élites both in the country and the cities. These disparate groups united to capture the bureaucratic mechanisms of the state. However, once ensconced at its centre they were co-opted into a ruling 'party' by the possession of the means of accumulation (Clapham 1985, 1986; Bayart 1993; Chabal 1994).

Decolonization in Africa has therefore largely been a struggle for the spoils of political power. In Africa's early democratic regimes party politics, lacking recognizable social classes with which to divide along, splintered into what western observers wrongly labelled tribal lines. This 'shadow theatre of ethnicity', as Bayart refers to it, concealed a more divisive development. Rather than tribal politics, clientelism was developing with the 'race for the spoils of power or of political office . . . [becoming] the motive force of these supposedly parliamentary systems' (Davidson 1992, p.207). Once new governments inherited the apparatus of the post-colonial state democracy increasingly gave way to authoritarianism. With the spoils of power secured, few regimes were willing to give it up. Thus '[b]ureaucracy ruled together with clientelism, and gradually became much the same thing' (ibid., p.209). It is this phenomenon that is referred to as 'neo-patrimonialism' and to which this chapter will now turn.

Politics in Africa has thus taken two broad forms. The first has been an attempt by social forces outside the historic bloc to penetrate the state apparatus and the second has adopted the establishment of a counter-hegemonic project to challenge the state. So long as the post-colonial African state could 'swell' to accommodate those forces outside it the former scenario was adopted. Hence state employment became a means to an end with those seeking state employment regarding it as their means to further political and economic hegemony. Such notions – what Bayart has called 'The Politics of the Belly' – suggest that corruption in Africa should be observed not as a sign of the failure of African states to approximate to the rational–legalism of the West but as a mechanism by which the legitimacy of the state is disseminated and wealth re-distributed.

Thus the pursuit of hegemony and the accumulation of wealth are inseparable in sub-Saharan Africa. To achieve power (and maintain it) groups must be co-opted by the creation of networks of patronage through which accumulated wealth is distributed. The saliency of corruption and clientelism is in part due to the carry-over of cultural values inherited from a pre-colonial patrimonial past which is only now being acknowledged as having a contemporary validity more systematic than previously accepted (Bayart 1993, p.107). 'The apparatus of the state is in itself a slice of the national cake . . . so that any actor worthy of the name tries to get a good mouthful' (p.90). For instance, the patrimonial act of gift-giving is easily transformed in the modern state into bribery and extortion. This is equally discernible in the deeply entrenched kinship loyalty and support. Clapham refers to this principle as extortion from below, a process where the extended family, caste or clan exerts moral pressure on a member who has achieved a degree of social elevation to use their position to the mutual benefit of the collectivity.

Because it is largely an external structure which has been appropriated by the ethnic/tribal groups that constitute the territory, it has been argued that the state may be swollen but it is 'soft'. The initial support given to the anti-colonial nationalists was by its nature not sustainable. Thus to function and retain legitimacy the ruling élites attempted to expand their support through the extension of clientelistic networks. Such a state 'functions as a rhizome of personal networks and assures the centralization of power through the agencies of family, alliance and friendship in the manner of ancient kingdoms' (Bayart 1993, pp.261–2). Support for the regime by the client is exchanged for security and reward by the patron. This security and reward vary from physical/legal protection to land, administrative posts, development assistance and so on. Because a neo-patrimonial state is one in which the main social cleavages exist between those within the state and those outside the state such clientelistic ties flourish. Control of the state ultimately carries with it the power to provide. Where the government is under no obligation to dispense office according to a public or universal criteria it does so at its own disposal to encourage political support (Clapham 1985, p.56). The only realistic alternative to clientelism in such states is repression. Clientelism is itself a form of corruption because it propagates the idea of government as the source of the satisfaction of private need. It is orientated towards the consumption of government services without supplying the means for their production. Ultimately, therefore, clientelism leads to a form of government by hand-out, and clientelism will remain effective *as long as* the state can deliver enough spoils for its clients. As one Cameroonian proverb states, 'goats eat where they are tethered'.

Consequently as the existing government bureaucracy became exhausted, state intervention in the economy continued with a wave of nationalizations and the creation of parastatals. Such policies were carried out with an express purpose, namely to allow the regime to co-opt a whole new group of 'claimants' to the apparatus of power into the existing regime. Thus neo-patrimonial linkages continued to spread inexorably, and as long as the state remained the only viable means of pursuing economic and political elevation in society, its legitimacy could be maintained.

Under such circumstances investment decisions become interwoven into a complex structure of kinship, favour and loyalty. The fact that such patron–client networks pervade the state so deeply leads to allocations very different from that produced by need; for example, a road will not be built to serve a place where it is most needed but to the village of a client. In addition, vast amounts of capital invested in such states have been appropriated by its statesmen and now reside in private bank accounts in the world's tax havens (see Chapter 8). For example, the private transfer of capital out of the Ivory Coast reached 7 per cent of GDP by 1980 (Bayart 1993, p.101).

Throughout the 1960s and 1970s therefore the African state grew excessively as the post-colonial African state was allowed to swell to meet the demands for state employment. For example, between 1960 and 1987 the bureaucracy of the Congo grew from 3000 to 73,000 employees (Davidson 1992, p.237) while in Nigeria federal expenditures rose from 12 per cent to 36 per cent of GDP between 1966 and 1977 and on the Ivory Coast from 32.6 per cent of GDP in 1976 to 42.7 per cent by 1978! (Bayart 1993). As the size of the bureaucracy increased, so too did the appropriations that legitimized its own survival. Thus while the military and urban areas necessary to the regime were maintained, the wider social and physical infrastructure of many states was allowed to fall into decay. The most immediate result of this was increasing impoverishment of rural areas. However, from the 1970s onwards it also had a less visible but more fundamental effect.

During the 1970s many farmers began to increasingly withdraw from the 'national' economy that both oppressed and demanded tribute from them. Instead, increasing numbers turned to self-sufficiency or to openings on the black market. Smuggling has become 'an almost universal response to the antirural discriminations of the official and city-based economy' (Davidson 1992, p.213). The extent of the scale and growth of these activities is difficult to measure, given the nature of the 'second economy' (MacGaffey 1991). However, a number of examples will demonstrate this phenomenon.

In 1988 in the state of Kano in Nigeria only 6 per cent of an estimated bumper wheat crop of 285,000 tons reached the state's mills, thus suggesting that 94 per cent went through illegal channels (Davidson 1992). In Tanzania some 30 per cent of economic activity is not accounted for in the official statistics; illegal activities in the Central African Republic are estimated to be worth approximately 75 per cent of the national budget while in Uganda the black market is estimated to be worth over 75 per cent of gross domestic product. Of all the states where studies of the such activities has been conducted nowhere is the phenomenon more rife than in Zaire. Adding black market activities to the GDP of Zaire triples the size of the economy! President Mobutu himself has remarked upon this:

> Everything is for sale, everything is bought in our country. And in this traffic holding any slice of public power constitutes a veritable exchange instrument, convertible into illicit acquisition of money or other goods, or the evasion of all sorts of obligations.
>
> (MacGaffey 1991, p.32, quoted in Callaghy 1984, p.190)

What began as a rural trend in the 1970s spread during the 1980s to become a general phenomenon. Today smugglers include plantation labour, teachers, pupils and housewives as well as the rich and powerful (MacGaffey 1991, pp.154–5). Goods and services often unavailable in the real economy are readily available in the black market, from gold (p.51), diamonds and ivory (p.89) to maize, flour (p.84) and even BMWs and other luxury cars (pp.85–6). On the more sinister side weapons and drug smuggling is also rife, often encouraged by military forces whose rank and file are increasingly finding their pay is overdue and inconsistent. Ironically the more elements within society 'drop out' of the formal economy, the more the resources of the state diminish, thereby encouraging appropriations to increase on the one hand and for yet more illegal activities to occur on the other.

Neo-patrimonialism refers therefore to a form of government for which regime survival is the primary goal and economic development or international competitiveness must therefore take a back-seat. As long as the established élite is able to maintain its hold on the levers of power and with it the means of wealth accumulation, the consequences for society as a whole and for the economic foundations of the state are disregarded. In Zaire, for example, the country's infrastructure has been allowed to rot. From 88,000 miles of usable road in 1960, Zaire today has less than 12,000 miles (Davidson 1992, p.257). As Davidson comments,

> So long as mining wealth could be sold for imported food to feed the Mobutist state – the bureaucracy and its clients, the towns, a few essential services, an army for internal use and a copious force of police – there could be no profit in helping peasants. The forests and savannah outside the state might fester in their brooding solitudes. . . . But who should care? The aircraft of the state and its beneficiaries flew high above the forests and savannah; passengers would not even notice that the roads below were drowned in all engulfing vegetation.
>
> (Davidson 1992, p.258)

Neo-patrimonialism as an inherently non-competitive political system

Neo-patrimonialism can be defined as a form of authority in which relationships of a broadly patrimonial type pervade an administrative system formally constructed on rational–legal lines. The concept derives from Weber who characterized three distinct forms of political authority: rational–legality, charisma and patrimony. For Weber the organization and the legitimacy of the modern (European) state rested on rational legal authority; that is, an authority in which power is exercised in accordance with a legally defined structure directed towards a publicly acknowledged goal.

The element of 'authority' is provided by goals that are themselves widely accepted, and structures that are likewise accepted as the means of achieving these goals. What is then necessary to make the structures work is a division between an individual's public role and a private role encapsulated in 'office'. When in office the individual acts simply as an official exercising the powers the office gives him, treating others in an impersonal manner. When outside the office the individual is a private citizen with personal ambitions but he is unable to use his public position to achieve them. Thus the state is divorced from the interests of its constituents. Obviously this description is an ideal type and one that Weber accepted was nowhere fully achieved. However, the rational–legal idea remains fundamentally important, because one of the means of ensuring that the enormous powers of the modern state are used both efficiently and legitimately, without the fear of their abuse, is through the acceptance of this division of roles.

It is clear from the post-colonial experience of successive regimes that the vast majority of states in Africa have failed to even approximate to a rational–legal idea. The removal of the legal framework of the colonially designed constitutions and their constant replacement and modification by ones that best suit the needs of the present incumbents bear testimony to this failure. It is also manifested by the lack of division between the public and private role of the state official who uses his public office to create clientelistic networks and extract 'tribute'.

Many scholars, especially of African politics, turned their attention to Weber's second ideal type of authority, namely charismatic authority. As Clapham defines it, 'Charisma was a form of authority inherent in an individual, who through his own virtue and example crystallised a new concept of authority' (1985, p.46). For Weber, the structures and processes of charismatic leadership become institutionalized and thus the accepted norm over time. The concept was therefore ideally suited to the leaders of the nationalist independence movements who, following their acquisition of the state, were at the height of their power and influence. However, successive overthrows of classic charismatic leaders such as Nkrumah in Ghana and Amin in Uganda suggested that such scholars had over-enthusiastically applied the idea. Charisma proved too fragile a base upon which any general analysis of political authority in the Third World could be based.

Weber's concept of patrimonialism offered the closest approximation of the exercise of authority in such states. The distinct feature of patrimony is that authority is imputed to a person and not an office, but in contrast to charismatic authority that person is rooted in a broader social and political order. Quoting Weber,

> The patrimonial office lacks the separation of the 'private' and 'official' sphere'. For the political administration, too, is treated as a purely personal affair of the ruler, and political power is considered part of his personal property. . . . The office and the exercise of public authority serve the ruler and the official on which the office was bestowed, they do not serve impersonal purposes.

(Weber 1968, pp.1028–9)

This is similar to feudalism, with those lower down the political order not being subordinates but vassals or retainers whose position depends upon the person to whom they owe their allegiance. Power is ill-defined and the whole system is held together by kinship or loyalty.

Neo-patrimonialism differs from patrimonialism in that it crafts a broadly patrimonial system of relationships on to a political and administrative system. Although traces of feudalism survive in the Third World, Third World states are clearly not feudal. Nevertheless, it is argued that officials exercise powers that are formally defined, but they carry out those powers as a form of private property, not as a public service. Hence the rational–legal division of office and individual is inverted. In addition, relationships with others fall into the patrimonial pattern of lord and vassal rather than the rational–legal one of superior and subordinate. In such a system the superior will consider that they have the right to intervene personally in any matter within their jurisdiction and that any subordinate who makes a decision without first referring it upwards to his superior will be regarded as snubbing the authority of that superior (Clapham 1985, p.49).

Like rational–legal authority, neo-patrimonialism is an ideal type but it is the most salient form of authority that can be identified in the Third World. This is for a number of reasons. First, neo-patrimonialism characterizes both tribal societies in which kinship loyalty is the primary social value and plural societies in which status and identity are determined by ethnicity or caste. Second, the artificiality of most Third World states, i.e. the state did not emerge organically from society but was crafted by external powers, and the incorporation of these states into the global economy have eroded a sense of common patrimonial values. In these circumstances neo-patrimonialism readily adapts itself, replacing the reciprocal obligations of patrimonialism with the neo-patrimonial considerations of the exchange of favours for personal benefit.

In all states, power is to varying degrees corruptly exercised, principally because of the artificiality of the private/public division when applied to human behaviour in office. However, in the neo-patrimonial state, because the distinction between these roles itself is scarcely acknowledged, public office becomes accepted as a means to personal enrichment and social elevation. Indeed, political office and its spoils are the very definition of success. Invariably corruption throughout the Third World is habitual. In extreme cases it is so endemic that the pursuit of power is no more than the pursuit of wealth with governments characterized as kleptocratic. Bayart estimates that in Zaire between 17 and 22 per cent of the national budget is for the personal use of President Mobutu. In his words, 'The apparatus of the state is in itself a slice of the national cake . . . so that any actor worthy of the name tries to get a good mouthful' (p.90).

It is important not to allow such features to disguise the role played in all this by the structural characteristics of the state in the Third World. Rational–legal ideas cannot be expected to be adhered to among public officials if the mechanisms of accountability are so weak. On the one

hand these states lack strong independent legal structures to curb corruption and on the other hand they are 'unchecked by countervailing
powers such as those produced by capitalism and private property'
(Clapham 1985, p.52). This is not to say that there is no business
class but rather that, as Bayart explains, '[t]he divisions between the two
activities, economic and politico-administrative do exist . . . [but] they
are expressed as antagonisms between roles rather than status groups or
classes' (1993, p.94). Thus the responsibility for maintaining a degree
of accountability lies in the behaviour and example of state officials.
Since corruption pervades every level of the state hierarchy, officials
are unchecked by their superiors. Thus even petty employees of the
state, such as traffic cops, use their position as a means to accumulate
wealth. Indeed perhaps the principal form of accumulation in these non-
competitive states has been the 'straddling' between office and private
investment such that positions of power become positions of predation.
Virtually every official decision carries with it some opportunity for
personal enrichment, from a simple signature to verify a document to
fiscal policy. It is no accident that the elevation of one individual to
a post of responsibility will often be followed by the emergence
of businessmen from that same individual's family/caste/tribe as a result
of business contracts awarded to them.

Non-competitive states and developments in the international political economy

The end of the cold war marks an epoch in world history particularly
for the Third World. Most evidently it has removed both the source of
political and financial support for many states while eliminating an alternative model of development. In addition, the removal of previously
established forms of control and hegemony has also released communal
tensions which are being fuelled by arms supplies accumulated both
during the cold war era and by arms traders deprived of the East–West
justifications for their industry (Halliday 1994, p.5).

The non-competitive state remains fragile and incomplete. The loss
of the external justification for state socialist development and the
removal of an alternative to the IMF and World Bank for financial
support is ensuring that the neo-liberal orthodoxy that has swept across
almost every corner of the developed world is now penetrating into the
heart of the Third World. The consequences that the conditionality of
monetarist economic policy has for non-competitive states challenge
the very foundations of neo-patrimonialism. Already this is altering the
social, economic and political environment of these states.

Perhaps the most fundamental of the IMF's conditions is a reduction
in the size of public expenditure. However, by beginning to 'roll back the
frontiers' of the swollen bureaucratic state in response to IMF loan
conditions the basis of this political legitimacy is being challenged in a
number of ways. First, as the state begins to disengage from certain

sectors of economic life, clients on the fringe of the patron–client network are beginning to fall away. Under such financial austerity it has
become increasingly difficult for the state to accommodate new groups
and counter-hegemonic élites are being 'rediscovered' with their own
political agendas and projects. Such alternative projects are identified
both with the explosion in black market activities across the continent
(already discussed) as well as with the revival of traditional religions,
trade unions and democratic pressures (Chabal 1986, 1994, pp.224–5;
Doornbos 1990, p.195).

Second, as civil servants' salaries diminish in real terms the extraction
of 'tribute' from their various clients increases to the point where today
the overwhelming bulk of a state official's income comes from such
prebends. As the state withdraws from various aspects of the public realm,
those outside the clientelistic networks become more impoverished; thus,
following the example of their leaders, they too have chosen to 'eat where
they graze' by establishing illegal trade in all sorts of commodities.

The erosion of the resources of the neo-patrimonial state has led to
increasing numbers of individuals and groups coalescing to form
counter-hegemonic élites. In most cases such groups merely aim to
capture the state and install their own patrimonial kinship networks.
The successive history of *coups* and counter-*coups* and the relative lack
of revolutionary upheaval in post-colonial Africa has been testimony
to this fact. However, as the ability of the state to provide its patrimonial function has dwindled with the onset of the debt crisis and
IMF 'conditionality', more state clients and counter-élites have turned
to an alternative source of economic elevation, namely the informal
economy or black market (MacGaffey 1991), which in turn has led
increasing numbers to attempt to disengage from the state, thus
challenging the existing political authorities (Davidson 1992, p.261).
This consists of

> all who may have become powerless or disenfranchised: not just villagers,
> fishermen, nomads, village councillors, or slum dwellers, but also profes-
> sionals, politicians, priests and mullahs, intellectuals, military officers and
> all others who are, or feel they are without access to the state . . . [this] is
> a constantly changing group of individuals whose only common ground
> is their being outside the State.
>
> (Chabal 1986, p.15)

The seizure of the colonial state by the nationalist counter-élite was a
one-off affair. As the new élites became embedded in the state structure
they became increasingly determined to maintain their hold on the levers
of power while precluding the development of a counter-hegemonic élite
that would challenge this position. As Bayart observes, 'Indigenous
dominant groups . . . never had at their disposal so many resources,
political, economic and military, with which to enforce their domination'
(1993, pp.110–11). Thus where this remained difficult, due to the post-
colonial state resting upon ethnic/cultural legitimacy, opposing ethnic
groups were viciously treated and repressed, for example, in Burundi in

1965 and 1972 when the Tutsi governments put down Hutu unrest by wholesale slaughter.

Conclusion

The real danger posed by such trends is that the neo-patrimonial state is in the process of disintegration either from a descent into increasing violence between rival kinship factions as in Somalia, or from a withering away of the state as the black market and civil society become increasingly autonomous. Indeed, one official recognition of the latter is the increasing quantities of aid from the West which are going direct to non-governmental organizations. Today about 10 per cent of development aid, approximately $8 billion, is distributed through NGOs, with the United States disbursing nearly a quarter of its aid this way. Such NGOs range from the globally famous such as Oxfam, Medicine Sans Frontiers and CARE to local indigenous groups (Chabal 1986; Doornbos 1990). While aid distributed in such a manner has proved to be less susceptible to appropriation by state officials, it is clearly encouraging the autonomy of those groups that have disengaged from the state.

Considering both developments it is difficult to see how those states that are today 'not in the game' can hope to find a niche for themselves in the global market in the near future. In this chapter we have argued that the specific nature of the neo-patrimonial state has ensured that the issue of international competitiveness has been peripheral for the vast majority of those states which we have classified as 'not in the game'. For the future, if the trends which are clearly evident across the African Continent today continue, the situation that such states face is likely to worsen. The inexorable drift of neo-liberal ideas to every corner of the globe will only accelerate such trends. Without the reform or replacement of the neo-patrimonial state, and greater constructive assistance from the West, the only 'game' that these states are likely to be influential players in is the illegal trade in commodities of all descriptions, and in particular of armaments and drugs.

Notes

1 See Sampson 1977; *Far Eastern Economic Review*, 28 June 1990, 28 March 1991, 20 February 1992, 5 November 1992, 3 June 1993. References refer to a number of articles in each issue dealing with drugs traffic and the impact of regional warlords in the Golden Triangle area of Burma, Laos and Thailand.

2 'It may be the case that relations with the outside world established long ago by certain agents (trading companies, military expeditions, etc.) proved not only acceptable but even useful to certain dominant groups, and that they became decisively important to the regime of accumulation insofar as the national social formation can no longer function without them because they resolve one or more of the contradictions inherent in its mode of reproduction' (Lipietz 1987, p.19).

Conclusion:
diversity and globalization

This study offers a number of specific conclusions which were detailed in the substantive chapters, and a few more general observations to which this short conclusion is devoted. First and foremost, it demonstrates the weaknesses of the two current contending positions on globalization in international relations. We have defined the state broadly as a mode of social organization. Basing ourselves on such criteria, we have demonstrated that there is little evidence that the state is about to disappear or wither away under the pressure of globalization. On the contrary, states are reacting vigrously and actively: while some of their functions, especially those associated with Fordism or Keynesianism are indeed threatened, the state, and more broadly, the system of states, is not. Indeed, this study demonstrates the degree by which the state remains an active participant in the new global political economy. None the less, this should not be interpreted as a sign that traditionalists in international relations have got it right. They have not. This book describes a plethora of profound and broad-ranging changes that go to the very heart of the 'system of states'. To argue that globalization is a hype and has so far had little or no impact on the state system appears to us grossly inaccurate.

We do not sense therefore that we are witnessing the demise of the state, nor do we feel that globalization is a passing or transitory phase. As opposed to some early predictions of the homogenizing impact of market forces, and the concomitant decline of the state and society, we have stressed instead the complex and multifaceted effect of growing competition and globalization. Instead of the rise of market forces and globalization generating a unified outcome, we are impressed by the sheer diversity of outcomes. The infrastructure of globalization, in the form of the 'competition state' and competitive strategies, has not evolved as a coordinated response to the changing global environment. It has evolved incrementally and partially, as a result of localized responses, largely determined by local conditions, specific socio-economic compromises, sectoral interests and so forth. The sum total of these incremental changes, pursued cither reactively or actively, each aimed either at forms of adjustment or survival, is fundamentally altering the entire political geography of accumulation.

As we argued in Chapter 1, this notion of adaptation and evolution is resonant with the ideas of neo-institutionalists and neo-structuralists. The modern state and, indeed, the modern state-system are not a static, unchanging entity. The effects of the new technologies of production and finance have had a significant impact upon states and social forces within such states. These impacts have generated a diversity of responses, from the broad societal compromise between labour and capital that distinguishes the shielders, to the attempt to harness and manage the productive forces of multinational enterprises that characterize the downwardly mobile states. Subsequently these responses themselves drive further forward the processes of globalization.

The principal conclusion that we draw in this book is that rather than negate the processes of globalization, or evaporate as a result of them, the system of states has accommodated itself and provides the institutional infrastructure upon which the globalization of the markets can proceed. In summing up, we provide a few examples of the relationship between institutionalization and globalization, examples that can surely be multiplied and repeated in other spheres of activities associated with globalization.

Perhaps one of the most visible forms of such structural change in recent years has been the deepening of the European Union and the formation of the North American Free Trade Area. Whether the drift towards regionalism is explained economically, strategically or in terms of parochial business, these institutions may be viewed in a broader context as being a functional necessity for modern capitalist accumulation. As we argued in Chapter 3, bloc formation involves creating and expanding networks of like-minded bureaucrats, politicians and corporate leaders into both the regional institutions and national governments. Bloc formation has been viewed (Sklar 1980, Overbeek and Van der Pijl 1993, Wilkinson 1993) as a step towards cementing transnational class interests, or conversely as the critical stage in the institutionalization of neo-liberalism and a commitment to global 'free trade', replacing the more limited achievements of GATT (Bhagwati 1993).

Thus the shift to regionalism or continental economic blocs represents tentative and incremental political responses to economic realities. The creation of specific institutions in order to manage and promote the expansion of the social, economic and political values of the actors within these regions represents the creation of an infrastructure. It is viewed as an instrument of social change, institutionalizing neo-liberal economic (i.e. pro-business) ideology. Mexico's and Canada's decisions to join in a 'bloc' with the US represent precisely such an intention. In this view regionalism is actually an instrument of *domestic restructuration* in a neoclassical framework. The institutional aspect of bloc formation in this sense serves to 'anchor in' the market-based rationale of the embedded liberal project.

Seen in this light it is difficult to picture how this trend could be halted or indeed reversed. While clearly support for regionalism has waned in Europe in recent years, giving rise to interest groups opposed to integration (such as the Eurosceptic wing of the British Conservative

Party, Phillipe de Villiers' and Jerry Goldsmith's *L'Autre Europe* in France and the Anti-European party in Denmark), the sheer weight of the institutional framework mitigates against a radical change in the EU structure. Similar trends can be observed in the United States, with the conversion of the Democrats to the NAFTA project during the 1992 presidential election campaign.

A similar infrastructural development can be observed with regard to the evolution of the global financial markets. The common depiction of this market is that of the sum total of global financial flows. Subsequently many conclude that a combined agreement among the major capitalist states could halt the globalization of finance and re-regulate these markets. (Whether the states want to or not is a separate question.) This depiction, however, ignores the entire 'infrastructure' which has developed in support of the global financial market. Such infrastructure is evident in the rise of global cities like London, New York and Tokyo, supported by an intricate web of financial legislation (the various acts passed during the Thatcher, Carter and Reagan administrations to de-regulate the financial markets and free capital flows) and the international banking facilities in the United States and Japan. In addition, the global financial market is also sustained by the plethora of tax havens around the world, through which half of the global stock of money is believed to pass (Kochen 1991), and the banking secrecy laws of states such as Switzerland, Luxembourg, and Austria. Hence government 'regulation' of transnational financial flows will not be effective unless this entire infrastructure is eliminated.

If one is to contemplate a reversal of this trend, it is not only some form of transnational re-regulation or the objections of business that one needs to deal with, but also the objections of such states who have essentially used their sovereignty as a shield. The tax havens will have to be abolished, as well as the entire legal infrastructure of the 'off-shore' financial centres. Hence the self-regulating City of London would have to become a thing of the past. This, of course, implies deep inroads into one of the central concepts of international law: sovereignty and sovereign equality. Even if it were contemplated, the action to reverse the trend would have to come about through an unprecedented degree of cooperation, for example, by groups of states in the OECD or the United Nations. No one state could achieve this because it would be regarded as a fundamental encroachment on one of the central institutions of the modern state system, namely sovereign equality. While collective action may seem more credible, any such action would represent a major evolution of the international state system from one based on the sovereign equality to one based on some sort of global governance. In present circumstances it is difficult to envisage this sort of co-operation taking place. The state system therefore, as opposed to any state in particular, effectively provides the legal and political support to global finance.

Similarly, our discussion of the downwardly mobile strategy has broader implications for an understanding of globalization. As we discussed in the Introduction, one of the popular interpretations of globalization is that it is clear that multinational enterprises need first a market and second a (semi-) skilled and disciplined labour force. Both of these can only be provided by the state. Without a territorial entity supported by a legal and political framework the market cannot function. Similarly the labour force itself has to be disciplined and regulated. This is not something that the MNE can achieve by itself although it can influence to some extent the form that the disciplining of the labour force takes. Second, we have seen that a growing number of developing world countries, appreciating these factors, have sought to take advantage of these requirements to manage their relationship with foreign capital. However, by doing so they of course provide these enterprises with the very legal and political structure they require which in turn offers companies additional opportunities to use the threat of relocation as a bargaining tool to wrest concessions from host governments.

The 'competition state' therefore can no longer be thought of as a debated response to a contested concept (globalization). Instead it has translated itself into a series of political structures embedded in the state. Therefore the debate as to whether 'states' can halt the process of global-ization is somewhat superfluous because what they will need collectively to halt, indeed reverse, is not simply trade flows and the de-regulated global financial markets, but also the very societal structures that have emerged over the past twenty years.

Bibliography

Abeywardene, Janaki, Romanye de Alwis, Jayasena, Asoka, Jayaweera, Swarna and Sanmugam, Thana, 1994, *Export Processing Zones in Sri Lanka: Economic Impact and Social Issues*, Multinational Enterprise Programme, Working Paper No. 69, Geneva, International Labour Office.

Abu-Lughod, Janet, 1989, *Before European Hegemony: The World System A.D. 1250–1350*, NY, Oxford University Press.

Adkogan, Haluk, 1995, *The Integration of International Capital Markets: Theory and Empirical Evidence*, Aldershot, Edward Elgar.

Aglietta, Michel, 1979, *A Theory of Capitalist Regulation: The US experience*, London, New Left Books.

Albert, M., 1993, *Capitalism against Capitalism*, NY, Four Windows.

Albert, M. and Ball, J., 1983, *Towards European Recovery in the 1980s*, Luxembourg, The European Parliament.

Albirtton, Robert, 1986, *A Japanese Reconstruction of Marxist Theory*, London, Macmillan.

Allen, Roy E., 1994, *Financial Crises and Recession in the Global Economy*, London, Edward Elgar.

Althusser, Louis, 1969, *For Marx*, London, New Left Books.

Amin, A., Palan, R. and Taylor, P., 1994, 'Forum for heterodox international political economy', *Review of International Political Economy*, 1 (1), 1–12.

Amin, A. and Thrift, N., 1995 'Institutional issues for the European regions: from markets and plans to socio-economics and power of association, *Economy and Society*, 24, 1.

Amin, Samir, 1974, *Unequal Development: An Essay on the Social Formations of Peripheral Capitalism*, Brighton, Harvester Press.

Amsden, A.H., 1979, 'Taiwan's economic history: a case of "etatisme" and a challenge to dependency theory', *Modern China*, 53, 341–79.

Amsden, A.H., 1985, 'The state and Taiwan's economic development', in P. Evans, D. Rueschemeyer and T. Skocpol, *Bringing the State Back In*, New York, Cambridge University Press.

Amsden, A.H., 1989, *Asia's Next Giant: South Korea and Late Industrialization*, New York and Oxford, Oxford University Press.

Amsden, A.H., 1994, 'Why isn't the whole world experimenting with the

East Asian model to develop? Review of *The East Asian Miracle*', *World Development*, 224, 627–33.

Anderson, Perry, 1974, *Lineages of the Absolutist State*, London, New Left Books.

Angel, Robert C., 1991, *Explaining Economic Policy Failure: Japan in the 1969–1971 International Monetary Crisis*, New York, Columbia University Press.

Appelbaum, R.B. and Henderson, J., 1992, *States and Development in the Asian Pacific Rim*, London, Sage.

Aris, Reinhold, 1965, *History of Political Thought in Germany From 1789 to 1815*, London, Frank Cass.

Armstrong, Philip, Glyn, Andrew and Harrison, John, 1984, *Capitalism Since World War II: The Making and Breakup of the Great Boom*, London, Fontana.

Arnold, W., 1985, 'Bureaucratic politics, state capacity, and Taiwan's automobile industrial policy', *Modern China*, 152, 178–214.

Arnold, W., 1991, 'Japanese economic presence in Taiwan: synergy and innocuous neglect', *Current Politics and Economics of Japan*, 12, 123–36.

Attali, Jacques, 1993, 'Asia's doing it. America's doing it. Let's do it here too', *The European*, 26 November.

Auster, Richard D. and Silver, Morris, 1979, *The State As A Firm: Economic Forces in Political Development*, Boston, Martin Nijhoff.

Barnes, Harry Elmar (ed.), 1948, *An Introduction to the History of Sociology*, Chicago, University of Chicago Press.

Barnet, Richard J. and Muller, Ronald E., 1974, *Global Reach: The Power of the Multinational Corporations*, New York, Simon & Schuster.

Bayart, Jean François, 1993, *The State in Africa: The Politics of the Belly*, London, Longman.

Beasley, W.G., 1990, *The Rise of Modern Japan: Political, Economic and Social Change since 1850*, London, Weidenfeld and Nicolson.

Beck, Ulrich, 1992, *Risk Society: Towards a New Modernity*, London, Sage.

Beidleman, Carl (ed.), 1987, *The Handbook of International Investing*, Chicago, Probus.

Bellah, Robert N., 1957, *Tokugawa Religion: The Values of Pre-Industrial Japan*, Glencoe, Tree Press.

Bello, Walden, 1992, *People and Power in the Pacific: The Struggle for the Post-Cold War Order*, London, Pluto Press.

Bello, Walden and Rosenfield, S., 1990, *Dragons in Distress: Asia's Miracle Economies in Crisis*, London, Penguin Books.

Berberoglu, Berch, 1992, *The Legacy of Empire: Economic Decline and Class Polarization in the United States*, Westport, CT, Praeger.

Berggren, Christian, 1992, *The Volvo Experience: Alternatives to Lean Production in the Swedish Auto Industry*, Ithaca, New York.

Bernard, M., 1989, 'Northeast Asia: The political economy of a postwar regional system', *Asia Papers No. 2*, Toronto, University of Toronto–York University, Joint Centre for Asian Pacific Studies.

Bernard, M., 1991, 'The post-Plaza political economy of Taiwanese Japanese relations', *The Pacific Review*, 44, 358–67.

Bernard, M. and Ravenhill, J., 1995, 'Beyond product cycles and flying geese: regionalization, hierachy, and the industrialization of East Asia', *World Politics*, 47, January, 171–209.

Bhagwati, Jagdish, 1993, 'Regionalism and multilateralism: an overview', in Jaime De Melo, Arvind Panagariya and Dani Rodrik (eds), *New Dimensions in Regional Integration*, Cambridge, Cambridge University Press.

Bienkowski, Wladyslaw, 1981, *Theory and Reality: Development of Social Systems*, London and New York, Allison & Busby.

Blair, Brook, George, David and Palan, Ronen, 1995, 'Ethical origins of the state in international relations', Unpublished.

Block, F. and Somers, M. J., 1984, 'Beyond the economistic fallacy: the holistic social science of Karl Polanyi', in Theda Skocpol (ed.), *Vision and Method in Historical Sociology*, London, Cambridge University Press.

Bodin, Jean, 1986/1576, *Les Six Livres de la republique*, Paris, Fayard.

Boling, P., 1990, 'Private interest and the public good in Japan', *The Pacific Review*, 32, 138–50.

Borrus M., D'Andrea Tyson, L. and Zysman, J., 1986, 'Creating advantage: how government policies shape international trade in the semiconductor industry', in Paul Krugman (ed.), *Strategic Trade Policy and the New International Economics*, Cambridge MA, MIT Press.

Bourdieu, Pierre, 1990, *The Logic of Practice*, trans. Richard Nice, Cambridge, Polity Press.

Boyer R. and Mistral J., 1978, *Accumulation, inflation et crise*. Paris, PUF., extended edition 1983.

Bracken, P., 1994, 'The military crisis of the nation state: will Asia be different from Europe?' *Political Studies*, XLII, 97–114.

Braudel, Fernand, 1979, *Civilization and Capitalism 15th–18th Century*, New York: Harper & Row.

Brogan, Hugh, 1985, *History of the United States of America*, London, Longman.

Bureau of National Affairs Inc., 1993, 'Study sees NAFTA as test case,' 12 October.

Cable, Vincent, 1995, 'The diminished nation-state', *Daedalus*, 124(2), 23–53.

Calder, K., 1993, *Strategic Capitalism: Private Business and Public Purpose in Japanese Industrial Finance*, Princeton, NJ, Princeton University Press.

Callaghy, T., 1984, *Hemmed In: Responses to Africa's Economic Decline*, Columbia, Columbia University Press.

Calleo, David, 1982, *The Imperious Economy*, Cambridge, MA, Harvard University Press.

Calleo, David, 1994, 'America's federal nation state: a crisis of post-imperial viablity?' *Political Studies*, 42, Special Issue.

Cardoso, F.H., 1974, 'Théorie de la dependence: ou analyse concrète des situations de dependence?', *L'Homme et la Société*, no. 33,4.

Cardoso, F.H. and Faletto, E., 1979, *Dependency and Development in Latin America*, Berkeley, University of California.

Castells, M., 1992, 'Four Asian tigers with a dragon head: a comparative analysis of the state, economy, and society in the Asian Pacific Rim', in R.B. Appelbaum and J. Henderson, *States and Development in the Asian Pacific Rim*, London, Sage.

Cecchini, Paolo, Catinat, Michael and Jacquemin, Alexis, 1988, *The European Challenge 1992: The Benefits of a Single Market*, Wildwood House for the EC Commission.

CEDETIM, 1978, *L'impérialisme française*, Paris, François Maspero.

Cerny, Philip G., 1990, *The Changing Architecture of Politics: Structure, Agency and the Future of the State*, London, Sage Publications.

Cerny, Philip G. (ed.), 1993, *Finance and World Politics: Markets, Regimes and States in the Post-Hegemonic Era*, London, Edward Elgar.

Cerny, Philip G., 1994a, 'The infrastructure of the infrastructure? Toward "embedded financial orthodoxy" in the international political economy', in R. Palan and B. Gills (eds), *Transcending the State–Global Divide: A Neo-Structuralist Agenda in International Relations*, Boulder, Lynne Reinner.

Cerny, Philip G., 1994b, 'The residual state', paper presented at the British International Studies Association Annual Conference, York, December.

Cerny, Philip G. 1995, Globalization and the Changing logic of Collective Action, International organizations, 34, 2

Chabal, Patrick, 1986, *Political Domination in Africa: Reflections on the Limits of Power*, Cambridge, Cambridge University Press.

Chabal, Patrick, 1994, *Power in Africa: An Essay in Political Interpretation*, London, Macmillan.

Chandler, Alfred, 1990, *Scale and Scope*, Cambridge, MA, Harvard University Press.

Chase-Dunn, C., 1994, 'Technology and the logic of world-systems', in R. Palan and B. Gills (eds), *Transcending the State–Global Divide: A Neo-Structuralist Agenda in International Relations*, Boulder, Lynne Reinner.

Chaudhuri, K.N., 1965, *The English East India Company: The Study of an Early Joint-Stock Company 1600–1640*, London, Frank Cass & Co.

Cheng, L. and Hsiung, P-C., 1992, 'Women, export oriented growth and the state: the case of Taiwan', in R.B. Appelbaum and J. Henderson, *States and Development in the Asian Pacific Rim*, London, Sage.

Chesnais, François, 1994, *La mondialisation du capital*, Paris, Syrus.

Cho, L.J. and Kim, Y. H., 1991, 'Political and economic antecedents of the 1960s', in Cho and Kim (eds), *Economic Development in the Republic of Korea: A Policy Perspective*, Honolulu: University of Hawaii Press.

Chomsky, Noam, 1991, *Deferring Democracy*, London, Verso.

Chomsky, Noam, 1993, 'Introduction, NAFTA, the new rules of corporate conquest', by Kristin Dawkins, The Open Magazine Pamphlet Series.

Chowdhury, I. and Islam, I., 1993, *The Newly Industrialising Economies of East Asia*, London and New York, Routledge.

CIA, 1994, *CIA World Factbook*, Brasseys, Washington, CIA Publications.

Clapham, C., 1985, *Third World Politics: An Introduction*, London, Routledge.

Clapham, C., 1986, *Private Patronage and Public Power: Political Clientelism in the Modern State*, London, Pinter.

Clark, C. and Chan, S., 1994, 'The developmental role of the state: moving beyond the developmental state in conceptualizing Asian political economies', *Governance: An International Journal of Policy and Administration*, 7(4), October, 333–59.

Clasters, Pierre, 1974, *La société contre l'état*, Paris, Minuit.

Clegg, L, 1987, *Multinational Corporations and World Competition*, London, Macmillan.

Cohen, Ronald, 1981, 'Evolution, fission, and the early state', in Henri J.M. Claessen and P. Skalnik (eds), *The Study of the State*, The Hague, Mouton Publishers.

Cohen, Stephen and Zysman, John, 1987, *Manufacturing Matters: The Myth of the Post-industrial Economy*, New York, Basic Books.

Commons, J., 1931, 'Institutional economics', in *The American Economic Review*, 21, December.

Cooper, Richard N., 1975, 'Prolegomena to the choice of an international monetary system', *IO*, 29(1), 63–97.

Cumings, B., 1987, 'The origins and development of the Northeast Asian political economy: industrial sectors, product cycles and political consequences', in F.C. Deyo, *The Political Economy of the New Asian Industrialism*, Ithaca and London, Cornell University Press.

Cumings, B., 1988, 'World system and authoritarian regimes in Korea, 1948–1984', in E. A. Winckler and S. Greenhalgh (eds), *Contending Approaches to the Political Economy of Taiwan*, Armonk and London, M. E. Sharpe.

Dalton, G. (ed.), 1968, *Primitive, Archaic and Modern Economies: Essays of Karl Polanyi*, New York, Doubleday.

Davidson, Basil, 1992, *The Black Man's Burden: Africa and the Curse of the Nation-State*, London, James Currey.

De Melo, Jaime, Panagariya, Arvind and Rodrik, Dani, 1993, 'The new regionalism: a country perspective', in De Melo *et al.* (eds), *New Dimensions in Regional Integration*, Cambridge, Cambridge University Press.

Deane, Phyllis, 1989, *The State and the Economic System: An Introduction to the History of Political Economy*, Oxford: Oxford University Press.

Demaio, Dennis, 1995, 'Hell in Mexican factories', *The Organiser*, 14 May.

Dendrinos, D., 1992, *The Dynamics of Cities: Ecological Determinism, Dualism and Chaos*, London, Routledge.

Denemark, Robert, 1994, 'On the demise of European socialism', *Review of International Political Economy*, 1, 2.

Dertouzos, Michael, Lester, Richard and Solow, Robert, 1989, *Made in America*, New York, Harper Perennial.

Deyo, F.C., 1987, *The Political Economy of the New Asian Industrialism*, Ithaca and London, Cornell University Press.

Deyo, F.C., 1989, *Beneath the Economic Miracle: Labour Subordination in the New Asian Industrialism*, Berkeley, University of California Press.

Dibben, Margaret, 1993, *Inter-City*, March, p.27.

Dicken, Peter, 1992, *Global Shift: The Internationalization of Economic Activity*, 2nd edn, London, Paul Chapman.

Doggart, Caroline, 1990, *Tax Havens and Their Uses*, 7th edn, London, *The Economist* Special Report No. 1191.

Dohlman, Ebba, 1989, *National Welfare and Economic Interdependence: The Case of Sweden's Foreign Trade Policy*, Oxford, Clarendon Press.

Dombusch, Rudriger (ed.), 1993, *Policymaking in the Open Economy: Concepts and Case studies in Economic Performance*, Oxford, Oxford University Press.

Doornbos, M., 1990, 'The African state in academic debate: retrospect and prospect', *The Journal of Modern African Studies*, 28, 2.

Drache, David, 1993, 'Assessing the benefits of free trade', in Ricardo Grinspun and Maxwell A. Cameron (eds), *The Political Economy of North American Free Trade*, London, Macmillan.

Drucker, Peter F., 1990, *The New Realities*, New York, Mandarin.

Duggan, Patrice, 1991, 'The mouse that wants to roar', *Forbes*, 4 March.

Dumont, Alain, 1990, 'Technology, competitiveness and cooperation in Europe', in Michael S. Steinberg (ed.), *The Technical Challenges and Opportunities of a United Europe*, London, Pinter.

Dunning, John H. (ed.), 1985, *Multinational Enterprises, Economic Structure and International Competitiveness*, London, John Wiley & Sons.

Easton, David, 1953, *The Political System*, Chicago and London, The University of Chicago Press.

Easton, David, 1981, 'The political system besieged by the state', *Political Theory*, 9, 3.

Elger, Tony and Smith, Chris, 1994, 'Convergence and competition in the organization of the labour process', in Elger and Smith (eds), *Global Japanization? The Transnational Transformation of the Labour Process*, London, Routledge.

Eringer, Robert, 1980, *The Global Manipulators: The Bilderberg Group, the Trilateral Commission, Covert Power Groups of the West*, Bristol, Pentacle Books.

Ernst, Dieter and O'Connor, David, 1989, *Technology and Global Competition: The Challenge for Newly Industrialising Economies*, Paris, Organisation for Economic Co-Operation and Development.

Esping-Anderson, Gosta, 1985, *Politics against Markets*, Princeton, Princeton University Press.

Esping-Anderson, Gosta, 1990, *The Three Worlds Of Welfare Capitalism*, Cambridge, Polity Press.

Evans, John, 1994, 'Currency trading hits new heights', *The European*, 13–19 May.

Fairbank, J.K., 1986, *The Great Chinese Revolution: 1800–1895*, London, Picador.

Fanon, Franz, 1965, *A Dying Colonialism*, trans. Haakon Chevalier, London, Writers and Readers.

Fanon, Franz, 1967, *The Wretched of the Earth*, trans. Constance Farrington, Harmondsworth, Penguin.

Faux, J. and Lee, T., 1991, *The Effect of George Bush's NAFTA on American Workers: Ladder Up or Ladder Down?*, Washington, Economic Policy Institute.

Faux, J. and Spriggs, W., 1991, *US Jobs and the Mexico Trade Proposal*, Washington, Economic Policy Institute.

Fehrenbach, R.R., 1966, *The Gnomes of Zurich*, London, Leslie Frewin.

Fingleton, E., 1995, 'Japan's invisible leviathan', *Foreign Affairs*, March/April, 69–85.

Flamm, Kenneth, 1990, 'Semiconductors', in Gary Clyde Hufbauer (ed.), *Europe 1992: An American Perspective*, Washington, DC, The Brookings Institution.

Fortes, Meyer, 1969, *Kinship and the Social Order: The Legacy of Lewis Henry Morgan*, London, Routledge and Kegan Paul.

Foucault, Michel, 1970, *The Order of Things: An Archeology of the Human Sciences*, London, Tavistock.

Frank, André Gunder, 1967, *Capitalism and Underdevelopment in Latin America: Historical Studies of Chile and Brazil*, New York, Monthly Review Press.

Frank, André Gunder, 1994a, 'Reply to Denmark, Hausner and Nove', *Review of International Political Economy*, vol. 1:2, 361–4.

Frank, André Gunder, 1994b, 'Soviet and East European : "Socialism"', *Review of International Political Economy*, vol.1:2

Franko, Lawrence, 1990, 'The impact of global corporate competition and multinational corporate strategy', in Michael S. Steinberg (ed.), *The Technical Challenges and Opportunities of a United Europe*, London, Pinter.

Freeman, Andrew, 1995, 'Other people's money: a survey of world street', *The Economist*, 15 April.

Fukui, Haruhiro, 1992, 'The Japanese state and economic development: A profile of a nationalist-paternalist capitalist state', in J. Henderson and R.P. Appelbaum, 1992, *States and Development in the Asian Pacific Rim*, London, Sage.

Galbraith, J.K., 1991, *The New Industrial State*, London, Penguin.

Garland, Peter, 1990, 'Finance and the family expatriates: avoiding the offshore traps', *Financial Times*, 3 March.

Gassman, Hanspeter, 1994, 'From industrial policy to competitiveness policies', *OECD Observer*, 187, April/May, 17.

GATT Executive Summary, 1993, 'Executive summary results of the GATT Uruguay round of multilateral trade negotiations. A report to President William Clinton', 15 December.

Geon, Jei Guk, 1992, 'The origins of the Northeast Asian NICs in retro-spect: the colonial political economy, Japan in Korea and Taiwan', *Asian Perspective*, 161, 71–101.

Gereffi, Gary, 1992, 'New realities of industrial development in East Asia and Latin America: global, regional and national trends', in Richard Applebaum and Jeffrey Henderson, *States and Development in the Asian Pacific Rim*, London, Sage.

Gerschenkron, A., 1962, *Economic Backwardness in Historical Perspective: A Book of Essays*, Cambridge, MA, Belknap Press of Harvard University Press.

Giddens, Anthony, 1984, *The Constitution of Society: Outline of the Theory of Structuration*, Cambridge, Polity Press.

Gierke, Otto, 1900, *Political Theories of the Middle Age*, Cambridge, Cambridge University Press.

Gierke, Otto, 1939, *The Development of Political Theory*, trans. Bernard Freyd, London, George Allen & Unwin.

Gill, Stephen, 1991, *American Hegemony and the Trilateral Commission*, Cambridge, Cambridge University Press.

Gill, Stephen and Law, David, 1988, *The Global Political Economy: Perspectives, Problems and Policies*, Brighton, Harvester Wheatsheaf.

Gills, Barry and Palan, Ronen, 1994, 'The Neostructuralist agenda in international relations', in Palan and Gills (eds), *Transcending the State–Global Divide: The Neo-Structuralist Agenda in International Relations*, Boulder, Lynne Rienner.

Gilmore, W.C. (ed.), 1992, *International Efforts to Combat Money Laundering*, Cambridge, Grotius Publications.

Gilpin, Robert, 1981, *War and Change in World Politics*, New York, Cambridge University Press.

Gilpin, Robert, 1987, *The Political Economy of International Relations*, Princton, Princeton University Press.

Gilpin, Robert, 1988, 'Implications of the changing trade regime for US–Japanese relations', in Inoguchi *et al.* (eds), *The Political Economy of Japan: The Changing International Context*, Vol. 2, Stanford, Stanford University Press.

Gilpin, Robert, 1993, 'The debate about the new world economic order', in Danny Unger and Paul Blackburn (eds), *Japan's Emerging Global Role*, Boulder, Lynne Rienner.

Giri-Deloison, Philippe, M., 1988, 'Vers un march-financier mondial: les rouages de la globalisation', *Revue Banque*, 485, July/August.

Gold, T.B., 1986, *State and Society in the Taiwan Miracle*, Armonk and London, M. E. Sharpe.

Gold, T.B., 1988, 'Colonial origins of Taiwanese capitalism', in E.A. Winckler and S. Greenhalgh (eds), *Contending Approaches to the Political Economy of Taiwan*, Armonk and London, M. E. Sharpe.

Goldsmith, James, 1995, 'The new utopia: GATT and global free trade', in J. Goldsmith, 1995, *The Response*, London, Macmillan.

Gonenc, R., 1994, 'From subsidies to structural adjustment', *OECD Observer*, October/November.

Gordon, R.A., 1981, *Tax Havens and Their Use by United States Taxpayers: An Overview*, Washington, DC, Tax Haven Study Group, Internal Revenue Service.

Gould, A., 1988, *Conflict and Control in Welfare Policy: The Swedish Experience*, London, Longman.

Gould, A., 1993, *Capitalist Welfare Systems: A Comparison of Japan, Britain and Sweden*, London, Longman.

Gregor, A. James, with Chang, M.H. and Zimmerman, A.B., 1981, *Ideology and Development: Sun Yat-sen and the Economic History of Taiwan*, Berkeley, CA, China Research Monograph 23; Institute of East Asian Studies, University of California, Berkeley, Center for Chinese Studies.

Grinspun, Ricardo and Cameron, Maxwell A., 1993, 'The political economy of North American integration: diverse perspectives, converging criticisms', in Grinspun and Maxwell (eds), *The Political Economy of North American Free Trade*, London, Macmillan.

Groenewegen, John, 1993, 'A changing Japanese market for corporate control', Paper presented at the EAEPE conference, Barcelona, October.

Grou, P., 1983, *La structure financière du capitalisme multinational*, Paris, Presses de la Fondation Nationale des Sciences Politiques.

Grubert, Harry and Mutti, John, 1991, 'Taxes, tariffs and transfer pricing in multinational corporation decision making', *The Review of Economics and Statistics*, February, No.1.

Grundy, Milton, 1984, *The World of International Tax Planning*, New York, Cambridge University Press.

Grundy, Milton, 1987, *Grundy's Tax Havens: A World Survey*, 5th edn, London, Sweet & Maxwell.

Guzzini, Stefano, 1995, 'The implosion of Italy', *Review of International Political Economy*, Vol. 2, 1.

Hamilton, Alexander, 1934, Papers on public credit, commerce, and finances,' ed. S. McKee, New York, Longmans Green.

Haggard, S., 1988, 'The newly industrialising countries in the international system', *World Politics*, 382, 343–70.

Haggard, S., 1990, *Pathways from the Periphery: Politics of Growth in the Newly Industrializing Countries*, Ithaca and New York, Cornell University Press.

Haggard, S. and Cheng, T., 1987, 'State and foreign capital in the East Asian NICs', in F.C. Deyo, *The Political Economy of the New Asian Industrialism*, Ithaca and London, Cornell University Press.

Halliday, Fred, 1983, *The Making of the Second Cold War*, London, New Left Books.

Halliday, Fred, 1992, 'A singular collapse: the Soviet Union, market pressures and interstate competition', Contention No. 2, Winter.

Halliday, Fred, 1994, *Rethinking International Relations*, London, Macmillan.

Hamel, G. and Prahalad, C., 1988, 'Creating global strategic capability', in N. Hood and J. Vahlne (eds), *Strategies in Global Competition*, London, Routledge.

Hamilton, E.J. 1934. *American Treasure and the Price of Revolution in Spain 1501–1650*. Harvard Economic Studies, vol. 42.

Hampton, Mark, 1994, 'Treasure islands or fool's gold: can and should small island economies copy Jersey?', *World Development*, 22(2), 237–50.

Hanzawa, Masamitu, 1991, 'The Tokyo Offshore Market', in *Japan's Financial Markets*, Tokyo, Foundation for Advanced Information and Research (FAIR), Japan.

Harrison, Benneth and Bluestone, Barry, 1988, *The Great U-Turn: Corporate Restructuring and the Polarizing of America*, NY, Basic Books.

Harrop, Jeffery, 1989, *The Political Economy of Integration in the European Community*, London, Edward Elgar.

Hart, Jeffrey A., 1992, *Rival Capitalists: International Competitiveness in the United States, Japan and Western Europe*, Ithaca, Cornell University Press.

Harvey, David, 1989, *The Condition of Post-modernity: An Enquiry into the Origins of Cultural Change*, Oxford, Blackwell.

Hausner, Jerzy, 1994, 'The collapse – an internal or external problem? A critique of Frank's approach', *Review of International Political Economy*, 1, 2.

Henderson, J., 1993a, 'The role of the state in the economic transformation of East Asia', in Chris Dixon and David Drakakis-Smith, *Economic and Social Development in Pacific Asia*, London and New York, Routledge.

Henderson, J., 1993b, 'Against the economic orthodoxy: on the making of the East Asian miracle', *Economy and Society*, 222, 200–17.

Henderson, J. and Appelbaum, R.P., 1992, 'Situating the state in the East Asian development process', in Appelbaum and Henderson, *States and Development in the Asian Pacific Rim*, London, Sage.

Hindess, Barry, 1977, *Philosophy and Methodology in the Social Sciences*, Brighton, Harvester.

Hindess, Barry, 1982, 'Power, interests and the outcome of struggles', *Sociology*, 16, 4.

Hintze, Otto, 1975, *The Historical Essays of Otto Hintze*, Felix Gilbert (ed.), Oxford, Oxford University Press.

Ho, S.P.S., 1984, 'Colonialism and development: Korea, Taiwan and Kwantung', in H. Ramon and Mark R. Peattie, *The Japanese Colonial Empire, 1895–1945*, Princeton, NJ, Princeton University Press.

Ho, S.P.S., 1987, 'Economics, economic bureaucracy, and Taiwan's economic development', *Pacific Affairs*, 602, Summer, 226–47.

Hobsbaum, Eric J., 1988, *The Age of Revolution 1789–1848*, London, Abacus.

Hobsbaum, Eric J., 1990, *Nations and Nationalism since 1780: Programme, Myth, Reality*, Cambridge, Cambridge University Press.

Hobsbaum, E., 1995, *Age of Extremes: The Short Twentieth Century, 1914–1991*, London, Abacus.

Hobson, J.A., 1988, *Imperialism: A Study*, 3rd edn, London, Unwin Hyman.

Hodgson, Geoffrey G., 1994a, 'The evolution of socioeconomic order in the move to a market economy', *Review of International Political Economy*, 1, 3, Autumn.

Hodgson, Geoffrey G., 1994b, 'The return of institutional economics', in Neil J. Smelser and Richard Swedberg, *The Handbook of Economic Sociology*, Princeton, NJ, Princeton University Press.

Holloway, John and Picciotto, Sol (eds), 1978, *State and Capital: A Marxist Debate*, London, Edward Arnold.

Hufbauer, Gary Clyde (ed.), 1990, *Europe 1992: An American Perspective*, Washington, DC, The Brookings Institution.

Hufbauer, Gary Clyde and Schott, Jeffrey J., 1993, *NAFTA: An Assessment*, London, Longman for Institute of International Economics.

Humbert, M., 1994, 'Strategic industrial policies in a global industrial system', *Review of International Political Economy*, 1, 3, Autumn.

Hung, Tran Q., 1987, 'The securitization of international finance', in Carl Beidleman (ed.), *The Handbook of International Investing*, Chicago, Probus.

Ingham, Geoffrey, 1985, *Capitalism Divided? The City and Industry in British Social Development*, London, Macmillan.

Itoh, Makoto, 1990, *The World Economic Crisis and Japanese Capitalism*, London, Macmillan.

Jackson, M. 1982, *Trade Unions*, Harlow, Longman.

Jackson, Robert, 1993, *Quasi States: Sovereignty, International Relations and the Third World*, Cambridge, Cambridge University Press.

Jackson, Robert H. and James, Alan (eds), 1994, *States in a Changing World*, Oxford, Oxford University Press.

Jackson, R. and Rosberg, C., 1982, *Personal Rule in Black Africa: Prince, Autocrat, Prophet, Tyrant*, Berkeley, University of California Press.

Jackson, Robert A. and Rosberg, Carl G., 1986, 'Why Africa's weak states persist: the empirical and the juridical in statehood', *World Politics*, XXXV, 1, 1–25.

Jacobs, E., 1973, *European Trade Unionism*, London, Croom Helm.

Jayasankaran, S., 1993, 'Made in Malaysia: The Proton car project', in Jomo, K.S., *Industrialising Malaysia: Performance and Prospects*, London, Routledge.

Jessop, Bob, 1985, *Nicos Poulantzas: Marxist Theory and Political Strategy*, London, Macmillan.

Jessop, Bob, 1990, *State Theory: Putting Capitalist States in Their Places*, London, Polity Press.

Jessop, Bob, 1993, 'Towards a Schumpeterian workfare state? Preliminary remarks on post-Fordist political economy', *Studies in Political Economy*, 40, Spring, 7–39.

Jessop, Bob, 1994, 'Post-Fordism and the state', in Ash Amin, *Post-Fordism: A Reader*, Oxford, Blackwell.

Johns, R.A., 1983, *Tax Havens and Offshore Finance: A Study of Transnational Economic Development*, New York, St Martin's Press.

Johns, R.A. and Le Marchant, C.M., 1993, *Finance Centres: British Isle*

Offshore Development Since 1979, London and New York, Pinter Publishers.

Johnson, C., 1978, 'Japan's Public Policy Companies,' Washington, American Enterprise Institute for Public Policy Research.

Johnson, C., 1980, '*Omote* explicit and *Ura* implicit: translating Japanese political terms', *Journal of Japanese Studies*, 61, 89–115.

Johnson, C., 1981, 'The Taiwan model', James C. Hsiung (ed.), *The Taiwan Experience, 1950–1980*, New York, Praeger.

Johnson, C., 1982, *MITI and the Japanese Miracle: The Growth of Industrial Policy, 1925–1975*, Stanford, CA, Stanford University Press.

Johnson, C., 1986a, '*La Serenissima* of the East', *Asian and African Studies*, 18, 57–73.

Johnson, C., 1986b, 'The patterns of Japanese relations with China, 1952–1982', *Pacific Affairs*, 593, 402–28.

Johnson, C., 1987, 'Political institutions and economic performance: the government–business relationship in Japan, Taiwan and South Korea', in F.C. Deyo, *The Political Economy of the New Asian Industrialism*, Ithaca, Cornell University Press.

Johnson, C., 1988, 'The Japanese political economy: a crisis in theory', *Ethics and International Affairs*, 2, 79–97.

Johnson, C., 1992, 'The people who invented the mechanical nightingale', Carol Gluck and Stephen R. Graubard (eds), *Showa: The Japan of Hirohito*, New York and London, W. W. Norton & Company.

Johnson, Harry G., 1974, *The New Mercantilism: Some Problems in International Trade, Money and Investment*, Oxford, Basil Blackwell.

Jomo, K.S., 1993, *Industrialising Malaysia: Performance and Prospects*, London, Routledge.

Kaldor, Mary, 1981, *The Disintegrating West*, Harmondsworth, Penguin.

Kann, Robert A., 1974, *A History of the Habsburg Empire 1526–1918*, Berkeley, University of California Press.

Kataoka, T. (ed.), 1992, *Creating Single Party Democracy: Japan's Postwar Political System*, Stanford, CA, Hoover Institution Press.

Katzenstein, Peter, 1984, *Corporatism and Change: Industrial Policy in Austria and Switzerland*, Ithaca, Cornell University Press.

Katzenstein, Peter, 1986, *Small States in World Markets*, Ithaca, Cornell University Press.

Kelsen, Hans, 1945, *General Theory of Law and State*, Cambridge, MA, Harvard University Press.

Kennedy, Paul, 1988, *The Rise and Fall of the Great Powers: Economic Change and Military Conflict from 1500 to 2000*, London, Fontana.

Khouri, J. Sarkis, 1990, *The Deregulation of the World Financial Markets*, London, Pinter.

Kochen, A., 1991., 'Cleaning up by cleaning up', *Euromoney*, April, 73–7.

Koechlin, Timothy, and Larudee, Mehrene, 1992, 'The high cost of NAFTA', *Challenge*, September/October.

Kolko, Joyce and Kolko, Gabriel, 1972, *The Limits of Power: The World and United States Foreign Policy, 1945–1954*, New York, Harper & Row.

Kornhauser, William, 1960, *The Politics of Mass Society*, London, Routledge & Kegan Paul.

Krasner, Stephan D. (ed.), 1978, *Defending the National Interest: Raw Materials Investments and U.S. Foreign Policy*, Princeton, NJ, Princeton University Press.

Krasner, S., 1994, 'International political economy: abiding discord', *Review of International Political Economy*, 1, 1, Spring, 13–20.

Krugman, P., 1986, *Strategic Trade Policy and the New International Economics*, Cambridge, MA, MIT Press.

Krugman, P., 1991, *New Thinking About Trade Policy*, in Clyde V. Prestowitz Jnr, Ronald A. Morse and Alan Toneson (eds), *Powernomics: Economics and Strategy After the Cold War*, New York, Madison Books.

Krugman, P., 1992, *The Age of Diminished Expectations: U.S. Economic Policy in the 1990s*, Cambridge, MA, MIT Press.

Krugman, P., 1993, 'Regionalism versus multilateralism: analytical notes', in De Melo *et al.*, *New Dimensions in Regional Integration*, Cambridge, Cambridge University Press.

Krugman, P., 1994, 'Does Third World growth hurt First World prosperity?', *Harvard Business Review*, July–August.

Kwan, C.H., 1994, *Economic Interdependence in the Asia-Pacific Region: Towards a Yen Bloc*, London and New York, Routledge.

Lake, David and Graham, John, 1990, *Global Corporate Financing in the 1990s: How to Succeed in an Era of Relationships and Cautious Credit*, *The Economist* Intelligence Unit.

Lasswell, Harold D., 1977, *On Political Sociology*, edited by Dwaine Marvick, Chicago and London, Chicago University Press.

Lauderbaugh, Richard, 1980, *American Steel Makers and the Coming of the Second World War*, Ann Arbor, MI, UMI Research Press.

Lee, E. (ed.), 1981, *Export Led Industrialisation and Development*, Geneva, ILO.

Lehmann, J-P., 1982, *The Roots of Modern Japan*, London, Macmillan.

Levi, Michael, 1991, 'Regulating money laundering: the death of bank secrecy in the UK', *The British Journal of Criminology*, Spring, 31, 2, 109–25.

Levinson, Charles, 1978, *Vodka-Cola*, published by Charles Levinson.

Levy, David J., 1993, *The Measure of Man: Incursions in Philosophical and Political Anthropology*, London, The Claridge Press.

Lewis, W.A., 1978, *The Evolution of the International Economic Order*, Princeton, NJ, Princeton University Press.

Lipietz, Alain, 1987, *Mirages and Miracles: The Crisis of Global Fordism*, London, Verso.

Lipietz, Alain, 1992, *Towards a New Economic Order: Postfordism, Ecology and Democracy*, trans. by Malcolm Slater, Cambridge, Polity Press.

Lipietz, Alain, 1994, 'The national and the regional: their autonomy vis-à-vis the global capitalist crisis', in Ronen Palan and Barry K. Gills K. (eds), *Transcending the State–Global Divide: The Neo-Structuralist Agenda in International Relations*, Boulder, Lynne Rienner.

List, F., 1904/1841, *The National System of Political Economy*, trans. Sampson S. Lloyd, New York, Longmans, Green.

Livingston, Steven G., 1992, 'The politics of international agenda-setting: Reagan and North-South relations', *International Studies Quarterly*, 36, 3, 313–29.

Lowith, Karl, 1964, *From Hegel to Nietzsche: the Revolution in Nineteenth-century Thought*, trans. David E. Green, New York, Columbia University Press.

MacGaffey, Janet, 1991, *The Real Economy of Zaire: The Contribution of Smuggling and other Unofficial Activities to National Wealth*, London, James Currey.

McCormick, Thomas J., 1989, *America's Half-Century: United States Foreign Policy in the Cold War*, Baltimore, Johns Hopkins University Press.

McGee, J. and Howards, T., 1988, 'Making sense of complex industries', in N. Hood and J. Vahlne (eds), *Strategies in Global Competition*, London, Routledge.

McKenzie, Richard B. and Lee, Dwight R., 1991, *Quicksilver Capital: How the Rapid Movement of Wealth Has Changed the World*, New York, Free Press.

Machlup, Fritz, 1977, *A History of Thought on Economic Integration*, London, Macmillan.

Maisonrouge, Jacques, 1989, *Inside IBM: A European's Story*, London, Fontana.

Mann, Michael, 1984, 'The autonomous power of the state: its origins, mechanisms and results', *Archives européennes de sociologie*, 25, 185–213.

Mann, Michael, 1986, *The Sources of Social Power*, Vol. I, *A History of Power from the Beginning to A.D. 1760*, Cambridge, Cambridge University Press.

Mann, Michael, 1994, *The Sources of Social Power*, Vol. II, *The Rise of Classes and Nation-States, 1760–1914*, Cambrige, Cambridge University Press.

Marklund, Steffan, 1988, *Paradise Lost? The Nordic Welfare States and the Recession 1975–1985*, Lund, Arkiv.

Marx, Karl, 1970, *Capital* Vol. I, London, New Left Books.

Marx, Karl, 1973, *The Revolution of 1848*, Harmondsworth, Penguin.

Mason, Terry B., 1987, 'Deregulation of the world capital markets', in Carl Beidleman (ed.), *The Handbook of International Investing*, Chicago, Probus.

Masumi, Junnosuke, 1988, 'The 1955 system in Japan and its subsequent development', *Asian Survey*, 28(3), March, 286–306.

Matsumoto, Sannosuke, 1978, 'The roots of political disillusionment: "public" and "private" in Japan', in J. Victor Koschmann (ed.), *Authority and the Individual in Japan*, Tokyo, University of Tokyo Press.

Mayhew, Anne, 1987, 'The beginnings of institutionalism', *The Journal of Economic Issues*, XXI (3), September, 971–96.

Meyer, John W. and Rowan, Brian, 1991, 'Institutionalized organizations: formal structure as myth and ceremony', in Walter Powell and Paul J. DiMaggio (eds), *The New Institutionalism in Organizational Analysis*, London and Chicago, Chicago University Press.

Mills, C. Wright, 1956, *The Power Elite*, Oxford, Oxford University Press.

Milner, Henry, 1994, *Social Democracy and Rational Choice*, London, Routledge.

Ministerial Communiqué, 1994, *OECD Observer*, August/September, 189.

Molyneux, Douglas and Storie, William R., 1995, 'Offshore mutual funds', Unpublished research paper.

Moore Jr, Barrington, 1984, *Privacy: Studies in Social and Cultural History*, Armonk and London, M. E. Sharpe.

Morgenthau, Hans J., 1967, *Politics among Nations: The Struggle for Power and Peace*, 4th edn, New York, Alfred A. Knopf.

Mornieau, Michel, 1985, *Incroyable Gazettes et Fabuleux Metaux: Les retours des tresor americanes d'apres les gazettes hollandaises*, Paris, Cambridge University Press.

Morishima, Michio, 1982, *Why Has Japan 'Succeeded'? Western Technology and the Japanese Ethos*, Cambridge, Cambridge University Press.

Morris-Suzuki, T., 1989a, *A History of Japanese Economic Thought*, London and New York, Routledge.

Morris-Suzuki, T., 1989b, 'Introduction: Japanese economic growth, images and ideologies', in T. Morris-Suzuki and T. Seiyama, *Japanese Capitalism Since 1945: Critical Perspectives*, Armonk and London, M. E. Sharpe.

Moulder, F.V., 1977, *Japan, China and the Modern World Economy: Towards a Reinterpretation of East Asian Development ca. 1600 to ca. 1918*, Cambridge and London, Cambridge University Press.

Muramatsu, M., 1993, 'Patterned pluralism under challenge: the policies of the 1980s', in G. D. Allinson and Y. Sone, *Political Dynamics in Contemporary Japan*, Ithaca and London, Cornell University Press.

Muramatsu, M. and Krauss, E.S., 1987, 'The conservative policy line and the development of patterned pluralism', in Kozo Yamamura and Yasukichi Yasuba, *The Political Economy of Japan, Volume One: The Domestic Transformation*, Stanford, CA, Stanford University Press.

Nairn, T., 1978, *The Break-up of Britain*, London, New Left Books.

Naylor, R.T., 1987, *Hot Money and the Politics of Debt*, London, Unwin Hyman.

Nester, W.R., 1990, *Japan's Growing Power over East Asia and the World Economy: Ends and Means*, London, Macmillan.

Nester, W.R., 1992, *Japan and the Third World*, London, Macmillan.

Nester, W.R., 1993, *American Power, The New World Order and the Japanese Challenge*, London, Macmillan.

Nisbeth, Robert, 1974, *The Social Philosphers: Community and Conflict in Western Thought*, London, Heinemann.

Nordic Social Statistical Committee (NOSCO), 1993, *Social Security in the Nordic Countries: Scope, Expenditure and Financing*, Oslo, NOSCO.

Norman, E.H., 1940, *Japan's Emergence as a Modern State: Political Problems of the Meiji Period*, New York, Institute of Pacific Relations.

Nove, Alec, 1994, 'What went wrong with André Gunder Frank', *Review of International Political Economy*, 1, 2.

O'Connor, D., 1993, 'Textiles and clothing: Sunrise or sunset industry?', in Jomo, K.S., *Industrialising Malaysia: Performance and Prospects*, London, Routledge.

O'Malley, W.J., 1988, 'Culture and industrialisation', in H. Hughes (ed.), *Achieving Industrialisation in East Asia*, Cambridge, Cambridge University Press.

OECD, 1977, *Restrictive Business Practices of Multinational Enterprises*, Reports of the Committee of Experts on Restrictive Business Practices, Paris, OECD.

OECD, 1991, 'Economic outlook', *Historical Statistics: 1960–1990*, Paris, OECD.

OECD, 1995, 'Figures: statistics on the member countries', *OECD Observer*, 194, June/July, supplement.

OECD Committee on Fiscal Affairs, 1987, *International Tax Avoidance and Evasion: Four Related Studies*, Issues in International Taxation, No. 1, Paris, OECD.

Oh, Won Sun, 1994, *Export Processing Zones in the Republic of Korea: Economic and Social Issues*, Multinational Enterprise Programme, Working Paper No. 75, Geneva, International Labour Office.

Ohmae, Kenichi, 1985, *Triad Power: The Coming Shape of Global Competition*, Basingstoke, Macmillan.

Ohmae, Kenichi, 1990, *The Borderless World: Power and Strategy in the Interlinked Economy*, London, Collins.

Ohmae, Kenichi, 1993, 'The Rise of the Region State', Foreign Affairs, Spring.

Ohmae, Kenichi, 1995, *The End of the Nation State: The Rise of Regional Economies*, London, HarperCollins.

Overbeek, H. and Van der Pijl, Kees, 1993, 'Restructuring capital and restructuring hegemony', in Overbeek, H., *Restructuring Hegemony in the Global Political Economy: The Rise of Transnational Neo-liberalism in the 1980s*, London, Routledge.

Owen Smith, E. (ed.), 1981, *Trade Unions in the Developed Economies*, London, Croom Helm.

Palan, Ronen, 1988, 'A non-Euclidian international relations?', *Millennium: Journal of International Studies*, 17, 1.

Palan, Ronen, 1991, 'Misguided nationalism: the causes and prospects for Slovenian independence', *Contemporary Review*, September, pp.119–27.

Palan, Ronen, 1993, 'Underconsumption and widening income inequalities: the dynamics of globalization', *Newcastle Discussion Paper*, No. 4.

Palan, Ronen, 1994, 'State and society in international relations', in Palan and Gills, *Transcending the State–Global Divide: A Neo-structuralist Agenda in International Relations*, Boulder, Lynne Reinner.

Palan, Ronen, 1995a, 'After the cold war: international relations in the period of the latest "New World Order"', in Hunter and Allen (eds), *Rethinking the Cold War: Essays on its Dynamics, Meaning and Morality*, Temple University Press for the A.E. Havens Center for the Study of Social Structure and Social Change.

Palan, Ronen, 1995b, 'The reluctant revolutionaries of the modern world', *Studies in Marxism*, Issue 2.

Palan, Ronen and Brook Blair, 1993, 'On the idealist origins of the realist theory of international relations', *Review of International Studies*, 19, 385–99.

Parboni, Ricardo, 1981, *The Dollar and its Rivals*, London, New Left Books.

Peagam, T., 1989, *Treasure Islands*, a supplement to *Euromoney*, May.

Pelkmans, Jacques, 1986, 'The bickering bigemony: GATT as an instrument in Atlantic trade policy', in Loukas Tsoukalis, *Europe, America and the World Economy*, London, Basil Blackwell.

Pempel, T.J., 1990, *Uncommon Democracies*, Ithaca, Cornel University Press.

Perot, Ross with Choate, Pat, 1993, *Save Your Job, Save Our Country: Why NAFTA Must be Stopped – Now!*, New York, Hyperion.

Pfaller, A., Gough, I. and Therborn, G., 1991, *Can the Welfare State Compete?*, Basingstoke, Macmillan.

Phillips, K.P., 1992, 'U.S. industrial policy: inevitable and ineffective', *Harvard Business Review*, July–August, 104–12.

Polanyi, K., 1957a [1944], *The Great Transformation: The Political and Economic Origins of our Time*, Boston, Beacon Hill.

Polanyi, K., 1957b, 'The economy as instituted process', in Karl Polanyi, Conrad M. Arensberg and Harry W. Pearson (eds) *Trade and Market in the Early Empires: Economies in History and in Theory*, New York, The Free Press.

Polanyi, K., 1977, *The Livelihood of Man*, Harry W. Pearson (ed.), New York, San Francisco and London, Academic Press.

Polanyi, K., Arensberg, C. and Pearson, H. (eds), 1971, *Trade and Market in Early Empires*, Chicago, Henry Regenery.

Porter, Michael E. (ed.), 1986, *Competition in Global Industries*, Cambridge, MA, Harvard Business School Press.

Porter, Michael, 1990, *The Competitive Advantage of Nations*, London, Macmillan.

Poulantzas, N., 1973, *Political Power and Social Classes*, London, Verso.

Poulantzas, N., 1978, *State, Power, Socialism*, London, New Left Books.

Powell, Walter W. and DiMaggio, Paul J. (eds), 1991, *The New Institutionalism in Organizational Analysis*, London and Chicago, Chicago University Press.

Prestowitz, C., Morse, R. and Tonelson, A., 1991, *Powernomics: Economics and Strategy After the Cold War*, Washington, Madison Books.

Pye, Lucian, 1985, *Asian Power and Politics: The Cultural Dimensions of Authority*, Cambridge, MA, Belknap Press of Harvard University Press.

Pye, Lucian, 1988, 'The new Asian capitalism: a political portrait', in P.L. Berger and H.M. Hsiao (eds), *In Search of An East Asian Development Model*, New Brunswick, Transaction Books.

Pyle, K.B., 1992, *The Japanese Question: Power and Purpose in a New Era*, Washington, DC, The AEI Press.

Pyo, H.K., 1993, 'The transition in the political economy of South Korean development', *Journal of Northeast Asian Studies*, Winter, 74–87.

Quigley, Carroll, 1966, *Tragedy and Hope: A History of the World in our Time*, London and Basingstoke, Macmillan.

Radcliffe-Brown, Alfred Reginald, 1952, *Structure and Function in Primitive Societies: Essays and Addresses*, London, Cohen and West.

Rees-Mogg, William, 1993, 'Down and out in trillionaire's row', *The Times*, 11 October, 14.

Reich, R., 1983, *The Next American Frontier*, New York, Times Books.

Reich, R., 1990, *The Work of Nations: Preparing Ourselves for Twenty-First Century Capitalism*, New York, Vintage Books.

Rueschmeyer, D., Huber Stephens, E. and Stephens, J.D., 1992, *Capitalist Development and Democracy*, Cambridge, Polity Press.

Rodney, Walter, 1972, *How Europe Underdeveloped Africa*, London, Bogle-L'ouverture Publications.

Romer, Paul M., 1986, 'Increasing returns and long-run growth', *Journal of Political Economy*, 94, 1002–37.

Rosencrance, Richard, 1986, *The Rise of the Trading State: Commerce and Conquest in the Modern World*, New York, Basic Books.

Rozman, G., 1990, 'The rise of the state in China and Japan', in Michael Mann, (ed.), *The Rise and Decline of the Nation State*, London, Basil Blackwell.

Ruhl, Sonja and Hughes, Janice, 1986, *Tokyo 2000: The World's Third International Financial Centre?*, *The Economist* Special Report no. 1055.

Ruggie, John G., 1982, 'International regimes, transactions, and change: embedded liberalism in the post-war order', *International Organization*, 36, Autumn, 379–415.

Rutherford, D., 1992, *Dictionary of Economics*, London and New York, Routledge.

Sabel, Charles F., 1994, 'Learning by monitoring: the institutions of economic development', in Neil J. Smelser and Richard Swedberg, *The Handbook of Economic Sociology*, Princeton, NJ, Princeton University Press.

Sabine, George H. and Shepard, Walter J., 1922, 'Translator's introduction' to H. Krabbe, *The Modern Idea of the State*, New York and London, Appleton and Co.

Salaff, J.W., 1992, 'Women, the family and the state in Hong Kong, Taiwan and Singapore', in Richard Appelbaum and Jeffrey Henderson, *States and Developments in the Asian Pacific Rim*, London, Sage.

Sally, Razeen, 1994, 'Multinational enterprises, political economy and institutional theory; domestic embeddedness in the context of internationalization', *Review of International Political Economy*, 1(1).

Sampson, Anthony, 1973, *The Sovereign State: The Secret History of ITT*, London, Hodder & Stoughton.

Sampson, Anthony, 1977, *The Arms Bazaar: Companies, The Dealers, the Bribes: From Vickers to Lockheed*, London, Hodder & Stoughton.

Samuels, R. J., 1994, *'Rich Nation, Strong Army': National Security and the Technological Transformation of Japan*, Ithaca, Cornell University Press.

Sassen, Saskia, 1991, *The Global City: New York, London, Tokyo*, Princeton, Princeton University Press.

Schaffer, J., 1995, 'Child labor remains global problem of huge proportions', *USIA East Asia Pacific Wireless File*, 22 May 1995.

Schissel, Howard, 1989, *Africa's Underground Economy*, Africa Report, January/February, 43–6.

Schmitter, P., 1979, 'Still the century of corporatism?', in G. Lehmbruch and P. Schmitter (eds), *Trends Towards Corporatist Intermediation*, London, Sage.

Schor, J., 1992, 'Introduction' to T. Banuri and J. Schor (eds), *Financial Openness and National Autonomy*, Oxford, Clarendon Press.

Schurmann, H. F., 1956, *Economic Structure of the Yuan Dynasty: Translation of Chapters 93 and 94 of the Yuan Shih*, Cambridge, MA, Harvard University Press.

Schwarzenberger, George, 1951, *Power Politics: A Study of International Society*, London, Stevens & Sons.

Sekine, Thomas, 1980, 'An essay on Uno's dialectic of capital', in Kozo Uno, *Principles of Political Economy: A Theory of Purely Capitalist Society*, Brighton, Harvester Press.

Shannon, T.R., 1990, *Introduction to the World System Perspective*, Boulder, CO, Westview Press.

Sheridan, K., 1993, *Governing the Japanese Economy*, Oxford and Cambridge, MA, Polity Press.

Silva, Michael and Sjogren, Bertil, 1990, *Europe 1992 and the New World Power Game*, New York, John Wiley & Sons.

Simiand, François, 1932, *Les Fluctuations économique a Longue Période et la Crise Mondiale*, Paris, Félix Alean.

Sinclair, Timothy, 1994, 'Passing judgement: credit rating processes as regulatory mechanisms of governance in the emerging world order', *Review of International Political Economy*, 1(1), 133–60.

Sivalingham, G., 1994, *The Economic and Social Impact of Export Processing Zones: The Case of Malaysia*, Multinational Enterprise Programme, Working Paper No. 66, Geneva, International Labour Office.

Sklar, H. (ed.), 1980, *Trilateralism*, Boston, MA, South End Press.

Skocpol, Theda, 1972, 'Wallerstein's world capitalist system: a theoretical and historical critique', *American Journal of Sociology* 82(5), 1075–90.

Smelser, Neil J. and Swedberg, Richard, 1994, *The Handbook of Economic Sociology*, Princeton, NJ, Princeton University Press.

Sorokin, Pitirim A., 1941, *Social and Cultural Dynamics 4*, New York, American Book.

Stallings, Barbara and Kaufman, R., 1990, *Death and Democracy in Latin America*, Boulder, CO, Westview Press.

Stein, P. and Dorfer, I., 1991, *The Death Knell of Social Democracy: Sweden's Dream Turns Sour*, London, Institute for European Defence and Strategic Studies.

Steinberg, Michael S. (ed.), 1990, *The Technical Challenges and Opportunities of a United Europe*, London, Pinter.

Stevens, Barrie, 1994, 'The social fabric under pressure', *The OECD Observer*, 189, August/September.

Stopford, J. and Strange, S., 1991, *Rival States, Rival Firms: Competition for World Market Shares*, Cambridge, Cambridge University Press.

Strange, S., 1986, *Casino Capitalism*, Oxford, Basil Blackwell.

Strange, S., 1987, 'The persistent myth of "lost" hegemony', *International Organization*, 41, 551–74.

Strange, S., 1988, *States and Markets*, London, Pinter.

Strange, S., 1994a, 'Wake up Krasner the world has changed!', *Review Of International Political Economy*, 1(2).

Strange, S., 1994b, 'From Bretton Woods to the Casino Economy', in Stuart Corbride, Ron Martin and Nigel Thrift (eds), *Money, Power and Space*, Oxford, Blackwell.

Strange, S., 1995, 'The defective state', *Daedalus*, 124(2), 55–74.

Swedberg, Richard, 1994, 'Markets as social structures', in Neil J. Smelser and Richard Swedberg, *The Handbook of Economic Sociology*, Princeton, NJ, Princeton University Press.

Tamburini, Tambio, 1994, 'Family affairs take a back seat in Italy', *The European*, 18–24 November.

Taplin, Grant B., 1992, 'Revitalizing UNCTAD', *Finance and Development*, June.

Taylor, P., 1993, *Political Geography: World Economy, Nation-State, Locality*, 3rd edn, London, Longman.

The Economist, 1989, 'Fading illusions: Austria, a survey', 25 February.

The Economist, 1991a, 'The cursed dole', 4 October, 16–17.

The Economist, 1991b, 'The ebb tide: a survey of international finance', 27 April.

The Economist, 1994, 'The Nordic countries: a survey', 5 November.

The Europa World Yearbook, 1995, London, Europa Publications Ltd.

Therborn, Goran, 1980, *What does the Ruling Class do when it Rules?*, London, New Left Books.

Therborn, Goran, 1991, 'Sweden', in Alfred Pfaffler, Ian Gough and Goran Therborn, *Can the Welfare State Compete? A Comparative Study of Five Advanced Capitalist Countries*, London, Macmillan.

Thompson, Paul and Sederblad, Per, 1994, 'The Swedish model of work organization in transition', in Tony Elger and Chris Smith (eds), *Global Japanization? The Transnational Transformation of the Labour Process*, London, Routledge.

Thomsen, Stephen and Nicolaides, Phedon, 1991, *The Evolution of*

Japanese Direct Investment in Europe: The Death of a Transistor Salesman, London, Harvester Wheatsheaf.

Tien, Hung-Mao, 1989, *The Great Transition: Political and Social Change in the Republic of China*, Stanford CA, Hoover Institution Press.

Tool, M., 1994, 'Institutional adjustment and instrumental value', *Review of International Political Economy*, 1(3), Autumn.

Trimberger, E.K., 1978, *Revolution from Above: Military Bureaucrats and Development in Japan, Turkey, Egypt and Peru*, New Brunswick, NJ, Transaction Books.

Tsoukalis, Loukas, 1986, *Europe, America and the World Economy*, London, Blackwell.

Ullmann, Walter, 1965, *A History of Political Thought: The Middle Ages*, London, Penguin.

Ullmann, Walter, 1975, *Law and Politics in the Middle Ages: An Introduction to the Sources of Medieval Political Ideas*, Ithaca, New York, Cornell University Press.

United Nations Centre on Transnational Corporations (UNCTC), 1991, *World Investment Report: The Triad in Foreign Direct Investment*, New York, United Nations, UNCTC.

United Nations Department of Economic Affairs, Research and Planning Division, 1948, *A Survey of The Economic Situation and Prospects of Europe, 1948*, Geneva, United Nations.

United Nations Department of International Economic and Social Affairs, 1995, World Economic Survey, New York, United Nations.

United Nations Development Programme (UNDP), 1991, *Human Development Report 1991*, Oxford, UNDP/Oxford University Press.

UNDP, 1992, *Human Development Report 1992*, Oxford, UNDP/Oxford University Press.

Uno, Kozo, 1980, *Principles of Political Economy: A Theory of Purely Capitalist Society*, Brighton, Harvester Press.

Van der Pijl, K., 1984, *The Making of an Atlantic Ruling Class*, London, Verso.

Van der Pijl, K. (ed.), 1989, 'Transnational relations and class strategy', *International Journal of Political Economy*, 19(3).

Van der Pijl, K., 1995, 'The second glorious revolution: globalising élites and historical change', in Bjorn Hettne (ed.) *International Political Economy: Understanding Global Disorder*, London, Zed Books.

Van Tulder, R. and Ruigrok, W. 1995, *The Logic of International Restructuration*, London: Routledge.

Van Wolferen, Karel, 1989, *The Enigma of Japanese Power: People and Politics in a Stateless Nation*, London, Macmillan.

Vattimo, Gianni, 1992, *The Transparent Society*, Cambridge, Polity Press.

Veblen, T., 1994/1899, *The Theory of the Leisure Class*, New York, Dover Press.

Vernon, Raymond, 1971, *Sovereignty at Bay: The Multinational Spread of US Enterprises*, London, Longman.

Vickey, G., 1993, 'Global industries and national policies', *OECD Observer*, February/March.

Viner, Jacob, 1950, *The Customs Union Issue*, New York, Carnegie Endowment for International Peace.

Vogel, S.K., 1994, 'The bureaucratic approach to financial revolution reform in Japan: Japan's Ministry of Finance and financial system reform', *Governance*, 7(3), July, 219–43.

Wade, R., 1988, 'The role of government in overcoming market failure: Taiwan, Republic of Korea and Japan', in Helen Hughes (ed.), *Achieving Industrialization in East Asia*, Cambridge, Cambridge University Press.

Wade, R., 1990, *Governing the Market: Economic Theory and the Role of Government in East Asian Industrialization*, Princeton, NJ, Princeton University Press.

Wakabayashi, Masahiro, 1992, *Taiwan: Bunretsu Kokka to Minshuka* (Taiwan: Democratisation in a Divided Country), Tokyo, Tokyo University Press.

Wallerstein, Immanuel, 1974, *The Modern World-System, Vol. I. Capitalist Agriculture and the Origins of the European World-Economy in the Sixteenth Century*, New York, Academic Press.

Wallerstein, Immanuel, 1979, *The Capitalist World Economy*, Cambridge, Cambridge University Press.

Wallerstein, Immanuel, 1980, *The Modern World-System. Vol. II. Mercantilism and the Consolidation of the European World-Economy, 1600–1750*, New York, Academic Press.

Waltz, K.N., 1979, *Theory of International Politics*, Reading, MA, Addison-Wesley.

Weaver, P.H., 1990, *The suicidal corporation: how big business fails America*, New York, Capstone Press.

Weber, Max, 1978, *Economy and Society: An Outline of Interpretive Sociology*, 2 vols. edited by Guenther Roth and Claus Wittich, Berkeley, University of California.

White, G. (ed.), 1988, *Developmental States in East Asia*, London, Macmillan.

White, G. and Wade, R., 1984, 'Developmental states in East Asia: editorial introduction', *Developmental States in East Asia: Capitalist and Socialist*, IDA Sussex Bulletin 15, April.

Whitely, R.D., 1990, 'Eastern Asian enterprise structures and the comparative analysis of forms of business organisations', *Organization Studies*, 111, 47–74.

Wilde, Lawrence, 1994a, *Modern European Socialism*, Aldershot, Dartmouth.

Wilde, Lawrence, 1994b, 'Swedish social democracy and the world market', in Ronen Palan, and Barry Gills (eds), *Transcending the State-Global Divide: The Neo-Structuralist Agenda in International Relations*, Boulder, Lynne Rienner.

Wilkinson, Bruce W, 1993, 'Trade liberalization, the market ideology, and morality: have we a sustainable system?', in Ricardo Grinspun and Maxwell Cameron (eds), *The Political Economy of North American Free Trade*, London, Macmillan.

Williams, Appleman William, 1972, *The Tragedy of American Diplomacy*, 2nd edn, New York, Delta Books.

Williams, D., 1994, *Japan: Beyond the End of History*, London and New York, Routledge.

Wilson, Dorothy, 1979, *The Welfare State in Sweden*, London, Heinemann.

Wolfe, Alan, 1977, *The Limits of Legitimacy: Political Contradictions of Contemporary Capitalism*, New York, The Free Press.

Woo, J.E., 1991, *Race to the Swift: State and Finance in Korean Industrialization*, New York, Columbia University Press.

Wood, Adrian, 1994, *North-South Trade, Employment and Inequality: Changing Fortunes in a Skill-driven World*, Oxford, Oxford University Press.

World Bank, 1983, *World Development Report*, New York, Oxford University Press.

World Bank, 1990, *World Development Report: Poverty*, New York, Oxford University Press.

World Bank, 1992, *World Development Report*, New York, Oxford University Press.

World Bank, 1993, *The East Asian Economic Miracle: Economic Growth and Public Policy*, New York, Oxford University Press.

World Development, 1994 22(4) pp.615–70, Oxford, Pergamon Press Ltd.

Yergin, Daniel, 1991, *The Prize*, New York, Simon & Schuster.

Zhang, Tien and Lin, Chuck, 1995, 'South Korea waste halts Nanjing port for 150 days', *China News Digest*, 28 February.

Zhao, Ding-xin and Hall, J., 1994, 'State power and patterns of late development: resolving the crisis of the sociology of development', *Sociology*, 28(1), February, 211–29.

Zysman, John, 1983, *Governments, Markets, and Growth: Financial Systems and the Politics of Industrial Change*, Ithaca, NY, Cornell University Press.

Index

Page numbers in bold denote major
section/chapter devoted to subject